TEACHING LANGUAGE ARTS CREATIVELY IN THE ELEMENTARY GRADES

A. BARBARA PILON
Professor of Elementary Education
Worcester State College
Worcester, Massachusetts

John Wiley & Sons
New York/Santa Barbara/London/Sydney/Toronto

Library of Congress Cataloging in Publication Data

Pilon, A., Barbara.
  Teaching language arts creatively in the elementary
grades.

  Includes bibliographies and index.
  1. Language arts (Elementary) 2. Creative thinking
(Education) I. Title.
LB1576.P578   372.6'044   77-23508
ISBN 0-471-68980-7

Printed in the United States of America

10 9 8 7 6 5 4 3 2

Teaching Language Arts Creatively in the Elementary Grades

To all of my students and to my husband, Al, who has always encouraged me to remain a student.

Acknowledgments

I gratefully acknowledge some very special people who gave me their thoughtful suggestions, time, and encouragement in the preparation of this book. Among them are Albert J. Pilon, Jr., Sam Sebesta, Bob Stewart, John Warren Stewig, Michael K. Sullivan, and James D. Walden, Susan Seibel. I also thank the following for reprint permission of copyrighted materials.

ADDISON-WESLEY PUBLISHING COMPANY. "Ain't," "O.K.," and "Spulling." Reprinted from HOORAY FOR CHOCOLATE, © 1960, by Lucia and James L. Hymes, Jr., a Young Scott Book, by permission of Addison-Wesley Publishing Company, Inc.

ATHENEUM PUBLISHERS, INC. "Pigeons." Text copyright © 1969 by Lilian Moore. From *I Thought I Heard the City*. Used by permission of Atheneum Publishers.

AVON. "Victor Y." Reprinted from THE ME NOBODY KNOWS, edited by Stephen M. Joseph. Copyright © 1969 by Stephen M. Joseph. Reprinted by arrangement with Avon Books. Non-United States and translation rights by permission of Stephen M. Joseph and Henry Morrison, Inc., his agents.

THOMAS Y. CROWELL, INC. "M," "V," and "X." From SONIA DELAUNAY'S ALPHABET by Sonia Delaunay, used by permission of Thomas Y. Crowell Company, Inc. Copyright © 1970 by Emme Edizione.

DOVER PUBLICATIONS, INC. From CREATIVE POWER: THE EDUCATION OF YOUTH IN THE CREATIVE ARTS by Hughes Mearns. Copyright © 1958 by Hughes Mearns. Reprinted by permission of Dover Publications.

DOVER PUBLICATIONS, INC. "Myself." From *The Children: Poems and Prose from Bedford Stuyvesant,* by Irving Benig. Reprinted by permission of Grove Press, Inc. Copyright © 1970 by Irving Benig.

HARCOURT BRACE JOVANOVICH, INC. "To Look At Any Thing." Copyright © 1961 by John Moffit. Reprinted from his volume, *The Living Seed,* by permission of Harcourt Brace Jovanovich, Inc.

HARPER & ROW PUBLISHERS, INC. "Invitation" from WHERE THE SIDEWALK ENDS, by Shel Silverstein. Reprinted by permission of Harper & Row, Publishers, Inc.

HOLT, RINEHART AND WINSTON. From "Riders" from THE POETRY OF ROBERT FROST edited by Edward Connery Lathem. Copyright1928, © 1969 by Holt, Rinehart and Winston. Copyright © 1956 by Robert Frost. Reprinted by permission of Holt, Rinehart and Winston, Publishers. Poems on pages 183, 193, 196, and 199. From *A Rocket in My Pocket*, by Carl Withers. Copyright © 1948 by Carl Withers. Reprinted by permission of Holt, Rinehart and Winston, Inc.

HOUGHTON MIFFLIN COMPANY. From TEACHER'S ANNOTATED EDITION OF ENGLISH FOR MEANING, 6 by Paul McKee and Annie McCowen. Copyright © 1962 by Paul McKee and Annie McCowen. Reprinted by permission of Houghton Mifflin Company.

JONATHAN CAPE LTD. "Riders." From the Estate of Robert Frost. In *The Poetry of Robert Frost*, edited by Edward Connery Lathem.

THE JUDSON PRESS. "I Like You As You Are," By Josie Carey. From WONDERING ABOUT US — Learner's Book — Second Edition, Perspective I by Harriet B. Dowdy and Muriel F. Lichtenwalner. Copyright 1969 by Judson Press.

BIL KEANE. For permission to include cartoons from "The Family Circus" by Bil Keane. Reprinted courtesy The Register and Tribune Syndicate.

MEL LAZARUS AND PUBLISHERS-HALL SYNDICATE, COPYRIGHT, FIELD ENTERPRISES. For permission to reprint three "Miss Peach" cartoons. Reprinted courtesy of Mel Lazarus and Publishers-Hall Syndicate, Copyright Field Enterprises.

J.B. LIPPINCOTT COMPANY. "I Keep Three Wishes Ready." From ALL THROUGH THE YEAR by Annette Wynne. Copyright 1932, © renewed 1960 by Annette Wynne. Reprinted by permission of J.B. Lippincott Company. "Sometimes at Night," from *Only the Moon and Me*, by Richard J. Margolis. Copyright © 1969 by Richard J. Margolis. Reprinted by permission of J.B. Lippincott Company.

THE MACMILLAN PUBLISHING COMPANY, INC. From THE CROCK OF GOLD by James Stephens. Copyright © 1912 by James Stephens. Reprinted by permission of Macmillan Publishing Company.

NATIONAL EDUCATION ASSOCIATION. From *Listening* by Stanford E. Taylor. Copyright © 1973 by the National Education Association of the United States. Reprinted by permission of NEA Publishing.

UNIVERSITY OF CALIFORNIA PRESS. "The Snail's Monologue." From CHRISTIAN MORGENSTEARN'S GALGENLIEDER: A SELECTION translated by Max Knight. Copyright © 1963 by Max E. Knight. Reprinted by permission of the University of California Press.

THE VIKING PRESS, INC. From BLUE WILLOW by Doris Gates. Copyright 1940, © 1968 by Doris Gates. Reprinted by permission of the Viking Press, Inc.

A.B.P.

Preface

One misty moisty morning,
When cloudy was the weather,
I chanced to meet an old man,
Clothed all in leather
He began to compliment
And I began to grin.
How do you do? And how do you do?
And how do you do again?
—Mother Goose

This Way, Delight, Herbert Read's title for a collection of poetry, expresses equally well the intent of my approach to language arts. Its underlying assumption is that learning can be pleasurable; that, in the words of the nursery rhyme, what is "learned with pleasure" is "learned full measure." Its principal goal is to help each child experience fully the joys of reading, listening, speaking and writing and sense the intimate relation of these arts of language. Its central theme is that good literature offers, in addition to its widely recognized value in enriching the lives of children , a pleasurable and effective entry into all aspects of language arts instruction. Children will read or listen to a story or poem that appeals to them. They will want to talk about it. Through reading, listening, and discussion, their vocabularies will grow along with their appreciation of the effective use of language. A selection that has been successful in getting children to express themselves will often also provide a springboard into writing. Writing comes easier to all of us once we have sorted out our ideas on a sub ect and heard the ideas of others.

This textbook does not advocate concentration on literature at the expense of writing, speaking, or the other arts and skills of language; nor does it suggest that you, the teacher, somehow find more time in the school day for teaching literature. The uses of literature suggested here are not meant to be *instead of* or *in addition to* anything; they represent pleasant and illuminating approaches to instruction in all aspects of language arts.

The language arts are most successful if they are taught in a unified program, not as separate subjects that are unrelated to each other. It has been my experience that good books, stories, and poems provide easy and effective access to all the language arts and that their use for this purpose highlights the essential unity of the subject. Literature (as I recommend that it be used in the classroom) is not only a way into the various language arts, but a way of connecting them as well.

Each selection suggested in this textbook was chosen because of its literary merit and because it can be used to develop a specific skill needed by elementary school children. (Many selections could be used to develop quite different skills. Sometimes this multiple use is specifically suggested; at other times connections will occur to you that will lead to new combinations of readings and skills.) The selection leads naturally to discussion and, from there, to activities that are appropriate to the relevant skill. Activities that kindle children's imaginations can be developed further with additional related activities. Those that awaken little interest in a particular group can be passed over quickly. You will find a variety of activities suggested, since not every one will appeal to every child.

Because children have different interests and different levels of competence, a wide range of selections has been suggested so that you can pick and choose to fit your own needs. Many of the recommended selections are appropriate for all age levels of elementary children. When level is important, an indication has been given. In general, however, I agree with C. S. Lewis "that the neat sorting out of books into age groups, so dear to publishers, has only a very sketchy relation with the habits of any real readers."* You are the best judge of what will work with your pupils, and you should be able to find suggestions here that will suit your needs. Whatever the ability level of your children, read aloud as much as you can. This gives children pleasure and avoids problems that might otherwise arise with poorer readers.

To repeat, the many suggested selections and activities are intended to give you choices; they are not meant as a body of material to be covered. It is far

---

*Footnote references for each chapter are located at the end of the book in the section, "References."

better to go slowly and respond to the reactions of your children. If you listen to them, you will know when to repeat, when to expand on an activity, and when to move on.

How suitable is this approach for children who are culturally different? In my view, all children can benefit from working with the materials and activities suggested here. Certainly all children need to find pleasure in learning, to develop a good opinion of themselves, and to experience success as often as possible. When differences in language or background raise obstacles to the fulfillment of these needs, an approach that puts a premium on their satisfaction is especially appropriate. Moreover, the special emphasis on literature can be of particular benefit to culturally different children. The ways and values of a culture are transmitted through its literature, not just from one generation to another within that culture, but from one culture to another. The broad objectives of this approach to language arts can be outlined as follows:

1. Making the learning of language arts skills a pleasurable experience.
2. Structuring the language arts experiences to help each child succeed.
3. Insuring that each child has ample opportunities for the expressive (output) phases of language, as well as the impressive (input) phases.
4. Engaging each child actively in the learning and language process.
5. Providing ideas for integrating the language arts as opposed to the more traditional practice of isolating each separate area of the language arts. To achieve this, trade books and other literary materials will serve as the prime catalyst to bring all the language arts skills together.

The purposes of this textbook, like the aspects of language arts that they reflect, are so intimately related that they can be treated in different combinations than those that I have chosen. Loving books and reading, reading and writing, writing and using the senses, sense impressions and writing and appreciating poetry—all flow into each other, and all are related to self-concept. I hope, as you read, that you will find that many ideas reach across the chapter boundaries and mingle to form the substance for a truly unified language arts program.

This is a new book only in an unimportant sense. I like to think of it as a "used" book. The ideas it contains have been used in working with elementary pupils of all backgrounds and abilities and in teaching prospective teachers at various colleges and universities throughout the country. Teachers have used these ideas in their classrooms, adding to them or adapting them to suit their pupils' needs. I hope you will try them also, giving them a rich and personal application of your own.

A. Barbara Pilon

Contents

125114

Come as You Are

What you believe, bring with you
    as you come.
If you have doubts, bring them with you also.
Come as you are, as inescapably you must come,
    if you would be yourself.
Of others, ask no more—or less.
Let us be what we are as best we can.
No one is perfect.
No one is better or worse than another,
For no one has lived the life of the other.
All are seekers, no matter how much they have found.
All are in need, no matter how much they resent it.
All are proud, no matter how humble they wish they were.
Let beliefs, doubts, shame, pride, humility, and the
    inescapability of self sit side by side in mutual
    and self-respect
Until there comes the feeling that,
    in depth of understanding and of feeling,
WE ARE ONE.

–Reverend J. Donald Johnston

1
Motivating Children to Love Reading

I have learned. . .that the head
does not hear anything until the
heart has listened. . . .
—James Stephens, *The Crock of
Gold*

Before we can use literature to unify and enliven language arts teaching, we must pose and answer a number of important questions. What makes a book good for children? Is there any one book that all children should read? What needs of children can literature satisfy? Are these needs the same as, or different from, the needs of adults? What can you, as the teacher, do to motivate children to love good books? The answers to these questions are most useful when presented in detail; therefore we will be returning to some of these questions throughout the textbook. However, these questions are so central to our purposes that we must seek at least preliminary answers now that can be refined or elaborated later on.

1. WHAT IS A GOOD BOOK FOR CHILDREN?

As Stephens' quotation suggests, the way to a child's head is through his or her heart. There are various routes that you can choose in making this journey of mutual discovery; the most direct and promising routes involve engaging children with books that they can enjoy and experience to the fullest. A good book for a particular child is one that he or she feels comfortable with. It is one in which the child can wiggle around, stretch, and grow. It offers, paradoxically, the possibility of forgetting personal problems and, at the same time, fulfilling private needs—needs for beauty, fun, security, and knowledge.

What's It About?

As Jean Karl observes in *From Childhood to Childhood: Children's Books and Their Creators,* "children are interested in as many subjects as adults, perhaps more."[1] (A moment's reflection on the importance of *why* in the child's vocabulary bears out this observation.) There is a *why* for most subjects and there are good books that have the answers for them. Often, one child can guide another to the answer to his or her question—or to a wholly new question that is just as interesting. By encouraging children to talk spontaneously and informally about their hobbies and interests, you can make use of each child's expertise—often quite considerable—to answer some *whys* and to generate some new ones.

Nancy Larrick[2] has some excellent suggestions as to ways of asking questions that will elicit children's interests, likes, and dislikes. You can also get much useful information by asking your pupils to complete open-ended sentences such as:

1. I love to read about. . . .
2. I am happy when. . . .
3. I like to. . . .
4. When I grow up, I want to be. . . .
5. I worry about. . . .
6. Wouldn't it be fun if. . . ?

Asking pupils to hand in a short list of "things I'd like to know about" will supply additional topics about which pupils are curious; when the lists are

discussed and compared, some common interests will be revealed. Finally, you might try reading Annette Wynne's "I Keep Three Wishes Ready" to your class and asking your pupils to tell—publicly or privately—what their wishes are.

I KEEP THREE WISHES READY

I keep three wishes ready,
Lest I should chance to meet,
Any day a fairy
Coming down the street.

I'd hate to have to stammer,
Or have to think them out,
For it's very hard to think things up
When a fairy is about.

And I'd hate to lose my wishes,
For fairies fly away,
And perhaps I'd never have a chance
On any other day.

So I keep three wishes ready,
Lest I should chance to meet,
Any day a fairy
Coming down the street.

—Annette Wynne

Vicarious Experience

Good books offer children the chance to live vicariously—to experience, understand, and sympathize with things to which they have never been, and may never be, exposed. The importance of extending and enriching children's lives vicariously can hardly be overestimated. The words that children learn during their earliest years are mainly related to their own firsthand experience; poems, stories, and book illustrations offer opportunities for enlarging their store of words and ideas. In dealing with the unfamiliar, children learn to draw on their own experience, using the familiar to help them to comprehend the new. Vicarious experience through books also enables children to sample lives whose quality and rhythms are very different from their own. The child whose living space is bounded by tenements and city streets can, in imagination, experience forests, fields, and country streams; the child who lives in a suburb or small town can gain a clearer understanding of what life in the city is like; all children can learn about and sympathize with the sometimes very different lives of children in other lands.

Illustrations

In the beginning of *Alice in Wonderland,* Alice wonders "What is the use of a book. . .without pictures or conversations?" Most children agree with Alice, at least as far as the pictures are concerned. Happily, there is a wealth of beautifully illustrated books with which children can satisfy this appetite.

Good illustrations are especially important for younger children and for children who are experiencing difficulties with reading. Such children are limited in the amount of information they can get from words alone, but they are able to take in and enjoy complex visual messages from pictures. A book need not be mainly a picture book in order for its illustrations to have an important role in carrying the story along.

The styles of book illustrators vary so widely that it is not possible to list criteria here that would be useful in judging their work. (However, you probably will find Patricia Cianciola's *Illustrations in Children's Books,* Second Edition, Dubuque, Iowa: William C. Brown Publishers, 1976, a very valuable source book to help you in this area.) In addition to the pleasing arrangement of color and design that an illustration for any audience might be expected to have, an illustration in a book for children should take into account the fresh and uninhibited way in which the child views the world.

Another consideration to ponder in evaluating illustrations is appropriateness to content. The child who is reading a fairy tale does not expect the characters to look like the people next door. Inconsistencies, although minor, can be distracting or upsetting to readers. For instance, the fairy tale "The Magic Fishbone" begins by mentioning that the king and queen have nineteen children. The first illustration, which appears to show all of the children, encourages young readers to count them. Alas, some of the princes and princesses are unaccountably missing.

Is It the Right Book, Right Now?

Some books are "ageless"—capable of being enjoyed by older children as well as younger ones. (Ruth Krauss's *A Hole is to Dig* is a good example.) But there are good books that a particular child may not be intellectually, emotionally, or socially ready for. As a teacher, you must guard against presenting a good book too soon. Consider, for instance, the case of Mary, an excellent reader in the third grade. Mary's mother suggested to her that she read *Caddie Woodlawn* by Brink. This book is written on a fifth- to sixth-grade reading level. Later, when Mary was asked how she and Caddie were

getting along, she replied apathetically, "Oh, I've got about sixty-two more pages to go."

Her answer was both revealing and sad. Surely, she will never look back to the book, *Caddie Woodlawn* and sigh (except, perhaps, for a sigh of relief). Certainly, Mary will not return to *Caddie Woodlawn* when she is older; when she was there the first time there was no delight, no fun, no shivers. No one goes back willingly to something that has held no joy.

Although you, as their teacher, can help children to find the right books, remember that they can often make good choices on their own, in the library or elsewhere. If a book is too difficult or fails to hold their interest, they put it down and find another. The ones that they can read and like, they relish. Perhaps the most important help you can give them is to increase the number of chances they have to make such choices.

2. WHAT YOU CAN DO

In order to start children off on a lifelong love affair with books, you must love books yourself, and you must be able to "sell" books to your pupils. This means, first, that books should be accessible and highly visible in the classroom—not boxed in or hidden away on dusty shelves. A policy of "look but don't touch" may preserve bindings, but it does little to encourage reading. Best-loved toys do not look new for long. It should be the same with books. Pack into your classroom as many books as you can—books standing on ledges or lying on tables, wherever they can be readily seen and sampled.

Book Jacket Displays

Publishers count on book jackets to attract readers, and you will find it worthwhile to follow their example. Most book jackets are visually appealing and can tempt a child to dip into a book, especially if the book itself is nearby waiting to be picked up. Many teachers ask their local or school librarians to save book jackets for them. Try this and you will soon have a handsome collection. The usefulness of the jackets can be further enhanced by supplying intriguing captions, descriptive phrases, or brief quotations to pique children's curiosity. You may also wish to designate a particular bulletin board for special displays that feature new books or books on subjects of special interest.

Help from Various Media

Much has been made of television as a rival of books. We should not overlook the fact that some television programs may entice chilren to read.

In addition to encouraging children to watch specific television programs (why not appoint a different child each week to be responsible for reporting to the class some programs that the children would not want to miss?), do not overlook the help and stimulation that commercially made materials can give you in motivating your youngsters to read. For example, Miller-Brody Productions, Inc., (342 Madison Avenue, New York, New York 10017) has records, sound filmstrips, and cassettes available of Newbery Award-winning books. Any of these may be purchased in a set or separately. For further information, write to Newbery Award Records, Inc. at 342 Madison Avenue, New York, New York 10017. If you would like information about starting a Newbery Award Record club for your students, they will send you the details.

Scholastic Book Services puts out record and book companion series. They are inexpensive and of excellent quality. Write to Scholastic Book Services for a free "Readers' Choice" catalogue. The address is 904 Sylvan Avenue, Englewood Cliffs, N.J. 07632.

Books in the Classroom

The importance of making books accessible cannot be overstated. You have probably had the experience of wanting to read a particular book, only to have your interest dwindle because you had difficulty in obtaining a copy. Obviously, there are limits to the number of books you can make a permanent part of your classroom library. But other resources are available. If you have a librarian in your school, you have a great potential ally. You can probably arrange to have a carton of books for use in your room for a month or so, which you can then exchange for another. If you do not have a school library, you may be able to work out a similar arrangement with a public library.

Paperback Book Clubs

In addition to providing a wide selection of good books at reasonable prices, paperback book clubs often have generous bonus plans, which provide another way of expanding your classroom library. (If you have enough paperbacks in your library, you may wish to encourage children to bring in a paperback of their own to exchange for one that has been in the classroom for a while.)

A word of caution is in order here regarding the so-called "Great Books" clubs; the selections offered are often inappropriate for the intended audience, and the accompanying apparatus is lethal to reading pleasure. (One such club offered Marc Connelly's Green Pastures at the fifth-grade level and suggested that it be read at least three times before being discussed!)

Book clubs can be wonderful resources for the teacher, but it is important to know what they are offering and whether or not the selections offered fit the needs of your pupils.

Library Trips

No matter how successful you are in building a classroom library, you will not, of course, be able to match the resources of a good public or school library. A trip to the library makes a valuable and enjoyable school excursion, particularly if you arrange in advance for the children's librarian to conduct a story hour for your pupils. (Many libraries offer such story hours as a regular feature. If yours does, you will want your pupils to know when and where they take place.) Encourage children who do not already have library cards to get them. It is a good idea to send parents a note pointing out the value of the child's having a library card, well in advance of the excursion.

THE FAMILY CIRCUS   **By Bil Keane**

"Daddy does that 'Fe, Fi, Fo, Fum' part better."

THE FAMILY CIRCUS, by Bill Keane, reprinted courtesy The Register and Tribune Syndicate, Inc.

3. STORYTELLING AND READING ALOUD

Book jacket displays and other promotional ideas may arouse a child's interest, and having the book readily available may capitalize on that interest. But the most direct way of involving children with books has so far only been implied. As much as possible, you should read aloud to your pupils or tell them stories. One well-known educator has observed that if parents read to their children more at an early age, they would be less concerned about their reading progress in school. If children from middle-class families are not read to enough, there are obviously other children who are not read to at all. All children share the need and desire to hear good books read well. The values of storytelling and reading to children are obvious and well known. However, they are so important that they should be stated explicitly.

First, children get the chance to hear their teacher's handling of the best that the English language has to offer. They learn that expression is that extra something that makes words capable of singing, snarling, running, crawling, sleeping, and leaping. The children then are not afraid to use good expression in their own reading. They have a good model before them continually.

They learn the delight that can be derived from deciphering all of those black symbols on the white paper. The decoding of these symbols gives them the magical key to the land of anyone, anytime, anywhere. They become eager to master the mysteries of these symbols so that they can read stories like the ones presented for themselves and when *they* want to.

There is the old debate of which comes first—interest or knowledge. Teachers who read to children soon discover that the two elements are tied together. By reading to children it is inevitable that interest will follow knowledge and that knowledge will follow interest. This will happen not only to the pupils but also to the teacher.

By being exposed to good literature, children's vocabularies and comprehension expand and take wing. The stories give them ideas for their own writings. Their imagination becomes stimulated and exercised.

Children's attitudes toward books and reading become firmly positive. The teacher has more rewards than those already mentioned. These is nothing quite so nice as when a child comes to her teacher and says, "Do you remember in *Twenty and Ten* when the Nazis questioned the French children about the Jewish children, and Sister Gabriel was in prison? Wasn't that scary?" Of course the teacher remembers and, for a moment, teacher and pupil share a moving recollection.

Who knows how many other wonderful things children are learning through being exposed to the best in literature for children? Perhaps they are learning the most important things anyone can teach—a love of life and beauty, a respect for all living creatures, and an admiration for the little engine who said, "I think I can—I think I can—I think I can," and discovered that he could, he could, he could![3]

Perhaps they may come to understand that other people have problems similar to those that they face. More important, they may realize that they can do something constructive about those problems. Thoreau once remarked that "to affect the quality of a day for others is one of the greatest of all arts." You can affect the quality of your pupils' days by giving time each day to the best in children's literature.

Storytelling

Everyone loves to hear a story—children most of all. From the earliest times, much of society's accumulated wisdom has been passed from one generation to the next through stories. Even today, although storytelling is unfortunately becoming less common in the home, some children are lucky enough to hear folk tales and personal anecdotes from grandparents. Anyone who has had the experience knows the warmth of such sharing.

As a teacher, you are in an excellent position to satisfy your pupils' appetite for stories. A fixed storytelling time is a popular feature in many elementary classrooms, but having established such a time should not prevent you from telling a story that is appropriate to whatever the class is reading or talking about. The spontaneous introduction of a story is one of the endearing traits of the true storyteller. Having a story ready for many different occasions calls, of course, for a good *repertoire*, but you will be surprised how quickly you develop one when you get into the storytelling habit. You will find a wealth of good suggestions in Ruth Sawyer's *The Way of the Storyteller*.[4]

There are a few things to remember in telling stories. When your source is a written story, it is usually enough to have a clear idea of the plot and the main features of the characterization. Whenever possible, use the writer's words for important characters and events. Make sure that you do not substitute inferior or inappropriate words for the words that the author has used. If you are telling a story about a giant, for example, do not refer to him as a "huge man," or even a "gigantic man." Do not say "tiny man" if what you really mean is an elf, or a gnome, or a dwarf. If the story is a fanciful one that takes place over the rainbow, behind the sun, and beyond the stars, it might begin with the beloved, familiar words, "Once upon a time," and not the words that predict a Washington Street, Main Street, or Walnut Street setting that might begin more realistically—"A long, long time ago, long before you were born. . . ." If it is a story such as those told by Kipling, do not try to tell it; read it. In all likelihood you will not be able to tell the story using your own words without losing the flavor that Kipling has so ably given it. Incidentally, stories like "The Cat That Walked by Himself" should be listened to first, like poetry, instead of being read first, even by children in the upper grades. Teachers should remember to read stories like these enough times so that when they are presented they can maintain eye contact and can read them expressively.

Reading Aloud

There are some who believe that once children can read for themselves, they no longer need to be read to. This notion would be silly if it were not so sad. The younger the child, the more occasions there should be for listening to stories and poems. But no one is ever too old to be read to. In the lower grades particularly, children should be encouraged to chime in on repetitive phrases in poems and stories; teachers should make sure that the pupils' favorites are "sung" to them periodically. Never take listening time away from your pupils as a punishment. Instead, provide more listening time as a reward. Of course, if the listening is to be really rewarding, you will have to read as well as you can. This does not mean that you have to try to match the accomplishments of the trained voices available on recordings, although you can always pick up a few pointers from them. But familiarity with the book, a little practice in reading aloud, and enthusiasm go a long way to make reading attractive. One good rule is never to read anything to children that you have not read before. Another rule is never to read anything you really do not like. Observing these two precepts will help you to avoid many pitfalls.

Teachers should try to memorize poems themselves so that they do not have to rush to a book when the first snowflakes sift down, or when the rain pounds angrily on the roof. Having a few poems in your head will help to convince your pupils that literature really matters to you.

In addition to reading regularly, make it a habit to announce what you will be reading the next day. You may find that this "sneak preview" technique has an amazingly good effect on reducing absences.

Reading Excerpts

Everyone knows the saying about leading a horse to water. If your objective is to make the horse drink, you have to make him thirsty. A good way to make children thirsty for a particular book is to read an excerpt that will give them the flavor and make them want to try some more. In general, it is a good idea to choose as excerpts chapters that are self-contained and satisfying in themselves. Chapters from the following books, for example, satisfy this requirement:

1. *Henry Huggins* by Beverly Cleary.
2. *The Saturdays* by Elizabeth Enright.
3. *The Peterkin Papers* by Lucretia P. Hale.

4. *Eddie's Pay Dirt* by Carolyn Haywood.
5. *Homer Price* by Robert McCloskey.
6. *More Homer Price* by Robert McCloskey (from *Centerburg Tales* by McCloskey, published by Scholastic Book Services, New York).
7. *Encyclopedia Brown: Boy Detective* by Donald J. Sobol.

In choosing a book to introduce in this way, you will want to consider both the availability of the whole book and the possibility that at least some of your students may not be able to read it easily. If you have picked a good story, be prepared to meet a considerable demand for the book. If you stimulate interest in children who may have difficulty in reading the selection, consider the suggestions in the following section.

Recorded Readings

Children love to hear their favorite stories and poems over and over again. To some extent, you will be able to indulge this taste by reading aloud; but you will also want to make provision for children to hear favorite selections over and over again on their own. For this purpose a tape recorder, which can be a lap surrogate for any age, is a boon. A number of companies offer professionally recorded materials that you might use. You can also record a chapter or two of a book yourself or ask some of your better readers to practice and then record a selection. (It is a good idea to have all of your students—good readers and not so good—practice and record readings of stories for children in lower grades.)

No matter whose voice is on the tape—a professional's, yours, or one of your pupil's—a recording provides an easy way to indulge a good reader's appetite for repetition and, even more important, a good way to help the child with reading difficulties. Reading along with a "voice over" helps with decoding problems and builds confidence. At least some of the excerpts you read to your classes should have recorded "next episodes" that your pupils can listen to.

MISS PEACH   By Mell Lazarus

YOUR UNCLE JUST GOT A NEW JOB, IRA?

YES, MISS PEACH. HE'S VERY SMART, AND THEY ALLOWED HIM TO NAME HIS OWN SALARY AND PICK HIS OWN HOURS AND TITLE...

ARTHUR, WILL YOU EVER BE SMART ENOUGH TO GET THAT KIND OF JOB OFFER?

SURE. AND I'D PICK A SALARY OF $50,000 A YEAR, MY HOURS WOULD BE 10 TO 3, AND MY TITLE WOULD BE "A TALE OF TWO CITIES."

4. TALKING ABOUT BOOKS

The books you and your pupils read will suggest activities that will involve your class with books. Ideas will stream from the books themselves, as well as from the children. Of these, no activity could be more natural than having children share their books. They like to talk over favorite books with their friends, just as adults do. But when children share their books, they should be permitted to do so informally. You may wish to have oral book reports from time to time, but you will want to be careful that the reports do not become long, boring, and mechanical. You should not take it to be a commandment that book reports have to be given on Friday afternoons.

Sharing Books

There are a number of varied and delightful ways in which children can share books with you and with others. You will find a wealth of suggested sharing activities in Larrick,[5] Huck,[6] and Yenson.[7] Another source you will find helpful is the paperback *100 Novel Ways with Book Reports* by Isabelle M. Decker (Citation Press, 1969).

Children whom I have worked with have come up with delightful and original ways to introduce books to other children. Their ideas gave joy to the children who were the "guests," and the children who were responsible for the innovative presentations also gained joy and a richer appreciation of the books they were introducing. One idea the children thought of was to have a wagon procession where children working individually or in small groups made stage settings in their wagons about a favorite book. They went to various rooms in their school with their wagons and gave "teasers" about the book they enjoyed. The displays were colorful and the presentations were impressive. Two sixth-grade girls decided to put on a puppet play of "The Owl and the Pussycat" by Edward Lear. They made their own stage, puppets, and costumes, and created their own dialogue. They put on their show for our literature and creative writing class and then decided to show their play to some children in third- and fourth-grade classes. All of the children who watched the play sat spellbound and were enthusiastic in their response to the girls' efforts. A whole group of children from the intermediate grades decided to put on individual skits and monologues for the school about their favorite storybook characters. Again, they made their costumes, created their own dialogue, and practiced on their lunch hour instead of going out to recess—a voluntary decision. They decided that they did not want to waste their literature class time practicing for any skit. They put on so many presentations during that school year and the next one that few ever did get out at noontime—but that was their decision. I decided, too, that I would rather spend my time with them than have my "recess." I will never forget one girl, Susan Hill, a sixth grader, who BECAME Pippi Longstocking. She was magnificent! When she was in college, I received a letter from her—we had kept in touch through the years. She asked me if I remembered the book, *Pippi Longstocking*. Susan told me she had just introduced it to her college roommate. I guess I was not the only one who did not forget Pippi. I wonder for how many children Pippi came to life because of Susan's love for her.

Books and Authors

Your children also will be interested in finding out how books come to be written. *Books* by Murray McCain and John Alcorn (Simon and Schuster, 1962) tells children about books in a highly readable and enjoyable way. Another resource is the series of books about books by Elizabeth Rider Montgomery: *The Story Behind Great Books, The Story Behind Great Stories,* and *The Story Behind Modern Books.*

A book of readings that contains some fascinating information on authors and excellent articles on children's literature in general is *Only Connect: Readings on Children's Literature.*[8] *Books Are by People*[9] by Lee Bennett Hopkins contains warm and interesting facts about 104 contemporary authors and illustrators of young people's books. This book should dispel some children's notions that writers go beyond the pale of human possibilities and that they are only paper creatures who turn up in places such as book spines, the title pages of books, and book blurbs. Hopkins' book includes a picture of each of the authors and illustrators discussed. Hopkins has written a sequel to this book—*More Books by More People* (New York, Citation Press, 1974). The periodicals *Language Arts* and *The Horn Book Magazine* also often carry insightful and entertaining articles about the works and lives of children's favorite authors.

You may wish to read a few books or poems by a particular author to the class and then make other works of the author available for children to look at and read. In this way, pupils will become acquainted with the styles and interests of various writers and illustrators. Be sure that you do not neglect humorous poems and stories by writers such as Dr. Seuss, Laura E. Richards, Jack Kent, Edward Lear, John Ciardi, Carl Withers, Lucia and James L. Hymes, and Ogden Nash, so that the children can see the fun of experimenting with words. One gifted boy, a former pupil of mine, after having been exposed to Nash and the limerick form, came up with this limerick about himself. He employed the same freedom that Nash displays in coining new words.

There once was a boy named Jim
Who found himself out on a limb
   Though he wanted to diet
   He'd much rather pie-it
So he wasn't exceedingly slim

—James

Jim's poem is but one example of the happy results that come from giving children good literature. There are really no limits to what children can do. We must be careful not to set limits for them.

5. TIPS FOR TEACHERS

In order to succeed in getting children to love books, you first must know and present children's books well. No reading list can be a substitute for a good, firsthand knowledge of the books themselves, especially if you want children to discuss books *with* you, not *for* you. Children are not slow to detect the fact that a teacher has not read the "wonderful" book that he or she has recommended. Knowing books well enables you to guide individuals to the books that are right for them and to establish a satisfying rapport when they are ready to discuss what they have chosen. You will also have to be resourceful in finding new and interesting ways to extend your pupils' experience with books. You will, of course, have to find out for yourself what approaches work best for you. However, the following suggestions may be helpful in taking some of the error out of what is necessarily a trial-and-error procedure.

Acting It Out

Children spend a lot of time at home and in the school yard in dramatic play. You can put this creative energy to work in the classroom as a natural follow-up to reading aloud, independent reading, or book sharing. Children should be encouraged to act out stories, episodes from stories, poems, or even words and phrases that they like. For younger children, you may wish to focus on more or less spontaneous acting out of stories or scenes that have well-defined plots and action. Older children will enjoy more playlike dramatizations involving simple settings and dialogue. You may also wish to experiment with pantomime and shadow plays. Shy pupils find it easier to get into dramatic activities when they are able to act without speaking. A valuable resource for drama is a collection of miscellaneous clothing and odds and ends that can serve as costumes and props. Pupils can add to this store with articles that they bring in or make themselves.

You will find many creative ideas and suggestions in G. B. Siks' *Creative Dramatics: An Art for Children*,[10] which will help you to turn your classroom into a place where drama happens. Another fine book with many excellent suggestions is John W. Stewig's *Spontaneous Drama: A Language Art* (Charles E. Merrill Publishing Company, Columbus, Ohio, 1973).

Contests and Awards

You can stimulate interest in books by suggesting that your class award its own Caldecott or Newbery prizes. As pupils give reasons why their favorites should be chosen, you will get some lively discussion and active sharing of books. A by-product of such a contest might be a list of suggested books "Too Good to Miss," which could be distributed to pupils in other rooms for vacation reading. There are, of course, contests and contests. You will want to avoid competitions that put undue emphasis on the number of books read. If children are to read for pleasure and enjoyment, reading a book should be its own reward, not a means of scoring points or collecting gold stars.

If You Want to Know How It Ends . . .

The reading of excerpts, discussed earlier in this chapter, is an obvious way of getting children interested in new books. However, before you say, after completing an exciting passage, "If you want to know how this story ends, you can find it at the library," you will want to be sure that they can, indeed, find it there. If the book you have excited your children about is a new one, perhaps the library does not have a copy. If it is a very popular book, what is the chance of the book being in the library when the children go to get it? No matter how popular a book is, no library is going to have enough copies for each of your children who descend en masse to get the book for themselves. What about children who cannot get to the library or who are not allowed to have a library card or who are not capable of reading the story by themselves? These are all questions that deserve our serious consideration. If a teacher uses this device, maybe the first time quite a few of his or her pupils would try hard to get a copy of the book but, after they have learned that the odds are overwhelmingly against them, they would not be apt to try again. I used this technique with graduate students to put them in the position of elementary pupils—to let them see what it felt like to have this trick played on them. I read them almost the entire book of Tops and Bottoms by Lesley Conger[11] and, when I reached the most critical point, I left them hanging. They were very upset. One teacher tried at three libraries to get the book and then gave up. Another teacher told me she could remember having teachers who used this method to get children to read books, and all of her classmates hated it. Of course, at our next meeting, I finished the story and we were satisfied.

You May Not Read . . .

A neighbor of mine once told me that her daughter, a fifth grader, was receiving terrible reading reports because she loved horse stories and wanted to read nothing else. I could see nothing wrong with reading horse books, and I have known many children of this age who have developed a passion for reading horse books. They adore everything Marguerite Henry has ever written. They read every horse book they can get their hands on, and they do not want to take their eyes away until every last word has been devoured and savored. Wonderful! However, since I did not want my friend to get into any more trouble, I suggested to her that she read Kate Seredy's *The Good Master*. The heroine in *The Good Master* was a girl quite like Sally. Additionally, there was a most exciting horse episode in the book that I thought would appeal to Sally. Later, she told me that *The Good Master* was the best book she had ever read.

Any teacher can widen the interests of a child by knowing books, knowing children, and reading books to children. How, for example, would children ever know how delicious Jamocha Almond Fudge ice cream is unless you introduce it to them? Some of your pupils might hate Jamocha Almond Fudge ice cream, but you as a teacher should know about other flavors that a child might enjoy. If one does not work, try another.

Parodies

You and your children can have a fine time with parodies of Mother Goose rhymes and other familiar poems and story ideas. In addition to its entertainment value, parody writing can be a good developer of imagination and creativity. Consider, for example, these two parodies of Little Miss Muffet, which were written by children.

Little Miss Muffet
Sat on a tuffet
Eating her curds and whey
Along came a spider
And sat down beside her
And said, "Is this seat taken?"

Little Miss Muffet
Sat on a tuffet
Eating her curves away!

Picture taken by Dr. Bob Stewart.

6. AFTERWORD

In our concern for making literature an important part of the language arts curriculum, we must not forget that a book can and often should be read just for the fun of it. Not every reading should result in a book report or diorama. Long, drawn-out discussion and analysis should not be the inevitable outcome of finishing a book. Children should be given opportunities when hearing stories to share their laughter, smile knowingly, and sometimes sigh.

What more could a teacher want? Some do, of course, want more, and they ask children to give the reasons they enjoyed a story. Such teachers can profit from Dickens' tale "The Magic Fishbone," in which the fairy Grandmarina stamps her foot and says to the king: "The reason for this, and the reason for that, indeed! You are always wanting the reason. No reason. There! . . . I am sick of your grown-up reasons."

Teachers who know children and remember what it was like to be a child will not fail to see Grandmarina's point.

Helps

Bissett, Donald J., "Literature in the Classroom," Urbana, Ill.: *Elementary English, 50* (5), 729–738, May 1973. Discusses the companies that are publishing children's paperbacks.

The Booklist, available from American Library Association, 50 East Huron Street, Chicago, Ill. 60611. Reviews books, tapes, films, records, multimedia kits, games, and so forth.

Bettelheim, Bruno, *The Uses of Enchantment: The Meaning and Importance of Fairy Tales,* New York: Alfred A. Knopf, 1976. A text for adults describing "the meaning and importance of fairy tales." Discusses how the reading of fairy tales promotes children's imaginative powers.

The Calendar, available from the Children's Book Council, Inc., 67 Irving Place, New York, N.Y. 10003. $5 for a subscription (paid once and only once). Highly recommended. Includes in its issues information on free and inexpensive materials and publications available; gives suggested new books for different months of the year; tells about book awards and prizes; calls to the readers' attention helpful professional books; and keeps the readers tuned in to other valuable book news.

Carmer, Carl, "American Folklore." Free pamphlet reprinted from *Compton's Pictured Encyclopedia,* 1961. F. E. Compton and Company, 1000 North Dearborn Street, Chicago, Ill. 60610.

Carmer, Carl, "A Channel Hopper's Guide to Kid Stuff That's Good," New York: *Saturday Review,* 60(38), 59–60, October 1972.

Chase, Mary Ellen, *Recipe for a Magic Childhood,* New York: The Macmillan Co., 1951. Delightful, slim book that tells the joys Mary Ellen Chase experienced by being fortunate enough to grow up in a house with people who loved books, shared their love, and planted that love deeply in Mary Ellen Chase's mind and spirit.

Cricket: The Magazine for Children, La Salle, Ill.: Open Court Publishing Co.

Darien House, Inc., Planetarium Station, P.O. Box 125, New York, N.Y. 10024 offers contemporary, cheerful children's posters. One offer includes huge, glossy pictures of *Little Red Riding Hood, Hansel and Gretel, Goldilocks,* and *Snow White's Seven Dwarfs.* The four prints in this series are done by Tomi Ungerer, copyright 1968.

Language Arts published September through May by the National Council of Teachers of English, 1111 Kenyon Road, Urbana, Ill. 61801. $20 per year.

Fader, Daniel N., *The Naked Children*, New York: The Macmillan Company, 1971.

Fader, Daniel N., *Hooked on Books*, New York: Berkley Medallion Books, 1976.

Fryatt, Norma R., editor, *A Horn Book Sampler*, Boston: The Horn Book, 1959.

Haviland, Virginia, compiler, *Children and Poetry: A Selective Annotated Bibliography*, Washington, D.C.: The Library of Congress, 1969.

Hazard, Paul, *Books, Children and Men*, translated by Marguerite Mitchell, Boston: The Horn Book, Inc., 1944.

Hopkins, Lee Bennett, *Books Are by People*, New York, Citation Press, 1969.

Hopkins, Lee Bennett, *Let Them Be Themselves*, New York: Citation Press, 1969. Second Edition, 1974.

Hopkins, Lee Bennett, *More Books by More People*, New York, Citation Press, 1974.

The Horn Book Magazine, published six times a year. Subscription prices $10.50 a year. Address: The Horn Book Incorporated, Park Square Building, Boston, Mass., 02116.

Huck, Charlotte S., "Discovering Poetry with Children," Chicago: Scott, Foresman and Company, 1964. Free pamphlet.

Huck, Charlotte S., *Children's Literature in the Elementary School*, Third Edition, New York: Holt, Rinehart and Winston, 1976.

Kennedy, Mary Lou, editor, *Paperbacks in the Elementary School: Their Place, Use and Future*, Middletown, Conn.: Xerox Corporation, 1969.

Landau, Elliott D., *Teaching Children's Literature in Colleges and Universities*, Champaign, Ill.: National Council of Teachers of English, 1968.

Lanes, Selma G., *Down the Rabbit Hole: Adventures and Misadventures in the Realm of Children's Literature*, New York: Atheneum, 1971.

Larrick, Nancy, *A Parent's Guide to Children's Reading*, Garden City, N.Y.: Doubleday and Co., Inc., 1975.

Meeker, Alice M., *Enjoying Literature with Children*, New York: The Odyssey Press, 1969.

Orff, Carl, and Keetman, Gunild, *Music for Children*, Album 3582-B (35650-651), New York: Angel Records, 1958.

Painter, Helen, *Poetry and Children*, Newark, Del.: International Reading Association, 1970.

Rasmussen, Margaret, editor, *Literature with Children*, Washington, D.C.: Association for Childhood Education International, 1961.

Riggs, Corinne W., compiler, *Bibliotherapy: An Annotated Bibliography*, Newark, Del.: International Reading Association, 1971.

Sayers, Francis Clarke, *A Bounty of Books*. Free pamphlet reprinted from *Compton's Pictured Encyclopedia*, 1964. F. E. Compton Co., 1000 N. Dearborn Street, Chicago, Ill. 60610.

Sawyer, Ruth, *The Way of the Storyteller*, New York: The Viking Press, 1962. F. E. Compton and Co. put out a free pamphlet based on Ruth Sawyer's book. Address inquiries to F. E. Compton Co., 1000 N. Dearborn Street, Chicago, Ill. 60610.

Scholastic Wall Charts. Colorful, delightful, large posters depicting children's poems and books. Note in particular Maurice Sendak's *Chicken Soup with Rice* and "Three Poems Poster Package." Write to Scholastic Book Services, 50 W. 44th Street, New York, N.Y. 10036. Other posters available.

Simmons, Beatrice, editor, *Paperback Books for Children,* New York: Citation Press, 1972.

Smith, Dora V., *The Children's Literary Heritage,* Urbana, Ill.: The National Council of Teachers of English, 1964. Pamphlet offered by N.C.T.E. 10 for $2. A $.40 billing charge will be added to orders without remittance.

Top of the News published four times a year by ALA. $15 subscription price, included in membership dues. 50 E. Huron Street, Chicago, Ill. 60611.

Weston Woods, Weston, Conn. Ask to be placed on their mailing list to receive catalogues of their latest sound filmstrips, tape cassettes, records, motion pictures, and book-recording packages. Weston Woods frequently offers quality free materials to teachers. All you need to do is request what they offer when you see it announced in one of their brochures. One fine film that you surely would enjoy seeing is *Libraries Are Kids' Stuff,* one of the films in their excellent "Signature Collection."

Literary Suggestions to Use to Lead Children to Love Reading

Brown, Beatrice Curtis, "Jonathan Bing" in *Jonathan Bing and Other Verses* by Beatrice Curtis Brown, New York: Oxford University Press, 1936.

Ciardi, John, "When I Went to Get a Drink" in *I Met a Man,* Boston: Houghton Mifflin Co., 1961.

Ciardi, John, "What Night Would It Be?" in *You Read to Me, I'll Read to You,* New York: J. B. Lippincott Co., 1962.

Cole, William, editor, drawings by Tomi Ungerer, *Oh, What Nonsense!,* New York: The Viking Press, 1969.

Clymer, Eleanor, editor *Arrow Book of Funny Poems* (selections), New York: Scholastic Book Services, 1961.

Ellentuck, Shan, *The Upside-Down Man,* New York: Doubleday and Co., Inc., 1965.

Farjeon, Eleanor, "Bedtime" in *Over the Garden Wall,* New York: J. B. Lippincott Co., 1933.

Fyleman, Rose, "What They Said," German nursery rhyme translated by Rose Fyleman in *Poems Children Will Sit Still For,* edited by Beatrice Schenk de Regniers, Eva Moore, and Mary Michaels White, New York: Scholastic Book Services, 1969.

Hymes, James L., and Hymes, Lucia, "Hooray for Chocolate," "Warning," "My Favorite Word," "TV," "I Don't Like Don't—I Don't, I Don't" in *Hooray for Chocolate,* New York: William R. Scott, Inc., Publisher, 1960.

Kahl, Virginia, *The Duchess Bakes a Cake,* New York: Charles Scribner's Sons, 1955.

Kahl, Virginia, *The Perfect Pancake,* New York: Charles Scribner's Sons, 1960.

Keller, Charles, compiler, *Going Bananas,* Englewood Cliffs, N.J.: Prentice-Hall, Inc., 1975.

Keller, Charles, and Baker, Richard, *The Star-Spangled Banana,* Englewood Cliffs, N.J.: Prentice-Hall, Inc., 1974.

Kent, Jack, *Clotilda,* New York: Random House, 1969.

Lewis, C.S., *The Lion, the Witch and the Wardrobe,* New York: The Macmillan Co., 1950.

McCain, Murray, drawings by John Alcorn, *Books,* New York: Simon and Schuster, 1962.

McCloskey, Robert, *Burt Dow: Deep-Water Man,* New York: The Viking Press, 1963.

McCord, David, "Jamboree" in *All Day Long,* 1966, appears in *Poems Children Will Sit Still For,* edited by Beatrice Schenk de Regniers, Eva Moore, Mary Michaels White, New York: Scholastic Book Services, 1969.

McGinley, Phyllis, *Boys Are Awful,* New York: Franklin Watts, Inc., 1962.

Masefield, John, "Sea-Fever" in *Story of a Round House,* New York: The Macmillan Co., 1940.

Merriam, Eve, "Mean Song" in *There Is No Rhyme for Silver,* New York: Atheneum, 1962.

Moore, Lilian, "Pigeons" in *I Thought I Heard the City,* New York: Atheneum, 1969.

Mosel, Arlene, illustrated by Blair Lent, *Tikki Tikki Tembo,* New York: Holt, Rinehart and Winston, 1968.

Nash, Ogden, "The Panther" in *I'm a Stranger Here Myself,* n.p.: Curtis Publishing Company, 1940.

Nash, Ogden, "The Tale of Custard the Dragon" in *The Face Is Familiar,* Boston: Little, Brown and Co., 1940.

Nash, Ogden, *A Boy Is a Boy,* New York: Franklin Watts, Inc., 1960.

Nash, Ogden, *Girls Are Silly,* New York: Franklin Watts, Inc., 1962.

Richards, Laura E., "Antonio," in "Time for Poetry" in *The Arbuthnot Anthology of Children's Literature,* edited by May Hill Arbuthnot, Glenview, Ill.: Scott, Foresman and Co., 1961.

Richards, Laura E., "Eletelephony" in *Tirra Lirra.* Boston: Little, Brown and Co., 1932.

Silverstein, Shel, *Where the Sidewalk Ends,* New York: Harper and Row, 1974.

Withers, Carl, compiler, "I Scream, You Scream," "Story without End," "Sound and Fury," "Do You Carrot All for Me?" "A Great Big Molicepan," "Smart Alec Oration," in *A Rocket in My Pocket,* New York: Henry Holt and Co., 1948.

2 Not Nobodies But Somebodies

I'm nobody! Who are you?
Are you nobody too?
Then there's a pair of us—don't
   tell!
They'd banish us, you know.
   —Emily Dickinson

There are so many children in our schools today who feel that they are nobodies. We need to start employing more practices that will help children to feel and say, "I'm SOMEBODY, and so are YOU." Positive self-concepts are not attained easily or magically. William Pitt, Earl of Chatham and Prime Minister of England, was correct when he said on January 14, 1776, "Confidence is a plant of slow growth." There are children who go to school day in and day out, year in and year out without ever experiencing success. The published writing of school children all too often echoes the melancholy observation made by Victor Y., a thirteen-year-old boy, from *The Me Nobody Knows:*

> When I first get up in the morning I feel fresh and it seems like it would be a good day to me. But after I get in school, things change and they seem to turn into problems for me. And by the end of the day I don't even feel like I'm young. I feel tired.[1]

One of the chief causes of discipline problems in school and at home is the low regard the children involved have for themselves. They feel that they are failures and that they are disliked because of it. Such children live in a climate of frustration. Their characteristic response to a homework task or a household chore is "I won't" or "I can't." *I won't* is a defense: you can't prove that I can't do what I refuse to do. *I can't* is a plea for help; if no help is offered, it soon becomes "I won't." Then, in frustration and rebellion, children express hostility toward the people who are unwilling or unable to help by resorting to attention-getting devices or—with even more serious consequences—they surrender and passively withdraw into themselves.

Paul Bowman observes that "persons who think negatively of themselves will behave in self-defeating ways."[2] Indeed, for such people, a dire, self-

fulfilling prophecy may be a way of being right: I know in advance I can't do or learn these things; I act accordingly; thus I demonstrate that I was right to hold myself in low regard.

1. PROMOTING POSITIVE SELF-CONCEPTS

Positive self-concepts are not easily attained. What is needed is a change in the way people think about themselves; usually, this involves a patient and systematic campaign to overcome their own estimates of themselves as failures or as worthless persons. A. H. Maslow provides valuable insights into the strategies to be employed in such a campaign by identifying and assigning priorities to basic human needs. He observes that "human needs arrange themselves in hierarchies of prepotency. That is to say, the appearance of one need usually rests on the prior satisfaction of another, more prepotent need."[3] In the order of the prepotency hierarchy, Maslow lists physiological needs, safety needs, love needs, esteem needs, and needs for self-actualization.[4] About self-esteem, Maslow writes that being thwarted leads to a person's feeling weak, inferior, and helpless. If individuals are to attain self-actualization (i.e., if they are to become what they can become), they must have satisfied the needs just mentioned. Maslow observes that "We shall call people who are satisfied in these needs (physiological, safety, love, and esteem) basically satisfied people, and it is from these that we may expect the fullest (and healthiest) creativeness."[5] Unfortunately, according to Maslow, the self-actualized person is all too rarely found in our society.

More concretely, Maslow lists the prerequisites for fulfilling these basic needs: "freedom to speak, freedom to do what one wishes so long as no harm is done to others, freedom to express one's self, freedom to investigate and seek for information, freedom to defend one's self, justice, fairness, honesty, and orderliness in the group."[6] The implications for those who teach or plan to teach are considerable. A poem handed in to his teacher by a Canadian high school student a few weeks before his suicide suggests the tragic consequences of failing to attend to these basic needs.

ABOUT SCHOOL

He always wanted to say things. But no one understood.
He always wanted to explain things. But no one cared.

Sometimes he would just draw and it wasn't anything.
He wanted to carve it in stone or write it in the
sky. He would lie out on the grass and look up in
the sky and it would be only him and the sky and
the things inside that needed saying.

And it was after that, that he drew the picture.
It was a beautiful picture. He kept it under the
pillow and would let no one see it.

And he would look at it every night and think about
it. And when it was dark, and his eyes were closed,
he could still see it.

And it was all of him. And he loved it.

When he started school he brought it with him.
Not to show anyone, but just to have with him like
a friend.

It was funny about school.
He sat in a square, brown desk like all the other
square, brown desks and he thought it should be red.
And his room was a square, brown room. Like all the
other rooms and it was tight and close. And stiff.

He hated to hold the pencil and the chalk, with his
arm stiff and his feet flat on the floor, stiff,
with the teacher watching and watching.
And then he had to write numbers. And they weren't
anything. They were worse than the letters that could
be something if you put them together.

And the numbers were tight and square and he hated
the whole thing.

The teacher came and spoke to him. She told him to
wear a tie like all the other boys. He said he
didn't like them and she said it didn't matter.
After that they drew. And he drew all yellow and it
was the way he felt about morning. And it was
beautiful.

The teacher came and smiled at him. "What's this?" she said. "Why don't you draw something like Ken's drawing? Isn't that beautiful?"
It was all questions.

After that his mother bought him a tie and he always drew airplanes and rocket ships like everyone else. And he threw the old picture away. And when he lay out alone looking at the sky, it was big and blue and all of everything, but he wasn't anymore.

He was square inside and brown, and his hands were stiff, and he was like anyone else. And the thing inside him that needed saying didn't need saying anymore.

It had stopped pushing. It was crushed. Stiff.
Like everything else.
—Anonymous

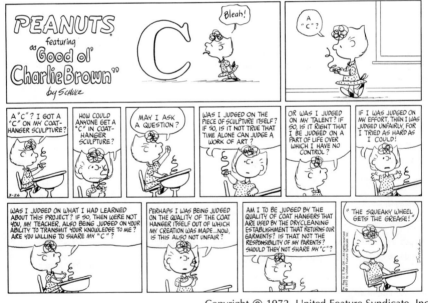

Copyright © 1972, United Feature Syndicate, Inc.

Eliminating Negative Feedback

Most people tend to see themselves as others see them or appear to see them. A derogatory remark overheard, consistent teasing, a sarcastic comment—these and similar instances of negative feedback can leave permanent wounds on the ego. Of course, the damaging news from outside does not have to be so directly stated. If a teacher says to a child who has not given the expected answer, "Obviously you haven't read Chapter Two," every other child in the room shudders empathetically. Maybe they do not have the right answer either, even though they may have read their lesson and done their homework. No one—adult or child—can learn new things without making some mistakes. It is important that learners be able to respond freely without fear of humiliation when their answer happens to be the "wrong" one. A more subtle and quite unconscious kind of negative feedback results from the not uncommon practice of giving a brighter child a longer time to answer a question than is given a slower or average pupil. The teacher is confident that his or her patience will be rewarded by the "right" answer, and often it is. But the message is not lost on the child passed quickly over who, like the third son in fairy tales, is rarely expected to succeed at the task at hand.

If possible, avoid using basal readers or workbooks that clearly indicate with stars or some other device that the material was intended for use at a lower level. Children soon figure out the system and read the message "dummy" all too clearly. It is also a good idea to make sure that children have the capability, the time, the necessary materials, and a suitable place to do homework at home before giving homework assignments.

One day when I was teaching an undergraduate class, I asked my students to try to recall their fondest and their most painful memories of elementary school days. Without exception, the best memories involved the enhancing of self-concepts and the most searing involved humiliation and the damaging of self-regard. Few teachers would consciously set out to undermine any child's self-respect; yet inadvertently we may sometimes confirm pupils' negative judgments about themselves or nip off tendrils of growing confidence.

Making Children Feel Good About Themselves

Children must fulfill their basic needs of worth and self-esteem before they can go on to satisfy their needs for self-actualization. Since we must expect that many children we work with will bring with them self-concepts already badly damaged, it is only reasonable to try to repair this damage. A good way to go about it is to find ways to help children feel good about themselves.

Charles Silberman[7] reports how one second-grade teacher used cameras to make the pupils feel good about themselves. In the room was a huge display that said:

"I'm the best one in the class in buttoning."

THE FAMILY CIRCUS, by Bill Keane, reprinted courtesy The Register and Tribune Syndicate, Inc.

We had our pictures taken by a photographer.
She used a camera.
How do you think you look?

Underneath their pictures the children made comments such as "Pretty," "Nice," and "Handsome." Below the display and the children's comments appeared the question, "Which words describe how we look?" The list included words such as *attractive, lovely, cute,* and *beautiful.* (Of course, the list need not be limited only to physically descriptive words.) This activity not only enhanced the children's self-concepts, but also made them more conscious of descriptive words and synonyms. Besides building egos, it helped to build vocabularies. Obviously, this kind of activity succeeds best if the children are encouraged to make positive statements about themselves. Too many of them, unfortunately, may already have been told that they are fat, ugly, or the like. Allowing them to use words like these in the activity would obviously defeat its main purpose.

To enhance each child's sense of his or her own identity and value, you might set aside a specific coat hook, cubby hole, or chair (whatever is possible) to be labeled with the child's name. Having an object or a place of their very own is extremely satisfying to children. Many children come from

homes where everything must be shared—bedrooms, beds, toys, bookcases, clothes—and for such children having something of their own is especially important. While you are putting names on things, you might try to tell children something about the meaning or origin of their names. Dictionaries and "name-the-baby" books are good resources for most first names, and many surnames mean something in the original language. Often, a member of the child's family may be able to provide interesting information about the meaning or origin of the family name. And do not neglect your own name; pupils will want to know about its meaning, too.

Boosting Birthdays

Everybody's birthday is a special day, and one good way of building egos is to make something of each child's birthday. You might want to try one or more of these ideas for boosting birthdays.

1. *A birthday calendar.* Have children write their names below their birth-dates on a school calendar or on one that they have made themselves. A birthday checker can be assigned the task of making sure that no one's birthday passes unnoticed. Special provisions must be made for children

SUN	MON	TUES	WED	THURS	FRI	SAT
			1 TERRY	2	3	4
5	6 JOSÉ	7	8	9	10	11
12	13 LEE	14 AL	15	16 MARIE	17	18
19	20	21	22	23	24	25 DONALD
26	27 SUE GEORGE	28	29	30		

whose birthdays fall during vacations, on weekends, or on school holidays. If the birthday is only a day or so away from a school day, celebrate it on the nearest possible one. Children whose birthdays fall in the summer should be granted the privilege of the Queen of England and be allowed to choose a suitable day for their birthday celebration.

2. *Celebrating the birthdays.* The main idea is noticing the birthday, and the details of the celebration—as long as they're fun and more or less the same from one birthday to another—are less important. Everyone should sing "Happy Birthday" on each occasion. You might consider designating a birthday chair for the birthday child to sit in. (If you wish, the chair can be decorated to serve for all birthdays or redecorated in a way that is appropriate for each particular child.) You will also want to grant some special privilege to the birthday child—perhaps the right to choose a favorite story or poem to be read to the class. If possible, you might post the child's photograph on a part of the bulletin board reserved for birth-

day use. (If you use the idea of a display of pictures of all children in the class, as suggested on pages 29-30, you can simply hold onto them and use them individually as birthdays come up.)

3. *Stories about birthdays.* You may wish to incorporate in your birthday celebrations at least some of the excellent birthday stories now available in children's books. A list of some good possibilities appears on pages 51-52.

Getting to Know Them

What else can we do to build confidence in our pupils? First, we might recall the words in the lovely Rogers and Hammerstein's song, "Getting to Know You," that Anna, the teacher, sings to her pupils in the play *The King and I.* Then we can follow the direction of the message the words to the song give and see where they can take us. Socrates realized that "One can teach only whom he loves." Our children must realize that we like them and hope that they, in turn, like us. A poem that you could recite to children that would let them know precisely what you think about them is called appropriately, "I Like You As You Are."[8]

I like you as you are, exactly and precisely;
I think you turned out nicely
And I like you as you are.

I like you as you are,
Without a doubt or question;
Or even a suggestion
'Cause I like you as you are.

I like your disposition,
Your facile composition;
And with your kind permission,
I'll shout it to a star.

I like you as you are,
I wouldn't want to change you;
Or even rearrange you, not by far.

I like you, I L-I-K-E - Y-O-U
I like you, Yes, I do,
I like you, Y-O-U.
I like you, like you as you are.

Handling Special Problems

An important part of getting to know children is to understand some of the problems that members of racial or ethnic minorities may face. An excellent resource for any teacher, but an especially valuable one for the white, middle-class teacher who may be unacquainted with some of the problems pupils face, is Charlemae Rollins' *We Build Together*,[9] an annotated bibliography of children's books that deal with the problems black children face. In addition to the stories from this bibliography that you may wish to use in class, there are certain books, such as Mary Hays Weik's *Jazz Man*, (Atheneum, 1966), that you may wish to read yourself to increase your own understanding. (You probably would not want to read *Jazz Man* to a group of children who have problems as overwhelming as Zeke's, the hero of this book.)

A book such as Shirley Burden's *I Wonder Why . . .* might produce some extremely thought-provoking discussions if used with white, middle-class children. The question that is so beautifully and simply illustrated in this book is why some children wouldn't like a child simply because she is black when she has the same loves as all children and all people everywhere.

A Success Story

In his excellent article, "Fostering Creative Behavior,"[10] E. Paul Torrance relates anecdotes that demonstrate how children's achievement in school flourishes when their sense of self-respect is enhanced. One of these stories concerns Maurice, a boy who had reading problems. Maurice's teacher described him in this way.

> Maurice was a large, passionate-eyed, blond who had been retained in third grade because he couldn't read and was thought to be "dull-minded." His interest seemed to be in science and in working with his delicate, sensitive hands. The class decided to make a dinosaur out of *papier-mâché*, so we made a table-sized brontosaurus, then a somewhat larger stegosaurus. Maurice didn't become very involved in either of these two projects. One day he said, "These dinosaurs are pretty good, but if I made one it would be the tyrannosaurus (king)." It then occurred to me that this boy wanted and needed to be leader, so I permitted this production. He worked on it for weeks. (I fought guilt feelings because now he was so absorbed that he didn't want to read at all, but he was involved, really involved, in this tyrannosaurus.) It was a big success—it was so big—8 feet tall, about 2 feet wide. He donated it to my future third graders. Shortly after this, I felt a growing confidence within this boy. His reading progress was a miracle. He lost his fear—and it was a fear that he would never read like the others. Maurice reads far above grade level and does a variety of interesting things.

2. USING LITERATURE TO IMPROVE SELF-CONCEPTS

In his introductory chapter to *Crisis in the Classroom,*[11] Charles E. Silberman observes that "... the false dichotomy between the 'cognitive' and the 'affective' domain ... can only cripple the development of thought and feeling ... poetry, music, painting, dance, and the other arts are not frills to be indulged in if time is left over from the real business of education; they *are* the business of education." Certainly, one important use for literature is the help it can provide in improving the self-concepts of children.

What kinds of books might you read to your children *every day* with the conscious purpose of using them to help to build up (or rebuild) the children's confidence in themselves, as well as to use them to try to increase their achievement motivation? Many fairy tales and folk tales are stocked with just the right elements that may help to do the kind of "magic" that is needed The beloved old stories of "Cinderella," "The Ugly Duckling," "The Little Red Hen," and "The Three Little Pigs" contain all the right ingredients. In these stories the downtrodden, the mistreated, the hardworking, and the persistent heroes and heroines triumph. What a vicarious feeling of success children can experience as they listen to these tales! How it can inspire them to emulate their best-loved story character!

Stories or poems where youngsters can feel superior to the silly characters they hear about can help to make children feel good about themselves. Stories or poems where children can anticipate or predict solutions to problems or questions posed in the storybooks faster than the main character in the books can inflate children's egos quickly.

Stories for older children that show bravery, courage, persistence, and faith in one's own self and one's individualism are plentiful. They can be read chapter by chapter to the class, introduced to the children by reading a few chapters; then the children who want to continue reading the story can be provided with paperback copies of the books. Some books for older children that stress the qualities just referred to are:

1. Claire Hutchet Bishop's *Twenty and Ten* (New York: The Viking Press, 1952).
2. Sheila Burnford's *The Incredible Journey* (Waltham, Ma.: Little, Brown, 1967, also available in a paperback edition by Bantam).
3. Alice Dalgliesh's *The Courage of Sarah Noble* (New York: Scribner, 1954).
4. Véronique Day's *Landslide!* (New York: Dell, 1961).
5. Walter D. Edmond's *The Matchlock Gun* (New York: Dodd, Mead, 1941).

6. Doris Gates's *Blue Willow* (New York: Scholastic Book Services, 1958).
7. Jean Craighead George's *Julie of the Wolves* (New York: Harper and Row, 1972).
8. Irene Hunt's *Across Five Aprils* (a Tempo paperback; New York: Grosset and Dunlap, 1964).
9. Irene Hunt's *Up a Road Slowly* (a Tempo paperback; New York: Grosset and Dunlap, 1968).
10. Madeline L'Engle's *A Wrinkle in Time* (New York: Farrar, Straus, & Giraux, 1962).
11. Marie McSwigan's *Snow Treasure* (New York: Scholastic Book Services, 1958).
12. Scott O'Dell's *Island of the Blue Dolphins* (Boston: Houghton Mifflin, 1960; available in a paperback edition by Dell).
13. Elizabeth Speare's *The Witch of Blackbird Pond* (Boston: Houghton Mifflin, 1958).
14. Armstrong Sperry's *Call It Courage* (New York: Macmillan, 1964; available in a paperback edition).

OUR HEROS AND HEROINES

15. Theodore Taylor's *The Cay* (New York: Doubleday and Co., 1969; available in a paperback edition from Avon Camelot also).
16. Maia Wojciechowska's *Shadow of a Bull* (New York: Atheneum, 1972; also available in paperback).

Additional suggested readings are listed on pages 49-51.

One more idea to try is suggested by a newspaper review of *The Moneymakers: or the Great Big New Rich in America.*[12] Three or four of the thirteen successful men interviewed spontaneously praised the Horatio Alger rags-to-riches stories and deplored the fact that these stories no longer inspired young men as they themselves were inspired. That is an impressive number of endorsements for a series not generally so highly regarded these days. You might try reading to your pupils success stories—stories that compare children's everyday successes to the successes of the story heroes or heroines. A project like this necessarily entails making sure that each pupil *does* succeed at something every day, but continuing success is so essential a factor in building positive self-concepts that you will want to assure such opportunities in any case.

3. REINFORCING POSITIVE SELF-CONCEPTS

All plants require careful nurture—especially plants of slow growth like confidence. Positive self-concepts cannot be developed and then forgotten; they need to be reinforced with daily successes. The ideas in this section are intended to suggest ways in which you can establish a climate of success in your classroom. Obviously, the suggestions do not exhaust the possibilities. But you may find some ideas that will work for you or some suggestions that you can develop in different ways.

Copyright © 1969, United Feature Syndicate, Inc.

Daily Successes

Your classroom provides numerous opportunities for simple tasks that can be easily accomplished and then praised. Children who show an interest can clean erasers, wash boards, sharpen pencils, lower or raise blinds, dust, water plants, collect milk money, and the like. Some children have never received a "perfect" mark in their lives and would like to—this wish is often expressed in the writings of school children. You might try following up a lesson with a reinforcement activity designed so that all can succeed. (If this is not possible, consider whether the children have had enough background or warm-up sessions to enable them to succeed with the assignment.)

Some teachers, even at the college level, tell students they never give 100s. Is it because the way they teach makes it impossible for their students to get 100? Do the professors feel that by giving the grade of 100 it means that the students know as much as they do—and this could never be? If there is such a grade as 100, then it should be possible to receive it. Listening to professors who claim otherwise has always puzzled me and makes me somewhat suspicious of them. If no one can reach a goal, any goal, and this is told to students, what is the point of trying? Psychologically, it is a good way to unmotivate most, if not all, students.

Success Notes Home

In his book *Our Children Are Dying*,[13] Nat Hentoff quotes a kindergarten teacher as saying: "You see five-year-olds already trying to play hooky. And some already tell lies. They take notes home, don't give them to their parents, but say they have. I tell them I don't like children who lie, because if they lie they'll eventually steal." It is my belief that any person who would make such comments has no business teaching! However, as these remarks suggest, even kindergarten children associate notes home with bad news. As an antidote, you might consider writing home occasional notes praising a pupil for a success in school—maybe for showing improvement, making a great effort, or making a special contribution. This kind of reward will be most effective if you write the note right after the success it celebrates has been achieved.

Simple Assignments

Keep your assignments simple—not insultingly simple, just simple enough so that they can be understood and carrried out successfully.

It is important to remember that what may be easy for you to do may be quite difficult, if not impossible, for your students to do. The reverse is just as true. The implication is a simple one. Do not expect children to do what is impossible for them to do. Children need to have pointed out to them that there are some things we can all do well and some things only certain people can do well. If you are not good in art, or music, or sports, tell your children that you are not. Develop a relationship of mutual help and respect in your classes. I know that when I was a reading workshop teacher and, before that, an elementary school teacher, I always did the art lessons with my children when the art supervisor came into the room. My pictures were never as good as my students', but they were displayed right along with all of the children's works. Once when I had to make a snowflake (during my student-teaching days), my children could tell the agony I was going through, so they helped me—and I truly needed it. The help came in a compassionate, generous, and uncondescending way. We should treat children in the same manner.

A book to read to young children in the early primary grades that conveys the idea that some activities are easy for some and difficult for others is Mary McBurney Green's *Is It Hard? Is It Easy?* It is published by Young Scott Books, New York, 1960 copyright.

Bil Keane, in the cartoon on the following page, "The Family Circus," which appeared on March 24, 1970 shows how relative the difficulty of tasks may be, depending on who is being asked to do the task.

If you have forgotten how difficult it is to learn how to read a new language and thus have forgotten what children feel and face in their classes, you could sign up for a crash course in a language you have never had before. I say "crash" because this way all the problems that children meet in reading come racing to crash in on you all at once. A course such as this can very quickly make you commiserate with children and give you an excellent insight into the problems that children may encounter with their language. Of course, this suggestion may prove completely infeasible. A very simple way to put yourself into your students' shoes is to go through as quickly as you can the pamphlet, "A Primer for Parents" by Paul McKee.[14] After reading this pamphlet, you may pledge to yourself that you will never again say to any child, "For heaven's sake, can't you do that? It's easy." Perhaps just reading the previous comment may bring back queasy sensations that you may have felt when a teacher said something along those lines to you or one of your classmates when you were in school.

If you suspect that some task is going to prove difficult for some of your pupils, anticipate their problems and help them to solve them; help them to conquer them. This cannot be done in a "hit and run" type of lesson. It will require time and ingenuity. I am reminded of a Peanuts cartoon that appeared on September 5, 1970.[15] In the cartoon by Schulz, Sally is complaining to Charlie Brown:

"Why do I have to go to school and learn the names of all those rivers? I've never even SEEN a river! They could at least take me to SEE a river."
Charlie Brown replies:

THE FAMILY CIRCUS   By Bil Keane

"Wowee! School was tough today! We tried to learn the first two lines of 'Here Comes Peter Cottontail'."

THE FAMILY CIRCUS, by Bill Keane, reprinted courtesy The Register and Tribune Syndicate, Inc.

"You have a good point there. . . ."

Sally continues her outcry:

"And mountains! I've never seen a mountain! Or a king! Or even a capital city! And we're supposed to know all those borders! I've never SEEN a border!"

Charlie Brown glumly responds:

"This may take more than one field trip to the zoo. . . ."

The Buddy System and Group Responses

You might try allowing children to confer with one or more buddies before having to answer questions, thus taking the pressure off any one child. Buddies can be assigned by drawing matching numbers or by some similar method to change the pairs or groups from day to day. It is often a good idea to give children some choices as to the questions they answer. You might tell two buddies or a team that they can answer one or two of a number of questions. You can then reward children who do more than was asked of them with extra credit.

Everybody Answers

Another idea is to try to get each child, as much as it is possible, to respond individually to every significant question that you pose. Every pupil in a small group might whisper the answer to you and you might make a non-committal comment such as, "Okay, now what do you think, John?" When all the children have given their answers you might say, "The answer (close-ended) was such and such because. . . ." You might explain why other answers that may have been given were not correct. No one in the small group feels bad about not knowing the answer. The children who did get the right answer will be rewarded intrinsically, and the other children will not be humiliated.

The "Pass" System

You can help to reinforce positive self-concepts by using the "pass" system, which permits any child who does not want to answer a particular question to hold up a "pass" card. If you find that many pupils are unwilling to respond, you may want to reconsider or rephrase your question. (Do not hesitate to use a "pass" card yourself from time to time if a pupil asks a question to which you do not know the answer.) The "pass" system is most effective after a bond of mutual trust has been established between you and your pupils. You may want to use some other techniques first.

Simple Lessons

Take pains to keep your lessons simple. When possible, make use of memory aids and dramatic techniques for making a word or idea stick in children's minds. For example, in teaching the names of the Great Lakes, it helps to have pupils remember that the first letters of the lakes spell HOMES. A reading consultant once told me that she remembered a teacher who introduced the word *impaled* by quickly thrusting a pencil through a sheet of paper while saying "Julius Caesar was *impaled*."

Reinforcers

For children who have enjoyed little success in school, tangible rewards offered as soon as something praiseworthy has been achieved can be very effective. (An especially good time to use such a reinforcer is when a pupil has improved on work done previously.) The kinds of reinforcers you use will depend on the age and interests of your class. Pennies, marbles, seashells, chestnuts, pieces of candy or gum—any of a number of small but desirable objects will do. Or you might try preparing a sign that says "Winner" or "Champ" to pin on the successful pupil.

Another kind of reinforcement that is critically important is enabling a child to see his or her progress through charts, graphs, comparison of papers, or tape recordings made at different stages.

A Reinforcement Table

When pupils have learned to delay gratification of their rewards, you might try using a reinforcement table. (The children themselves should have a voice in how long they are willing to delay their reward; with some children, as with some adults, "A bird in the hand is worth two in the bush.") On the table are displayed a number of items in taped paper bags or in wrappings or boxes made of construction paper. Each item is marked with the number of points required to obtain it; the points are won in the same way as the small reinforcement prizes previously mentioned. Children might contribute to the

reinforcement table by bringing in a seashell, a record, toy, book, or something they have created themselves. You will probably want to find other ways of obtaining objects. You might also work out a swap system with other teachers using reinforcement tables, thus making it possible to eliminate duplication or objects inappropriate to the age of your class.

4. AFTERWORD

There are too many children in our schools today who feel like nobodies. We must do everything we can to make all of our pupils feel as good about themselves as the eleven-year-old who wrote this poem.

MYSELF

Myself is lovely.
I am nothing but myself.
Myself, I think, is handsome.
I am lovely like a flower,
Myself is a black boy.
—Randy Cook

HELPS

American Friends Service Committee, Anti-Defamation League, *Books Are Bridges,* 1957. A bibliography of trade books that focuses on members of minority groups as the main characters. Included are selections appropriate for kindergarten children through junior high school youngsters. For copies, address orders to "Books Are Bridges" Department, Anti-Defamation League of B'nai B'rith, 515 Madison Ave., New York, N.Y. 10022, or "Books Are Bridges" Department, American Friends Service Committee (Quakers), 20 South 12th St., Philadelphia, Pa. (c/o EMC).

Associated Publishers, Inc. 1538 Ninth St., N.W., Washington, D.C. 20001. They have available: 100 pictures of distinguished Negroes 5½ × 7½ inches—$5; 24 pictures of distinguished Negroes 8½ × 11 inches—$3; 24 pictures of distinguished Negroes 11 × 14inches—$7.

Bowmar Early Childhood Series, Glendale, Cal.: Bowmar Publishing Co., 1969. Fine series of picture books. There are seven books in Part One: "About Myself." See particularly the books entitled, *Do You Know That . . .?* and *What Is a Birthday Child?* Very attractive and enticing books. Address: 622 Rodier Drive, Glendale, Cal. 91201.

Banfield, Beryle, *Africa in the Curriculum,* New York: Edward W. Blyden Press, Inc., 1968. P.O. Box 621 Manhattanville Station, New York, N.Y. 10027.

Black, Irma Simonton, senior editor, *The Bank Street Readers,* New York: The Macmillan Co., 1965. A series of reading books designed for children of the elementary grades that include as main characters in their stories children who represent members of minority groups instead of portraying just white children from middle-class backgrounds and environments. White children who are presented are shown as living in highrise city dwellings instead of just the stereotyped "white picket fence" setting that children have seen for so long in their school and library books.

Boning, Richard A., illustrated by Joseph Forte, *Profiles of Black Americans, Volumes 1 and 2,* New York: Dexter and Westbrook, Ltd., 1969. Address: 111 South Centre Ave., Rockville Centre, New York, N.Y. 11571. A series of 250 glossy, colored pictures and biographical notes on leading black Americans. Each picture is 6½ × 9½ inches and is made of durable oaktag.

Broderick, Dorothy M., *Image of the Black in Children's Fiction,* New York: R.R. Bowker Company, 1973. A critical analysis of the portrait of the black that emerges from children's books published between 1827 and 1967. This book is an adaptation of Broderick's dissertation done at Columbia University.

Carlson, Ruth Kearney, *Emerging Humanity: Multi-Ethnic Literature for Children and Adolescents,* Dubuque, Iowa: William C. Brown Publishers, 1972.

Fitzgerald, Bertram A., Jr., editor, *Golden Legacy,* New York: Fitzgerald Publishing Co., Inc., 1970. Address: 527 Madison Avenue, New York, N.Y. 10022. The *Golden Legacy* magazine is done in the style of a comic book; therefore, many children who may have been labeled "reluctant readers" may not be reluctant about picking it up. Its focus is on people who have made significant contributions to black history. There are eleven volumes in all. Address all inquiries to: Golden Legacy, P.O. Box 4989, Clinton, Iowa 52732.

Hall, Elvajean, compiler, Boston, Mass.: Campbell and Hall, n.d. Paperback bibliographies briefly annotated that you may find helpful—"Books They Can Really Read," January 1971; "Black Heritage," April 1972; "Personal Problems of Children," May 1970; "The Saga of the North American Indians," n.d. The cost is $.20 each or $.10 each for ten or more of a title. Address: Campbell and Hall, P.O. Box 350, Boston, Mass. 02117.

Harris, Larry A., *Reports on Reading and the Disadvantaged: Elementary Level,* Bloomington, Ind.: Eric Crier Reading Review Series, Volume 1, Bibliography, Indiana University, 1968. Well-annotated bibliography of "reading projects and reports related to educational programs for the disadvantaged."

Hayes, Ruth M., compiler, *The Black Experience: Books for Children.* Boston Public Library, Boston, n.d. This free, briefly annotated bibliography has books suitable for children from the early primary grades through the junior high school level. The paperback pamphlet is divided into sections such as "Picture Books and Easy Reading," "Stories for Young Readers," "Fiction for the Older Boy and Girl," "Poetry, Music and Art," "Africa-History," "Africa in Stories," "The Magic of Folklore: Tales from Africa," and "Courageous Lives." The Boston Public Library continually updates its free bibliographies. One (1976) is *Black on Black.* Black authors write on the black experience. It is for young adults. A bibliography teachers would find helpful is *Black Is. . .1977.*

Heinrich, June Sark, *Black ABC's* Chicago: Society for Visual Education, Inc. *Black ABC's* includes 26 study prints. They are enclosed in a vinyl portfolio. The glossy pictures, each 18 × 13 inches, are visual delights. They are done in full color and include capital and lower-case letters with captions such as "A is for Afro." Letters to be emphasized are printed in red. On the back of each card are suggestions that can be used in teaching and reinforcing the letters. The set—PSSP 1200—sells for $26. Address: SVE, 1345 Diversey Parkway, Chicago, Ill. 60614.

Hentoff, Nat, *Our Children Are Dying,* New York: Four Winds Press, 1966. Hentoff tells the touching and powerful true story of Dr. Elliott Shapiro, the principal of Harlem's P.S. 119. Shapiro's love of children and the courage and unswerving devotion he shows in his attempts to make possible what could be possible for all of our country's inner-city schools causes this paperback to stamp a lingering, memorable impression on its readers. It is a book well worth reading.

Holt, John, *How Children Fail,* New York: Dell Publishing Co., Inc., 1964. An excellent paperback that describes some of the approaches used with children in school that ensure their failure.

Holt, John, *How Children Learn,* New York: Pitman Publishing Corporation, 1969. A follow-up to Holt's *How Children Fail* that gives some practical suggestions that anyone interested in children can use to good advantage to help children learn *and* like learning. Also available in paperback by Dell Publishing Co.

Hopkins, Lee Bennett, *Let Them Be Themselves,* Second Edition, New York: Scholastic Magazines, Inc., 1974. This very fine paperback has an excellent chapter on self-concept, pages 1–31. On pages 21–23 Hopkins includes an annotated bibliography of books that can be used with birthday children to make their day a happy one.

Interracial Books for Children, New York: Council on Interracial Books for Children, Inc., n.d. Interracial Books for Children is a paper published quarterly. Twenty-five copies can be obtained for $.30 each and fifty copies or more can be purchased for $.20 each. Address requests to the Council on Interracial Books for Children, Inc., 9 East 40th Street, New York, N.Y. 10016.

Keating, Charlotte Matthews, Building Bridges of Understanding, Tuscon: Palo Verde Publishing Co., Inc., 1967. A thoroughly annotated bibliography of trade books to use with children of preschool age through high-school age. Keating divides her book into six main sections. These sections cover books on "Negroes," "American Indians," "Spanish-speaking Ethnic Groups," "Chinese-Americans," "Japanese-Americans," "Hawaiians, Jews, Selections with Multi-ethnic Representation, and Other Minority Groups." Within each one of these divisions the author subdivides the sections into three levels—preschool and primary, upper-elementary, and junior high and high school. There are blank pages inserted in the books so that the reader may record titles of books that she or he has found that may be appealing to students.

Klugherz, Dan, America's Crises (Marked for Failure), Bloomington: Ind., 1965. Indiana University Audio-Visual Center. Bloomington, Ind. 47401. Sixteen millimeter, sixty minute, black and white film. Sale price is $200, rental price is $9.15, and preview is free except for return postage. Excellent film that focuses on reading problems of culturally divergent children.

Laskey, Harold H., director, Red, White, Black, Brown and Yellow: Minorities in America, No. 4. New York: The Combined Book Exhibit, Inc., n.d. A free pamphlet that lists titles of some books that teachers may find helpful to use with their students. Pages 12–15 probably would be most valuable to teachers of children in the elementary grades. The books referred to are not annotated.

Martin, Bill, Jr., Freedom Books, Glendale, Cal.,: Bowmar Publishing Co., 1970. An exceptionally fine series of books that help children (and adults) realize the worth and uniqueness of each individual in addition to developing a joy in reading. The books are beautifully written and illustrated. Two in particular that you might want to investigate are I Am Freedom's Child, illustrations by Symeon Shimin, and I Reach Out to the Morning, illustrations by Henry Markowitz.

Mathis, Sharon Bell, illustrated by Charles Bible, Brooklyn Story, New York: Hill and Wang, 1970. Brooklyn Story is one of a series of Challenger paperbacks written for upper elementary or junior high school students. Brooklyn Story uses the language that many black children in our country customarily hear and use themselves. "Each Challenger Book is an original story written with special sensitivity to the needs of the black or the Spanish-speaking communities of the United States." The editors of the series are helped to select manuscripts by "black and Spanish-speaking consultants, who are librarians, educators, and community leaders."

Meeker, Alice M., Enjoying Literature with Children, New York: The Odyssey Press, 1969. Meeker's second chapter of her paperback focuses on culturally deprived children—pages 13–39. Her suggestions that are found on these pages are as helpful to teachers who do not work with "culturally deprived" children as those who do. On pages 29–37 she includes references to books that can be used with "culturally deprived" children from preschool through the sixth grade. Most of the books mentioned can be used most beneficially with children from all backgrounds.

Reid, Virginia M., editor, *Reading Ladders for Human Relations,* Washington, D.C.: American Council of Education, 1972. Annotated book lists and section introductions. Paperback.

Robinson, Matt, and Cash, Rosalind, *The Year of Roosevelt Franklin: Gordon's Friend from Sesame Street,* New York: Columbia Records/CBS, Inc., 1970. Particularly fine to improve young children's self-concepts are the songs "Keep on Trying," number 4, and "The Skin I'm In," number 7.

Ross, David P., Jr., editor, Winslow, Eugene, illustrator, and Adams, Russell L., author, *Afro-Am Portfolios.* Chicago: Afro-Am Publishing Co., Inc., 1969. In all, Afro-Am Publishing Company offers nine picture portfolios. In each portfolio there are twenty-four 11 × 14 inch glossy pictures that have on them a brief biography of the person represented. Each print is made of durable stock. Each portfolio costs $4.95. The ones that I have examined are "Negroes in Our History"—T43B, "Modern Negro Contributions"—T43C, and "Negroes of Achievement"—T43D. For further information write to Afro-Am Publishing Company, 1727 South Indiana Avenue, Chicago, Ill. 60616.

Schneider, Kathryn Jackson, *Let's Start Picture Boxes* (Box 2), New York: Scholastic Magazines, Inc., 1968. Twenty-one black and white photos of multiracial groups of young children involved in familiar classroom activities. They come in durable containers and can be used to stimulate discussions. The item number is LS-6. There are two other *Let's Start Picture Boxes* available. For further information write to Scholastic Magazines, Inc., Department WAM70, 900 Sylvan Avenue, Englewood Cliffs, N.J. 07632.

Spache, George D., *Good Reading for the Disadvantaged Reader,* Champaign, Ill.: Garrard Publishing Co., 1970. Spache's first two chapters in this book concentrate on the importance of self-concept and the means by which it can be built. Other chapters in the book focus on the black American today, the American Indian today, Mexican-American and migrant workers, Puerto-Ricans, and Orientals. There is a chapter on audiovisual resources and one on professional resources. In all, Spache has eighteen chapters in his book. The chapters that deal with suggested reading materials will make children of various minority groups feel important and that they count (and make middle-class white children aware of that fact, too). Spache divides his lists into suggestions for the primary, intermediate, and the junior and senior high school level. Each citation is annotated briefly, and the approximate reading level is indicated. It might be pointed out here that children who are not able to read for themselves a book of a particular grade level can listen to it, understand it, and enjoy it immensely. So many of these books can be read *to* children.

Thoburn, Tina, and Hedges, Betty Lou, art by Harry McNaught, *My Story About Me,* New York: Western Publishing Co., Inc., 1970. This is a paperback workbook in which children are invited to draw objects, activities, and people they like or in some way are asked to reveal something about themselves, their ideas, and their opinions. For example, on one page it says "And here is something I don't like to touch." Underneath the words is a white rectangle where the children can draw what they wish. On another page it says, "People who like each other are friends. Here is a picture of my friend." There then follows a large blank circle where they can draw their friends. Beneath this picture on the same page it says, "My friend's name is ————." Besides making a child feel important, this paper workbook can be used to get children to open up and talk willingly and happily. It also is a fine resource to use to motivate children to read. When a child has finished the workbook, he or she has a book all about himself or herself. This paperbook is part of the fine *Adventures in Discovery* program published by Western Publishing Co., Inc.

Torrance, E. Paul. "Creative Positives of Disadvantaged Children and Youth," *The Gifted Child Quarterly, 13,* 71–81, Summer 1969. Torrance's article describes the positive talents of "disadvantaged" children and young people. He suggests that more needs to be done to discover and develop the creative youngsters who come from "disadvantaged" environments. What can be emphasized are those positive attributes which such youngsters are known to have.

Triple "I" Series, New York: American Book Co., 1970, 7 volumes. Controlled vocabulary books from levels 1–4. "The vocabulary falls generally one year below a standard reading series." Self-concept and interpersonal relationships, intersocial relationships, and values are stressed in each book. "Famous Americans from minority groups are featured in each unit to help the children achieve positive ethnic identification."

Whipple, Gertrude, et al., *All About Me: A Prereading Book,* Chicago: Follett Education Corporation, 1969. For the most part this is a traditional prereading workbook. However, occasionally, there are pages where children are asked to show what they like to do or are asked to draw their families or show their friends, thus making them personal and important parts of the workbook. The workbook has fully colored pictures on each page and, therefore, is visually appealing. It also shows pictures of black and oriental children playing and working with white children throughout the book and so cannot be considered as a placebo-type "integrated" text.

White, Doris, compiler, *Multi-ethnic Books for Head Start Children, Part I: Black and Integrated Literature,* Urbana, Ill.: ERIC Clearinghouse on Early Childhood Education, National Laboratory on Early Childhood Education, 1969. Well-annotated paperback that is a fine resource book for teachers working with young elementary school children and Head Start children. There are resources included for adult reading and books that can be used with children. Textbooks and trade books are mentioned in this paperback. For further information write to 805 West Pennsylvania Avenue, Urbana, Ill. 61801.

Wolfe, Ann G., *About 100 Books,* New York: The American Jewish Committee, Institute of Human Relations, November 1969. A well-annotated list of books to use with children as young as three up to young adults of seventeen years of age.

Again, it must be remembered that a book can be read by a child of one age and listened to and enjoyed by a younger child; so age ranges as they are given in most bibliographies must be used only as marginal indicators of what books a child may like and understand. It is all a matter of each child's background, interests, and ability, and the age range indicated should not ever be considered to be as straitjacketed as it most often appears to be.

Literary Suggestions to Present to Children to Increase Their Positive Self-Concepts

Adoff, Arnold, editor, drawings by Benny Andrews, *I Am the Darker Brother: An Anthology of Modern Poems by Negro Americans,* New York: The Macmillan Company, 1968.

Aldis, Dorothy, "Everybody Says" in *Favorite Poems Old and New,* selected by Helen Ferris, New York: Doubleday and Company, Inc., 1957.

Aliki, *My Hands,* New York: Thomas Y. Crowell Co., 1962.

Berends, Polly Berrien, illustrated by Lilian Obligado, *Who's That in the Mirror?,* New York: Random House, 1968.

Beskow, Elsa, pictures by George Wilde, *Pelle's New Suit,* New York: Wonder Books, 1962.

Bradfield, Joan, and Bradfield, Roger, *Who Are You?,* Racine, Wis.: Whitman Publishing Co., 1966.

Cameron, Polly, *"I Can't" said the ant,* New York: Scholastic Book Services, 1963.

Cameron, Polly, drawings by Consuelo Joerns, *The Green Machine,* New York: Coward-McCann Inc., 1969.

Crossen, Stacy J., and Covell, Natalie Anne, illustrated by Victoria de Larrea, *Me Is How I Feel: Poems,* New York: The McCall Publishing Co., 1970. See particularly poems entitled "Happy," "Eddie," "I'm a Boy," and "I'm a Girl."

De la Mare, Walter, "Me," from *Favorite Poems Old and New,* selected by Helen Ferris, New York: Doubleday and Company, Inc., 1957.

Elkin, Benjamin, pictures by Bernice Myers, *Six Foolish Fishermen,* New York: Scholastic Book Services, 1968.

Frost, Frances M., "The Little Whistler" in *The Little Whistler,* Whittlesey House, New York: McGraw-Hill Co., 1949.

Gruenberg, Sidonie Matsner, compiler, illustrated by Dagmar Wilson, *Let's Read More Stories,* New York: Garden City Books, 1960. See particularly story entitled "Pancho."

Hopkins, Lee Bennett, compiler, woodcuts by Ann Grifalconi, *Don't You Turn Back: Poems by Langston Hughes,* New York: Alfred A. Knopf, 1969.

Hopkins, Lee Bennett, compiler, illustrated by Emily McCully, *Girls Can Too!,* New York: Franklin Watts, Inc., 1972. See particularly "Bea's Bee" by Melanie Ray and the title poem.

Hopkins, Lee Bennett, compiler, photographs by David Parks, *On Our Way: Poems of Pride and Love,* New York: Alfred A. Knopf, 1974.

Keats, Ezra Jack, *The Snowy Day,* New York: Scholastic Book Services, 1967.

Keats, Ezra Jack, *Whistle for Willie*, New York: The Viking Press, 1969.

Keats, Ezra Jack, *Hi, Cat!*, New York: The Macmillan Co., 1970. Ask librarian for a list of other books written by Keats. One excellent book is *John Henry*.

Keats, Ezra Jack, *Pet Show!*, New York: The Macmillan Co., 1972. Exceptionally fine for its idea of showing how everyone can feel important.

Klein, Leonore, pictures by John Fischetti, *Brave Daniel*, New York: Scholastic Book Services, 1970.

Konigsburg, E.L., *Jennifer, Hecate, MacBeth, William McKinley, and Me, Elizabeth*, New York: Atheneum, 1967.

Krauss, Ruth, pictures by Crockett Johnson, *The Carrot Seed*, New York: Scholastic Book Services, 1966.

Krauss, Ruth, pictures by Mary Blair, *I Can Fly*, New York: Golden Press, 1966.

Lawrence, Jacob, *Harriet and the Promised Land*, New York: Simon and Schuster, Inc., 1968.

Leaf, Munro, *Gordon and the Goat*, New York: Scholastic Book Services, 1968.

Lewis, Shari, and Reinach, Jacquelyn, design and illustration by Kent Salisbury and Adrina Zanazanian, *The Headstart Book of Knowing and Naming*, New York: McGraw-Hill Book Co., 1966. See particularly "The King and ——— (Your Child's Name)."

Lexau, Joan M., illustrated by Don Bolognese, *Benjie on His Own*, New York: The Dial Press, 1970.

Merriam, Eve, "What in the World?" in *There is No Rhyme for Silver*, New York: Atheneum, 1962.

McGovern, Ann, pictures by Nola Langner, *Stone Soup*, New York: Scholastic Book Services, 1968.

McGovern, Ann, photographs by Hope Wurmfeld, *Black Is Beautiful*, New York: Four Winds Press, 1969.

Palmer, T.H., "Try, Try Again" in Helen Ferris' *Favorite Poems Old and New*, New York: Doubleday and Company, 1957.

Payne, Joan Balfour, *The Raven and Other Fairy Tales*, New York: Hastings House Publishers, 1969.

Piper, Watty, *The Little Engine That Could*, New York: Platt and Munk, Publishers, 1961.

Scott, Louise Binder, and Thompson, J.J., *Talking Time*, St. Louis: McGraw-Hill Book Co., 1966. See story entitled "The Threap."

Scott, Louise Binder, *Learning Time with Language Experiences for Young Children*, St. Louis: McGraw-Hill Book Co., 1968. See poems entitled "Identifying Me," and "Who Is Me?"

Seuss, Dr., *Horton Hears a Who*, New York: Random House, 1954.

Seuss, Dr., and McKie, Roy, *My Book About Me*, New York: Random House, 1969.

Seuss, Dr., *I Can Draw It Myself*, New York: Random House, 1970.

Shecter, Ben, *Conrad's Castle*, New York: Harper and Row, Publishers, 1967.

Steptoe, John, *Stevie*, New York: Harper and Row, Publishers, 1969. Ask librarian for other books written by John Steptoe, a talented, young, black writer. One book you may like is his book called *Birthday*, which is published by Holt, Rinehart and Winston.

Taylor, Theordore, *The Cay,* New York: Doubleday and Company, Inc., 1969.

Udry, Janice May, pictures by Eleanor Mill, *What Mary Jo Shared,* New York: Scholastic Book Services, 1967. Ask librarian for other books written by Udry about Mary Jo.

Walker, Barbara, illustrated by Harold Berson, *Pigs and Pirates: A Greek Tale,* New York: David White, 1969.

Walley, Dean, illustrated by Vivian Taylor, *There's Only One You,* Kansas City, Mo.: Hallmark Cards, Inc., 1970.

Walter, Nina Willia, "We Are Bright" in *Let Them Write Poetry,* New York: Holt, Rinehart and Winston, 1962.

White, Anne Terry, *George Washington Carver,* New York: Random House, 1963.

Yates, Elizabeth, *Amos Fortune, Free Man,* New York: Dell Publishing Co., 1971.

Literary Suggestions to Help Celebrate Birthdays

Averill, Esther, *Jenny's Birthday Book,* New York: Harper and Row Publishers, 1954.

Banner, Angela, illustrated by Bryan Ward, *Happy Birthday with Ant and Bee,* New York: Franklin Watts, Inc., 1968. Delightful to read to celebrate an "unbirthday" or a child's birthday that falls on a holiday or weekend.

Bannon, Laura, *Manuela's Birthday,* Chicago: Albert Whitman and Co., 1972.

Buckley, Helen E., illustrated by Paul Galdone, *The Little Boy and the Birthdays,* New York: Lothrop, Lee, and Shepard Co., Inc., 1966.

Chalmers, Mary, *The Happy Birthday Present,* New York: Harper and Brothers, Publishers, 1952.

Chance, E.B., pictures by Arline Meyer, *Just in Time for the King's Birthday,* New York: Scholastic Book Services, 1970.

Chute, Marchette, "Birthdays" in *Around and About,* New York: E.P. Dutton, Ltd., 1957.

Collier, Ethel, *The Birthday Tree,* pictures by Honoré Guilbeau, New York: William R. Scott, Inc., Publishers, 1961.

Farjeon, Eleanor, "Choosing" in *Over the Garden Wall,* Philadelphia: J.B. Lippincott Co., 1933.

Fisher, Aileen, "Birthday Cake" in *Runny Days, Sunny Days,* New York: Abelard-Schuman, Ltd., 1958.

Fyleman, Rose, "The Birthday Child" in *Favorite Poems Old and New,* selected by Helen Ferris, New York: Doubleday and Company, Inc., 1957.

Ginglerd, David R., and Winifred E. Stiles, "Birthday Song" in *Music Activities for Retarded Children,* Nashville: Abingdon Press, 1965.

Hoban, Russell, pictures by Lillian Hoban, *A Birthday for Frances,* New York: Harper and Row, Publishers, 1968.

Hopkins, Lee Bennett, *Happy Birthday to Me,* New York: Scholastic Book Services, 1972.

Johnson, Lois S., illustrated by Genia, *Happy Birthdays Round the World,* Chicago: Rand McNally and Co., 1963.

Lobel, Anita, *A Birthday for the Princess,* New York: Harper and Row, Publishers, 1973.

Martin, Bill, Jr., "Happy Birthday, Henry!" in *Sounds of Home,* New York: Holt, Rinehart and Winston, Inc., 1966.

Maskin, Marietta D., with line drawings by Morton Garchik, *The Best Birthday Party,* New York: The John Day Co., 1964.

Munari, Bruno, *The Birthday Present,* Cleveland: The World Publishing Co., 1959.

Seuss, Dr., *Happy Birthday to You,* New York: Random House, 1959.

Steptoe, John, *Birthday,* New York: Holt, Rinehart and Winston, 1972.

3 Listen, My Children

Sometimes at night
When the house is dark
things I think about get so loud
I can't even sleep.
—Richard J. Margolis

As the familiar words "Listen, my children and you shall hear" suggest, listening, unlike hearing, is a voluntary act by which a listener participates in spoken communication. Taken for granted until about twenty-five years ago when extensive research in the area began to be conducted, listening skills are only now beginning to assume their proper place among the other language arts. The important role of listening is suggested by Stanford E. Taylor[1] as follows:

As early as 1926, research had established that 70 percent of the average adult's working day was spent in verbal communication, with 45 percent of that time spent in listening acts. Reading, on the other hand, occupied only 16 percent of the verbal communication time. In 1949, explorations of listening in the elementary classroom led to the discovery that 57.5 percent of class time was spent in listening. Recently, researchers have estimated that close to 90 percent of the class time in high schools and colleges is spent in listening to discussions and lectures.

Certainly listening has always occupied a good portion of our communication time, and since the advent of TV the proportion of time spent in listening has been increasing.

Despite the amount of time we spend in listening, it is evident that we do not always listen efficiently. Every teacher knows that many children have problems in following spoken directions, in retaining information delivered orally, and in interpreting and appreciating features of spoken discourse. The obvious answer is to make an intelligent program for developing listening skills a part of language arts instruction, and it is to this end that this chapter addresses itself. A necessary first step, however, is to consider the circumstances under which people do and do not listen.

Copyright © 1976, United Feature Syndicate, Inc.

1. WHEN PEOPLE LISTEN AND WHEN THEY DON'T

Some of the situations in which people, including teachers, listen are listed below. People listen when:

1. They can listen—that is, when there is no hearing impairment and when the speaking can be heard and understood.
2. They are interested and involved in the subject matter.
3. They like the person who is speaking.
4. They are motivated to want to respond.
5. They know that they will be expected to respond individually.
6. They can follow the speaker's presentation because it is organized in a clear and forceful way.
7. They do not have to listen for too long.
8. They have some other special motivation for listening. (For example, a mother, who might have preferred to ignore her child's clamoring at the door, listened when she heard him scream "Cott tam it, I want to come in!" Her motivation was her wish that the child not repeat his demand, particularly within hearing of the neighbors.)

Many of the occasions that prompt people not to listen are the reverse of those mentioned above, but reviewing them briefly permits mentioning some specific "turn-offs" of which every speaker can afford to be reminded. People do not listen when:
1. They cannot easily hear the speaker—either because he/she is speaking too softly or because there is distracting noise.

THE FAMILY CIRCUS   **By Bil Keane**

"Read slower, Daddy. I can't listen that fast."

THE FAMILY CIRCUS, by Bill Keane, reprinted courtesy The Register and Tribune Syndicate, Inc.

2. They find his/her manner of speaking monotonous.
3. They find the speaker's mannerisms annoying or distracting.
4. They are conditioned not to listen. (For example, a teacher who always gives (or reads) the same directions in exactly the same way or who habitually repeats all instructions conditions his/her listener to think there is no reason to listen attentively.)
5. They disagree with the speaker and stop listening as they think about their own objections to a point he/she just made.
6. They may find the speaker's vocabulary or syntax too difficult to comprehend.
7. They respond in a predictable but undesirable way to psychologically unsound remarks. (For instance, a teacher who knows that most of the class hates poetry would be ill advised to say, "I know that many of you hate poetry. We are going to read lots of poetry so that you will learn to love it.")
8. They know that the speaker is going to call on only one listener to respond. (If a teacher habitually calls on one, or one of several, to answer questions, the rest of the class is likely to tune out.)

9. They are reminded by the speaker's words of a personal experience or concern and start thinking about that.
10. They anticipate incorrectly what the speaker is going to say. (For example, if a person responds to the question "How are you?" with "Terrible!" the person who asked may reply with "Good.")

2. TECHNIQUES FOR DEVELOPING LISTENING SKILLS

A study published in 1967[2] indicates that "less than one percent of the content of texts for children is devoted to lessons on listening." Although texts published in the last few years have improved on this ratio, you will probably want to think about ways in which you can develop listening skills quite independently of text materials that may be available. A good way to start is to bear in mind the general reasons already suggested for listening or not listening. You may find it useful to incorporate into your speech in the classroom random statements such as "Johnny has only five arithmetic problems to do today;" "If Mary's group will remind me at 10:15, I'll show all of you how to play a new game;" "Let's all stop what we're doing at eleven o'clock because I have a funny story to read to you. Please remind me, or I may forget;" or "Don't let me forget to pass out lollipops today to those who improved in any of their work yesterday." (Everyone, of course.)

If you praise children for work well done, they will begin to listen for their names. Whenever possible, the praise should actively involve the children. For instance, you could say, "Billy, Sue, Mary, and Tommy, would you read the poems you did for us yesterday this afternoon at 2:15 p.m?;" "Bobby's group—I was talking to Mrs. _____ in the third grade the other day, and she wanted to know if you could come down to her room on Wednesday and show her pupils the posters you did for Book Week."

On a holiday such as Halloween, or near a holiday such as Thanksgiving or Christmas or Hanukkah, you might have a chart with each child's name on it and a time he or she could come to you for some directions. When a child's turn comes, tell the child to follow a certain number of directions given orally in order to find a "treasure." The number would depend on the ability of the child. You might wish to call up small groups of children so that they could listen and follow vicariously the directions given to one child. They might help the child by calling out words such as "hot," "warm," "cool," or "cold" for every direction the child was attempting to follow. Some children might want to make treasures for others to find. Some could be silly notes or sayings or inexpensively made fun objects. You could provide inexpensive treasures or the children could collect interesting "found" objects they thought other children in the class might enjoy finding and keeping. Naturally, children would be allowed to swap treasures.

It's fun to ask children to practice giving instructions on a game they would like to play and then introduce the game to the class. Tell them you will be glad to listen to their directions or else tell them to choose some friend from the class to practice with to make sure the directions given are clear. The games can be made up by children (individually or in small groups) or they can be games that are familiar to all. They can be used for indoor activities in language arts, reading, or any other subject, or outdoor activities. Other groups can volunteer to team up and listen to the directions and see which teams are the best listeners.

If a game is familiar to all of the children, the directions might be changed by the children to assure that everyone would need to listen. Not only would this sort of activity motivate children to listen, but it would also help children to realize how important it is to give clear directions. Teams might be rewarded for giving the best directions as well as being rewarded for listening the best.

Children might enjoy some chuckles together while practicing when they realize how funny or confusing it can be if directions are not given clearly, simply, and in the right order. Children should be given the opportunity to talk about what makes it easy for them to listen and understand. They could be guided to discuss what they would do to help each child understand so that a task such as tying one's shoe could be carried out by listening to someone giving directions.

3. LISTENING GAMES

There are a number of listening games that can be used to reinforce other language arts skills as well as to develop skills for listening. Those suggested in the following section are only a few possibilities, but they will suggest variations that you will think of and want to use. You will need to adapt some of the games to suit the age level of your pupils. When you are introducing a new listening game, remember to make the directions as clear as you can. After all, being able to listen and respond appropriately to oral instructions is an important listening skill that can be reinforced as each new game is described.

Simon Says

In addition to providing practice in following directions, this familiar game can be adapted to review learnings in reading and the other language arts. For example, if you have been working on the sound /m/ in initial position, you can instruct children to act out only the commands that begin with this sound. (If you wish to retain the game feature that only commands beginning "Simon says" are to be followed, then you will have to explain that the players should act out a command only if you say these words and the command begins with an /m/ sound. It is obviously simpler to drop "Simon says.") The children would then act out commands such as:

Mow a lawn.
Mew like a kitten.
Make a cake.

They would not respond to commands such as:

Sweep the floor.
Take a big step.
Jump in place.

With older children who are learning more complex reading skills, the same game can be used in other ways. For example, to review one or more "short" vowels, the rules can be changed so that only commands in which the first word had a "short" vowel should be followed. (You will want to restrict the first words of your commands to words of one syllable.) Sample commands might be:

Bat a ball.
Hug yourself.
Sit on the floor.
Hop in a circle.
Pet a kitten.

Many variations can be created, particularly if you encourage the children to think of words and directions that would zero in on a particular skill. Give them time to think and then let them take turns being leader of the game.

Lucy Lockett

This Mother Goose rhyme can be adapted to get children to listen to and recognize initial consonant sounds. The original verse goes like this:

Lucy Lockett lost her pocket,
Kitty Fisher found it.
Not a penny was there in it,
Only ribbons round it.

Decide on five or six initial consonants you want to review and prepare (or have the children prepare) a set of oaktag cards, each of which has one of the corresponding letters on it. Each child should have a complete set. Then say the rhyme, each time using a new alliterative name beginning with one of the sounds you are working with (Tim Tuttle, Susan Simpson, and so on.)

You may wish to introduce another alliterative name in the second line (e.g., "Kitty Kelly found it"). When the children hear and recognize the sound being emphasized, they are to point to or hold up the appropriate letter card.

As a follow-up activity, you might give each child a card on which a known word beginning with one of the sounds being reviewed is written. If the child can say the word and match it with the appropriate letter card, he or she earns a point. Games, incidentally, offer good oppprtunities for achieving the small successes discussed in the previous chapter. You may want to have each pupil keep a daily score card on which he or she records the points earned.

The Place Game

You or one of the children can start the game by naming a city, state, or country. The first player thinks of another place that starts with the *sound* of the letter that the first word ends with. Thus, Kansas, Sweden, New York would be a possible sequence. If a player mistakes the last letter, he/she should have the choice of trying again or passing.

Rhyming Games

Divide the class into teams. Have one team supply a word. The other team must give a rhyming word in a matter of seconds. If the second team cannot supply a rhyming word, the first team gets a point if it can supply one. The first team keeps the "serve" until the other team has successfully answered. Then it is their turn. Only the serving team can score points.

Guessing Games

If you have a tape recorder available, you can easily develop an interesting game that provides good experience in auditory analysis. For instance, you might record the sound of paper being crushed, the sound of crumpling cellophane (a good sound effect for fire crackling), and the sound of the school duplicating machine. Children who guess the sound correctly are awarded a point. Do not insist on exact identification of each sound. If paper being crumbled sounds like fire to someone, accept the answer and award the point. You will get freer and more imaginative answers in this way.

Cat and Dog

The players sit in a circle. The player who starts the game has two small objects—a piece of chalk and an eraser will do. He/she passes the first to his/her right, saying "I found a cat." The second player says, "A what?" and the first repeats "A cat." The second player then repeats the process with the player to the right. Immediately after starting the first object, the first player starts the second one to the left around the circle, saying "I found a dog." The distractions increase as the objects get closer together. When one object gets back to the starting player, he/she repeats the process, naming a new object—"I found a dollar (a rabbit, or whatever)." This game works best in fairly small groups and with pupils adept enough at listening skills to cope with the distraction.

The Minister's Cat

In this game, the first child starts off by saying something like this: "The minister's cat is active." Then the second player must add an adjective beginning with *b*: "The minister's cat is active and brave." The players go as far as they can through the alphabet, repeating what has been said before and adding a new adjective each time. As a variation, you might call on a child to give the next adjective instead of going around the class in a predictable way.

Miss Fussbudget

This game calls for good observation as well as listening skills. You can begin by explaining that Miss Fussbudget is very picky about things she likes and does not like. Then give some statements such as:

Miss Fussbudget likes lo*ll*ipops but does not like fudge.
Miss Fussbudget likes je*ll*y but hates jam.
Miss Fussbudget likes dre*ss*es but hates slacks.
Miss Fussbudget likes swi*mm*ing but dislikes skating.
Miss Fussbudget likes pe*pp*er but does not like salt.

After giving four or five examples, ask children whether they know how Miss Fussbudget decides on her likes and dislikes. If a child raises his/her hand, have him/her give an example of another thing Miss Fussbudget would like. Continue giving examples until most of the children have solved the puzzle. Be sure the examples you give are words where each of the double consonants in the stimuli provided can be *heard*.

Since you can only use Miss Fussbudget's likes and dislikes once, you might want to use a variant later. This time, Miss Fussbudget is planning a trip and deciding what to take with her. The game is played like "The Place Game" (described on page 61). For instance, she might pack a necklace, salt, a telescope, a pipe, and so on. As before, give examples until most children have guessed the system. Remember that it is a listening game and not a spelling game and thus depends on sounds heard.

Ear Scavenger Hunt

As in a regular scavenger hunt, the children take partners. If possible, all of the pairs should be given instructions as to what to look for at the same time, each pair getting different instructions. You can manage this by having some pupils give instructions and then play in the next round. All of the objects on the list are, of course, hidden about the room. The first pair to return with their assigned objects wins. You will probably want to start out with only a few objects and extend the listening list as the children become more expert.

The Question-Asking Game

Carl Bereiter and Siegfried Engelmann[3] suggest a game that encourages children to ask questions. The game is played like Simon says, but the idea is to include some directions that children will not be able to carry out without asking questions. One such instruction might be "Touch your cranium." Bereiter and Englemann suggest that instead of letting children guess, it is better to ask them if they know what to do. If they do not, the teacher leads the children to realize that they cannot follow a direction without knowing the meaning of a key word, and they must ask the teacher a question such as "What is a cranium?"

4. USING LITERARY MATERIAL IN LISTENING

Literary selections are a rich source of listening activities. The suggestions that follow are only a few of the possibilities.

Copycat Games

Literary selections that entice children to act out certain words that they hear in the selections not only motivate them to listen and get them actively involved but also introduce or deepen their concepts of certain words or phrases used in the materials. Children who initially may not know a word's meaning will feel no shame or sense of failure if they imitate the actions of other children and the teacher who are acting out the pieces. As in choral reading, children who are more shy will not be intimidated, and the more

extroverted children can open up their dramatic vent all the way and help others to express themselves more freely.

Vachel Lindsay's "The Little Turtle"[4] is a three-stanza verse that should appeal to early primary children. They can move around and be encouraged to show how they would look if they "lived in a box." They can act out words such as "swimming," "climbing," "snapping," and "catching." It is very possible that they will act out other words, also. Do not set limits for them; instead, limber up their limits so that their limits will always be lengthening.

Older children who are familiar with Lindsay's "The Little Turtle" should respond gleefully to Shel Silverstein's parody called "Not Me."[5]

Eve Merriam's[6] poem, "On Our Way," has many phrases in it that will invite children to get up out of their seats and act out their thoughts. They can "stretch like a turtle with a poking-out neck" and "plod like a camel with an up-and-down hump." Northrop Frye[7] has said that listening to stories is basic to the training of one's imagination. Certainly, listening to particular kinds of poems will also train the imagination. If one of our goals is to stimulate and develop each child's creative abilities, then we must use the materials that we feel will be most likely to accomplish that goal.

Another poem to use to get children to listen and then act out certain words is Evelyn Beyer's[8] "Jump or Jiggle." This very simple poem tells how different creatures get about. Six of the seven stanzas are done as couplets, and each couplet includes only a "couple" of words such as "snakes slide." The last stanza is written in three lines to give emphasis to the point that "I walk!" These last two words are written in italics.

Not only is this poem a fine one to encourage children to listen and then respond to what they hear, but it is also a good one to use to get children to make up their own poems based on Beyer's writing. You could start off by providing some first lines and the first words to the second lines. Children could listen and suggest to the teacher some rhyming words that would complete each couplet. Children would be helped in this exercise to listen to words that sound alike at the end. The words the children give need not sound identically alike at the ending. That is, words such as "kids" and "cribs" are rhyming words. They are examples of *slant verse* or *approximate verse*. You might write on the board the various words that the children volunteer, and then the group might decide which words they like best in the various slots. On ditto sheets children could write in the ones they like and, after a sufficient warm-up, some children might want to try to contribute orally or write down their own original couplets. The words you choose to write on the board and on the children's mimeograph sheets should be words the children already know.

After you have supplied a few first lines and the first word for the second line and feel that the children have the idea, you can simply supply the first words to each line. The next step is to see if children can help each other in composing their own couplets. The last step is to see if anyone would like to do his/her own individually.

Examples of the stages are:

Cows moo._____
Dogs _____.

Boys wiggle_____
Girls _____.

Birds fly_____   ____
I _____.

Ants _____.
Worms _____.

Cats _____
Fish_____.

_____ _____
_____ _____.
_____ _____
_____ _____.

Perhaps children might think, after working with these examples, that they are limited in their responses to sharing their thoughts on animals. To prevent such thinking, you might put the beginnings of a few other couplets on the board, such as:

At the end of the school day,

_____.

    or

My favorite thing that I can make,

_____.

    or

One thing that I really like

_____.

More Literature Selections for Listening

Some devices that authors employ that entice children to listen and then participate include the use of:

1. Cumulative verses.
2. Repetitive refrains.
3. The structuring of a story or poem so that children begin to anticipate what is going to come next in the literary selection.
4. Rhyming words that, when combined with the creative structure and format of the book, trigger children's instinct to respond and to become a part of the story or poem.
5. Questions that arouse a child's desire to respond.
6. Plots or topics that implicitly or explicitly invite the listener to suggest answers.

Examples of literary materials that use the techniques just mentioned are:

1. *The House That Jack Built*

This is the house that Jack built.
This is the malt
That lay in the house that Jack built.
This is the rat,
That ate the malt
That lay in the house that Jack built.
This is the cat,
That killed the rat,
That ate the malt
That lay in the house that Jack built.
This is the dog,
That worried the cat,
That killed the rat,
That ate the malt
That lay in the house that Jack built.

2. *I Know an Old Lady* by Rose Bonne, music by Alan Mills, pictures by Abner Graboff (New York: Scholastic Book Services, 1968).
3. *Do You Hear What I Hear?* by Helen Borten (New York: Abelard-Schuman, 1960).
4. *Listen! And Help Tell the Story* by Bernice Wells Carlson, illustrations by Burmah Burris (Nashville: Abingdon Press, 1965).
5. "What Did You Put in Your Pocket?" and "What's the Funniest Thing?" in *Something Special* by Beatrice Schenk de Regniers, drawings by Irene Haas (New York: Harcourt Brace Jovanovich, 1958).
6. *Did You Ever See?* by Walter Einsel (New York: Scholastic Book Services, 1962).
7. *What Is Your Favorite Thing to Hear?* by Myra Tomback Gibson (New York: Grosset and Dunlap, Inc., 1966).
8. *I Had a Little. . .* by Norma Levarie, illustrated by John Wright (New York: Random House, 1961).
9. "The Birthday Party" and "Pick a Word" in *The Headstart Book of Thinking and Imagining* by Shari Lewis and Jacquelyn Reinach, design and illustration by Alex D'Amato and Art Seiden, pp. 22–29 (New York: McGraw-Hill Book Company, 1966).
10. *What Is That Sound?* by Mary L. O'Neill, drawings by Lois Ehlert (New York: Atheneum, 1966).
11. *Time for a Rhyme* by Ellen Wilkie, illustrated by Sharon Kane (Chicago: Rand McNally and Company, 1966).

Onomatopoeia

Some introductory materials to use:
A very simply written book, mentioned previously, is *The Listening Walk* by

Paul Showers, illustrated by Aliki (New York: Thomas Y. Crowell Company, 1961). A "listening walk" is a walk on which not one word is spoken, since it is essential to let nothing interrupt one's listening power. This story tells of a little boy who takes such a walk and describes all the onomatopoeic sounds that he hears and likes. You may wish to tell your pupils that words like the many words referred to in the book are called "onomatopoeic" sounds. They are words that imitate real sounds. At the conclusion of the book, the reader is told to listen and see how many sounds he/she can hear "RIGHT NOW." You also can suggest that the children take a "listening walk" after school and then report the sounds that they heard the next day.

A fine poem to present to children is the "Song of the Train," by David McCord. This poem can be found in the *Anthology of Children's Literature,* compiled by Edna Johnson, Evelyn R. Sickels, and Frances Clarke Sayers (Boston: Houghton Mifflin Company, 1959). McCord repeats again and again the words "clickety-clack." When a teacher reads this poem, she/he can start out very slowly repeating "clickety-clack" and gradually increase the speed until the children can "see" and "hear" the train speeding along its tracks. A good idea would be to allow the children to tape-record themselves saying this poem, listen to it, and suggest ideas for improving their delivery.

All Sizes of Noises by Karla Kuskin (New York: Harper and Brothers, Publishers, 1962) is a book in rhyme form that is filled with onomatopoeic sounds. The illustrations of the onomatopoeic sounds are done creatively. The presentation of this book might induce some children to try to arrange cleverly the onomatopoeic sounds that they hear.

In *Roar and More,* also written by Karla Kuskin (New York: Harper and Row, Publishers, 1956), the focal point is the sounds made by various animals. Once more, the onomatopoeic sounds are illustrated very ingeniously.

Another book that emphasizes onomatopoeic sounds is *The Sound of Things,* by William Wondriska (New York: Pantheon, 1958). On one page of this book is a picture of an object such as a horn. Opposite it is its sound. Like Kuskin, Wondriska is very inventive and imaginative in the depictions of onomatopoeic words. Children's attention should be drawn to these clever illustrations.

Other materials that can be presented to children so that they can become familiar with onomatopoeic words include:

1. "The Motor Boat Song," and "Toaster Time," by Eve Merriam in *There Is No Rhyme for Silver* (New York: Atheneum, 1962), pp. 36, 10.
2. "Our Washing Machine," by Patricia Hubbell, and "Sleet Storm," by James Tippett, in *Poetry Keepsake,* compiled by Louise Markert (Boston: Ginn and Company, 1968), pp. 6, 7.

3. Any excerpt from *Sparkle and Spin* by Ann Rand and Paul Rand (New York: Harcourt Brace Jovanovich, 1957).
4. "Galoshes" by Rhoda W. Bacmeister in *The Arbuthnot Anthology of Children's Literature* by May Hill Arbuthnot (Chicago: Scott, Foresman and Company, 1957), p. 103.
5. "Different Bicycles," by Dorothy Baruch in *The Arbuthnot Anthology of Children's Literature,* p. 65.
6. "Ears Hear," by Lucia and James Hymes in *Oodles of Noodles* (New York: Young Scott Books, 1964), pp. 16–17.
7. "Ululation," by Eve Merriam in *It Doesn't Always Have to Rhyme* (New York: Atheneum, 1966), p. 18.

Using onomatopoeic words in writing or in speech vivifies the language and makes the listener feel that he/she is there. This fact will become quite obvious to the children after they have had some of the previous materials read to them. The feeling of reality that these words produce should be brought to the attention of the children. They should become aware of the effect of these words. Perhaps you will want to guide your pupils in describing this effect in their own words.

Sounds and Feelings

Helen Borten's book, *Do You Hear What I Hear?* is beautifully illustrated and written. It tells the effect that sounds can have on people—how sounds can make a person feel. It is crowded with descriptions of what different sounds are like. Thus, it is stocked with similes, and the similes are fresh and original. Throughout the selection, the author asks questions of her readers. In dealing with very quiet sounds Borten asks her readers whether they have heard things such as a falling star or the petals falling from a daisy.

Borten discusses near and far sounds, short and long sounds, low, high, and harsh sounds. She also suggests that sometimes it is not the sound but what makes the sound that causes a person to feel a certain way. A hiss from a snake has a different effect on a person than a hiss from a collapsing balloon. Children will naturally use Borten's thoughts as a springboard to thinking and talking about their own ideas concerning sounds.

You might have the children talk together about the quietest, loudest, most frightening, or funniest sounds they have ever heard. The teacher should start the children off, perhaps suggesting the following quiet sounds.

As quiet as the last thread breaking on a button.
As quiet as grass growing.
As quiet as a country night after a freshly fallen snow.
As quiet as my face gets red when I get embarrassed.
As quietly as a sliver of glass can cut your hand.

By using Borten's book, children are coaxed into using similes and original ways of expressing themselves.

De Regniers, in her *Something Special,* includes a delightful unrhymed poem entitled, "Little Sounds." She tells children to "listen for the little secret sounds." She then offers many examples of such little quiet sounds. At the end of the poem the reader is directed to listen to more little sounds. This poem would fit in very nicely with Borten's book.

In *What Is That Sound?* O'Neill writes many pieces on topics such as the "Sound of Water" and the "Sound of Fire." Both of the poems mentioned are unrhymed. In the "Sound of Water" O'Neill, using single words, all verbs with the exception of the word "rain," describes how water sounds to her. Similarly, in "Sound of Fire," she tells what fire is by listing two words, the word "a" followed by a descriptive noun such as "hiss." Some of her other selections in this book include "Country Sounds," "Sounds of the City," "The Sound of Day," "The Sound of Night," and "The Sound of Air." These poems could induce children to tell about sounds they have heard and some of their favorite sounds.

A poem that relates the noises one poet likes is entitled "Noise." It is written by J. Pope and can be found in *Poetry Keepsake,* compiled by Louise Markert (Boston: Ginn and Company, 1964).

Special Sounds

Another suggestion is to read Eleanor Farjeon's "The Sounds in the Morning." This poem can be found in the *Anthology of Children's Literature,* edited by Johnson, Sickels, and Sayers. "The Sounds in the Morning" presents a listing of all the country sounds that the speaker hears in the morning. The persona of the poem mentions that she becomes aware of each new day first through her ears. Then this sense diminishes in importance and the world of her eyes takes the dominant role.

Children now could work together on an unrhymed contribution. Titles might include "House Sounds," "School Sounds," "The Sound of Children," "The Sound of Happiness," or "The Sound of Sadness."

Children, after having some of the previous pieces presented to them, can be made aware of the sounds right around them in their environment. You might try passing out to each pupil a piece of paper with a certain time of day printed on it. Precisely at the individually appointed time, children can put their heads on their desks and just listen for approximately five minutes. Then the children would think about what they heard going on around them and could record their "noises" as well as possible. At a later time, perhaps the next day, the children can share their written observations and comment on the "reality," the vividness of each one.

Myra Gibson's *What Is Your Favorite Thing To Hear?* should be able to provoke children into responding to the author's question quite easily. Gibson includes some favorite sounds in verse form. Toward the end of the book, after referring to many sounds the speaker of the book loves to hear, the title question is posed. In a discussion period, children can be encouraged to talk about their favorite sounds. After talking about them, some may want to write their own. A poem that might fit in well at this time is Myra Cohn Livingston's "Whispers" in *Whispers and Other Poems,* illustrated by Jacqueline Chwast (New York: Harcourt, Brace and World, Inc., 1958).

Special Words for Special Effects

As children gain more experience with poetry, they come to realize that poets choose each of their words with care in order to establish a mood, express a particular shade of meaning, or achieve a special effect. With younger children, this realization will come sooner if they are exposed to some poems in which the choice of words for special effects is particularly noticeable. For instance, you might try a poem intended to make a reader feel dizzy—"Merry-Go-Round" by Dorothy Baruch.[9] The arrangement of the words on the page and the repetition of *around* and *round, up* and *down* combine to achieve the desired effect. (This selection is a good one to have children record; they will enjoy trying to read it in a way that produces a dizzying effect on listeners.) Another poem that children like to play with on a tape recorder is "Raccoon" by William Jay Smith.[10] The recital of the many animals the raccoon would prefer to be instead of being himself is bound to leave a reader breathless.

In "Little Charlie Chipmunk,"[11] Helen LeCron uses the word chattered so many times that the reader feels the urge to stifle the talkative Charlie.

An excellent way to prove that words can make a reader laugh is to read the superb nonsense poems of Laura E. Richards. Her works are widely anthologized. You may want to try to get a copy of *Tirra Lirra*. Richards revels in using coined words and sprightly rhythms. In addition, the *Poetry Keepsake* compiled by Louise Markert includes two poems that children can delight in. In "Parrot," by William Jay Smith, the author presents some of the phrases that the parrot uses that sound "terribly bad." Some of the *verboten* exclamations the parrot from Trinidad uses include "Lolloping Lumberjack" and "Cold Kamchatka." Children *might* be encouraged to think of some more forbidden remarks that could be attributed to the hero of the poem. David McCord, in the poem "Up from Down Under," combines rollicking words like *billabong, boomerang, kangaroo,* and *collibah,* which are sure to amuse readers.

Sound and Sense

One of the ways in which poetry achieves its rhythmic, musical quality is through the use of alliteration. Alliteration is simply the repetition of the same sound, whether it be a consonant or a vowel. If consonants are repeated, as in the phrase by Rudyard Kipling in "The Cat That Walked by Himself"—"and they walked in the Wet Wild Woods by their wild lones," the precise term for the repetition of the consonant sound of *w* is *consonance*. If vowel sounds are repeated, as in "Jane gazed lazily at the lacy sky," the reoccurrence of the vowel sound *a* is called *assonance*.

Besides producing a lyrical quality, certain consonant sounds can produce a "soft" or "languid" mood. In the quotation from Kipling, for instance, the reiteration of the w sound causes a slow, leisurely tone or sensation. Other consonants that can create similar feelings are the letters l, m, v, and s. Some consonants create an explosive, fast, humorous, or harsh feeling; they include the hard sound of the letter c, and the letters q, k, p, d, and b.

Short vowel sounds tend to give a writing a clipped tone, while long vowel sounds and vowel combinations such as the sound of "oo" in "moon" and "too" cause words to linger and echo making them seem longer. One poem that repeatedly uses long "oo" sounds is "Choosing Shoes" by Ffrida Wolfe.[12] This sound is employed eighteen times in seventeen lines.

To demonstrate these points inductively to students, you may wish to read some specific poems to children and ask them what they notice about the contrasting groups of selections. Ask them to pay particular attention to specific groups of words.

To prove the humorous outcome of utilizing repeated hard or gutteral consonants, you can read choices such as Rands's[13] poem, "Godfrey Gordon Gustavus Gore," the fellow who would never shut a door, or "Old Quin Queeribus" by Turner.[14] This latter poem tells about a strange character who loved his garden products so much that he could never eat them, he could only watch them grow. Of course, a book of tongue twisters such as Peter Piper's Alphabet, illustrated by Marcia Brown,[15] would be an excellent resource to demonstrate the pervasive comic effect of repeated consonant sounds.

Merriam,[16] in It Doesn't Always Have to Rhyme, includes an interesting free verse poem titled, "A Jamboree for J." Using mainly j words, the point she makes is that it is difficult to make a j sound anything else but happy. She employs thirty-eight joyful j words. The effect is, indeed, delightful. After hearing the effect that j's have on Merriam, some children might want to talk or write about the effects that other letters have on them. Some letters, such as the explosive ones, may tickle their funny bones, while others, like l may give them lumps in their throats or turn their smiles upside down.

A Mother Goose poem that begins with the words, "One misty moisty morning," gives at the same time a humorous tone plus a soft, dreamylike feeling because of the specific use of the consonant m.

Poems that truly cast a spell of softness, peace, and quietude include Cane's[17] "Snow Toward Evening," de la Mare's[18] "Silver," and Wylie's[19] "Velvet Shoes." After reading the poems aloud, you could pass out copies and let the children see what words are creating the many long vowel sounds. They can note also the great use that the poets make of *s* sounds. Ten out of fourteen lines in "Silver" and thirteen out of twenty lines in "Velvet Shoes" end in long vowel sounds. The use of long vowel sounds in lines and at the ends of lines seems to produce a long, lingering feeling. (Although all vowels resound, the "echoes" made by long vowels cast longer shadows.) You might also have children observe the effect that using words such as "slowly," "silently," "soft," "sleep," and "still" in these poems have on the reader. The point is that certain words in and of themselves, because of the meanings that they convey, the connotations that they hold, create a mood or tone. This can be discussed and lists of words that would contribute to eliciting or evoking specific feelings could be compiled. In "Velvet Shoes," by Wylie, children again may be asked to note the number of times the author uses *s* words in particular, and peaceful, quiet words in general.

Having been exposed to the suggestions given so far, children would already have met "coined" words and would be aware of the humorous effect that they cause. Teachers may elect to read some of Kipling's stories in his book, *The Just So Stories,* to expose children to the beautiful alliterative language that Kipling so frequently uses. In addition, like Laura E. Richards and Ogden Nash, Kipling occasionally uses nonsense words. For example, in "How the Whale Got His Throat," one line the Mariner speaks is—"By means of grating/I have stopped your ating." In this same story there is a wonderful paragraph that through the employment of twenty-two rhyming verbs, tells exactly what the Mariner did as soon as he found himself in the "Whale's . . . inside cupboards."

A very similar technique has been utilized by Fyleman[20] in the poem "The Goblin." It tells, by employing many rhyming verbs, what the goblin does in "OUR house." From hearing these two selections children could be encouraged to work together, compiling a series of rhymed verbs that might be appropriate to use when talking about boys, girls, babies, parents, dogs, or cats.

Other Features of Verse

Besides the use of specific vowels and consonants, the length of the words used in the writing of poems and the length of the lines themselves in the works contribute to the mood of the writings. A poem mentioned previously, "Raccoon" by William Jay Smith, produces a fast pace because of its very short lines. In addition, the poem's tempo is increased because Smith employs more than twice as many monosyllabic words as polysyllabic words. Another poem that would help children to realize the effect of short lines on the poem's pace is "Timothy Boon" by Ivy O. Eastwick.[21] Only one line out of thirty has more than four words in it, and that one line has six words. It might be appropriate in working with this poem to point out to the children that quite a few lines in this poem do not end with punctuation marks. There are many lines, in other words, that are not "end-stopped." They are run-on lines. This technique of using run-on lines, or *enjambment,* helps to move any piece along briskly. Because the lines are so short, there is no need of punctuation within each line which, if used, would help to slow down a work. "Timothy Boon" may be contrasted with "Godfrey Gordon Gustavus Gore," in which only three lines out of twenty-six are not end-stopped. Moreover, several of the lines in this latter poem have internal punctuation.

Occasionally, however, there may be a poem that uses so much internal punctuation that the result is a choppy, very fast-moving piece of writing. It seems as though each word or phrase is a different line. An example of such a piece is "For a Mocking Voice" by Farjeon.[22] In this poem every line is end-stopped and abounds in internal punctuation. The poem includes many questions and exclamations, and those questions and exclamations are repeated either partially or wholly. This might be an excellent poem to use with pupils for choral reading. You might ask the children how they think it should be handled and then permit them to do it in various ways and tape-record their presentations. They could then decide which way sounded best, and perhaps they could think of other ways to improve the poem's dramatic qualities further. Another example of such a poem is "A Sure Sign" by Nancy Byrd Turner,[23] where the internal punctuation provides a heightened feeling of excitement and the sensation of pressing urgency. It recreates the scene a person acts out in sorting the mail near Valentine's Day when he/she is hoping to find a Valentine among the assorted pieces of mail.

One poem that very appropriately seems to move on, not impeded by much punctuation at all, is Harry Behn's "The Kite."[24] Behn helps to promote a feeling of ease, motion, and speed in this poem by including only one multisyllabic word out of one hundred and seven words.

Four poems that are over almost as soon as they are begun are Dickinson's[25] "A Word," Sir Henry Newbolt's[26] "Finis," Robert Frost's[27] "Dust of Snow," and James Guthrie's[28] "Last Song." These poems have very short lines and a preponderance of monosyllabic words that contribute to their mood of brevity and fleetingness. In "Dust of Snow" the only action that takes place is that a crow shakes down just a "dust," just a little suspicion of snow, on the speaker of the poem and thus helps save some part of his day. This little action befits a little poem. After hearing, seeing, and talking about these poems, some children at least will be able to realize how these authors used short lines and one-syllable words to establish a certain mood.

Why Bother With All That?

It may be objected that the last part of the discussion—the part relating to sound and sense in poetry—has little practical value for elementary school. And certainly every teacher must decide how much attention to pay to the inner workings of poetry. John Ciardi writes that analysis of a poem can help a reader "enter the poem more perceptively."[29] In my experience, thinking and talking about the sounds of poetry and how the sounds match the sense can enhance the appreciation of children who are ready for it. As Ciardi points out, poetry is a game with some difficulties in it. He also points out that a game with no difficulties—no challenge—is not much fun.

Helps

Daly, Brian, Neville, Mary H., and Pugh, A.K., *Reading While Listening: An Annotated Bibliography of Materials and Research, Paper No. 13*, The University of Leeds Institute of Education, 1975.

Duker, Sam, compiler, *Teaching Listening in the Elementary School: Readings*, Metuchen, N.J.: The Scarecrow Press, 1971.

Rasmussen, Carrie, *Choral Speaking for Speech Improvement*, Magnolia, Mass.: Expression Company—Publishers, 1953. This small book includes a selection of poems and notes on how to use them with elementary school-age children. There are poems that stress particular vowel sounds that the teacher may find helpful to use as listening reinforcement activities after particular vowel sounds are introduced. Because of the date when the book was published, there is a poem that teachers should avoid using. It is the "Story of Creation," page 52.

Russell, David H., and Russell, Elizabeth F. *Listening Aids through the Grades*, New York: Columbia University, Bureau of Publications Teachers College, 1959. *Listening Aids through the Grades* is a paperback that, in addition to including one hundred and ninety listening acitivities for the teacher to select from, includes listening references and materials arranged according to "general references and sources," "specific teaching techniques and materials," "teaching with audiovisual aids," and "tests of auding abilities." The booklet ends with four blank sheets of paper on which the teacher can record his/her own listening ideas and activities. A most worthwhile resource tool.

Schoolfield, Lucille D., and Timberlake, Josephine B., *Sounds the Letters Make*, Boston: Little, Brown and Company, 1940. This unpaged book contains poems each of which emphasizes a certain letter or letter combination sound. Many of the poems include short suggestions for children to involve themselves in after the poem has been presented to them. As one example, after the short poem that has several long *i* sounds in it is introduced the following suggestion is offered: "Can you draw a kite and put some other Long I words on it?"

Wagner, Guy, Hosier, Max, and Blackman, Mildred, *Listening Games: Building Listening Skills with Instructional Games*, Darien, Conn.: Teachers Publishing Corporation, 1962. Similar to the Russells' paperback, this paperback describes one hundred and forty-one listening games and activities. There is a section devoted to "Other Ways of Developing Listening Power," a section that includes an annotated "bibliography of professional references," and an "index of skills." The "index of game titles" is divided so that a reader can pick activities suitable for the needs and abilities of the pupils.

Withers, Carl, illustrated by Garry Mackenzie, *A Treasury of Games*, New York: Grosset and Dunlap, Publishers, 1964. Delightful! Filled with all kinds of games sure to please children. Two listening activities that children probably would want to play are "Aunt Jemima's Trunk," a more complex variation of "The Minister's Cat" game (p. 156), and "New Names," a game where everyone is given a new name for a certain period of time. Players must remember to call that person by *whatever* name they choose to give (nonsense name, animal name, vegetable name, and so forth). If a teacher wanted to make the game more complex after the children became familiar with this version, she/he could have the children give different names to objects given in the classroom (e.g., books, blackboard, chairs) and see if the children and she/he could remember the new names. A good story to read along with this activity is "Master of All Masters." It can be found in "Time for Magic," pp. 157–158 in *The Arbuthnot Anthology of Children's Literature*, Fourth Edition (Glenview, Ill.: Scott, Foresman and Company, 1976). Another fine literary motivator for these activities is the poem, "Blum," by Dorothy Aldis in *Here, There and Everywhere* (New York: G.P. Putnam's Sons, 1956).

Literary Suggestions to Help Children Enjoy Listening

Carlson, Bernice Wells, "Our Thanksgiving Dinner" in *Listen! And Help Tell the Story*, Nashville: New York, 1965. "Our Thanksgiving Dinner" is a cumulative poem that can be used to stimulate children to listen and chime in on the lines that they remember. It is a fine poem that children can be encouraged to adapt to use for other special occasions such as their birthdays or Christmas.

Dale, Ralph Alan, pictures by Olivia H.H. Cole, *Games to Sing and Play*, New York: Scholastic Book Services, 1971. A delightful paperback that contains songs and verses that invite children to listen and then participate actively in the singing. Fun!

Flack, Marjorie, "Ask Mr. Bear" in "Time for Fairy Tales" in *The Arbuthnot Anthology of Children's Literature*, Chicago: Scott, Foresman and Company, 1961. A short story that a teacher can read to pupils and give them chances to participate in by answering questions posed in the tale.

Guilfoyle, Elizabeth, pictures by Mary Stevens, *Nobody Listens to Andrew*, New York: Scholastic Book Services, 1957. What happens in this paperback because "nobody listens to Andrew" should help to promote the attitude that people, young and old alike, should listen to what others are saying to them or else the consequences could be disastrous.

Heide, Florence Parry, pictures by Kenneth Longtemps, *Sound of Sunshine, Sound of Rain*, New York: Parents' Magazine Press, 1970. A beautifully written and illustrated book about a young black boy who is blind but who listens for all the lovely sounds around him that so many of us miss. He listens for the sound of sunshine, the sound of rain, the sounds of leaves, the sounds of life and love. A sensitive book.

Holl, Adelaide, literary editor, pictures by Art Seiden, *Listening for Sounds,* New York: Western Publishing Company, Inc., 1970. This is a book that uses many onomatopoeic sounds and that asks questions of its listeners. A book that is appropriate for children in the primary grades.

Hutchins, Pat, *The Surprise Party,* New York: Collier Books, 1969. *The Surprise Party* is a story that tells how Rabbit first tells his friend Owl that he is having a surprise party. Owl relays a distorted message to Squirrel and, in turn, Squirrel relays another distorted message to Duck. Each creature hears an entirely different message from what Rabbit originally said. When the time comes for Rabbit to invite his friends to his party personally, they all refuse. Rabbit has to straighten the whole mess out and everyone does come to a nice party that, indeed, is a surprise party for all.

After hearing this paperback, the teacher can whisper a message to one of the children in the group who can pass it to the next. The last child in the group can tell what he or she thinks the original message was. The teacher can then repeat the original comment and the children can see whether or not they "passed" correctly. This passing game is more fun if a group of about twelve to fifteen children are involved. As the children become more adept at playing this game, the message passed can become more complex.

Weston Woods in Weston, Connecticut offers for sale or for rent a filmstrip based on Pat Hutchins' *The Surprise Party* that may excite some reluctant readers to read the book.

Podendorf, Illa, illustrations by Darrell Wiskur, *Sounds All About,* Chicago: Children's Press, 1970.

Rand, Ann, and Rand, Paul, *Listen! Listen!,* New York: Harcourt, Brace and World, Inc., 1970.

Sicotte, Virginia, illustrated by Edward Ardizzone, *A Riot of Quiet,* New York: Holt, Rinehart and Winston, 1969.

Victor, Joan Berg, *Sh-H! Listen Again! Sounds of the Seasons,* Cleveland: The World Publishing Company, 1969.

Wessells, Katherine Tyler, selector and arranger, pictures by June Goldsborough, *Songs and Singing Games.* New York: Western Publishing Company, Inc., 1970.

Winn, Marie, collector and editor, musical arrangements by Allan Miller, pictures by Karla Kuskin, *What Shall We Do and Allee Galloo!,* New York: Harper and Row, Publishers, 1970.

4 Bringing Children to Their Senses

TO LOOK AT ANY THING

To look at any thing,
If you would know that thing,
You must look at it long:
To look at this green and say
"I have seen spring in these
Woods," will not do-you must
Be the thing you see;
You must be the dark snakes of
Stems and ferny plumes of
    leaves,
You must enter in
To the small silences between
The leaves,
You must take your time
And touch the very peace
They issue from.
—John Moffitt

Educators who recognize the importance of listening in the language arts are not always aware of the role of the other senses in developing a child's creative abilities. It is essential to help childen to develop all of their senses. They must be given opportunities to see things, smell things, taste things, and touch things and be given many opportunities to talk about their reactions to these things. They need opportunities to let their imaginations reach out and explore, and they should be able to follow where their imaginations take them. They can be helped in this journey by listening to poems and literary selections that appeal to the senses, that will invade their senses, and that will foster in them a desire to express themselves, whether it be in an oral or written form, so that their listeners or readers will be touched by what they are thinking. Edward L. Mattil[1] reminds us that every small child's senses are acutely developed. Our job as teachers is to keep our pupils receptive to the messages from their senses and to help them to develop sensitivity and selectivity.

The activities discussed in this chapter have two broad objectives: (1) to make children aware of all their senses and to use them as they speak and write, and (2) to use their senses to achieve what Dwight Burton refers to as "imaginative entry"[2] when they read. Without imaginative entry or empathy there can be no "reading" of literature. Burton insists that every teacher can promote imaginative entry by first choosing selections for children that will give them a running chance to utilize their own experiences as the "touchstone" for imaginative entry. In introducing specific works to children a teacher should consciously and overtly help the students to relate their experiences to those described in the selections.

A simple book that can be used to introduce students to an awareness of all of their senses is *My Five Senses* by Aliki.[3] *My Five Senses* helps a child to notice that there are times when he/she uses all five senses, while at other times only one or two may be important.

Another book that can be used in starting work on developing children's senses is *About Four Seasons and Five Senses* by Radlauer.[4] In rhyme, the book concentrates its attention on the five senses of seeing, hearing, smelling, tasting, and feeling. Radlauer takes each season, one by one, and describes what everyone can see, hear, smell, taste, and feel. After each section has been covered (e.g., what feelings a person may experience in the springtime, a question is always posed such as, "What other feelings do you have in spring?" This is a book that a teacher can use throughout the year. *About Four Seasons and Five Senses* encourages much thinking, discussing, and participating on the part of both the teacher presenting it and the pupils listening to it.

Learning How to Use the Five Senses by Fuller and Ellis[5] is one more resource that can be referred to throughout the school year. This book is filled with suggestions of activities to use in helping children become involved in a series of explicit sensory experiences.

1. SIGHT

The objective in working with the sense of sight should not be only to help children become accurate observers, important as that goal is. We also want them to be imaginative viewers who are able to see things differently and freshly. Small children begin by noticing everything but, as they grow older and have more to compete for their attention, children fall into the grown-up habit of looking without seeing. No one remains acutely observant by chance. It is a skill that must be learned, worked on, practiced. The suggestions in this section are intended to encourage children to see when they look.

Getting Started

A good first book for helping children build perception skills is *Snail, Where Are You?* by Ungerer.[6] This book contains no text, just colorful pictures; each picture is incorporated with at least one snail. As a follow-up activity, your children might enjoy drawing pictures of their own in which they conceal the shape of something.

A book that might further excite the pupils about the possibilities of shapes is *The Wing on a Flea*[7] by Ed Emberley. It is similar to Ungerer's book in that it tickles a child's imagination, curiosity, and ideational and associational fluency; it deals most ingeniously with triangles, circles, and rectangles. Throughout the book Emberley tells his readers to look and see.

It is a very simply written selection in verse form with charming and detailed illustrations. You will find some imaginative exercises involving shapes and testing powers of observation in *Invitations to Speaking and Writing* by Myers and Torrance.[8] In "Figure It Out," they suggest giving children drawings of geometrical shapes with other shapes enclosed and asking them to figure out how many squares, triangles, and so on there are.

You can find additional visual material for sharpening observation in *The Arrow Book of Brain Teasers*,[9] which contains illustrations in which mistakes have been made and a good puzzle called "Jane's Patchwork Quilt," in which ten girl's names are concealed in the design.

You may also want to consider some introductory activities suggested by Myers and Torrance that do not involve books or pictures. One such idea is to have children try, for a given period, to look at objects as though they were seeing them for the first time. Later, the children are asked to list five items and tell what was "new" about them. Another possibility is to ask a series of questions that require careful observation to answer (e.g., which shoe do you put on first in the morning?).

An exciting book for both children and teachers is Marilyn Burns's *The Book of Think: Or How to Solve a Problem Twice Your Size* (Boston: Little, Brown and Company, 1976). Part One; "Getting Out of Your Own Way," is especially valuable to use to sharpen our powers of observation.

Observation Games

Games provide an entertaining way of building observation skills. The possibilities suggested here obviously lend themselves to variation.

Sometime, with no advance warning, you might ask your pupils to cover their eyes and describe what someone in front of or beside them is wearing. At another time, you might ask your pupils to enumerate as many objects in the classroom as possible—again without looking. In these and other gamelike acitivities, award points liberally for accurate observation.

You can set up a good activity by displaying a random collection of objects on a table top and giving the children a minute or so to examine them. Then, without looking, they can be asked to list as many of the displayed objects as they can remember. This activity can be repeated from time to time, using an increasing number of objects as the children's powers of observation increase.

A variant on this activity is "What's Missing?" This time, you leave the displayed objects around for most of the day and remove one when no one is looking. The idea is to remember what was there in order to tell what is missing. A similar game can be played by randomly grouping pupils in a circle with their eyes closed. You tap one child, who will then quietly leave the room. Have the remaining children hold hands to make the circle smaller and then open their eyes. The first child to notice who is missing wins.

Awareness Books

"Awareness books"—books expressly designed to make their young readers aware of the quality of their experience—can be useful for developing all of the senses. We will deal with them here because sight always receives the main emphasis.

Alvin Tresselt has written some excellent awareness books that you will want to investigate. In *Rain Drop Splash,*[10] he explores what happens on a day that it rains a lot. Of particular interest is the way in which the book employs typographical devices to suggest the different kinds of rain. If you use this book, give your pupils plenty of time to examine it and encourage them to try their hands at arranging words in a way that reinforces their ideas.

White Snow, Bright Snow,[11] another of Tresselt's books, helps children to be aware of what happens when it snows, the effect that snow has on people, and what snow looks like. While the children still have the author's evocative images in mind, you may want to follow up with discussions intended to encourage pupils to record their own impressions of a rainy or snowy day.

Can You Imagine? by Myers and Torrance[12] contains some excellent activities designed to lead children to take a closer look at the world around them. You will find activities that ask children to think of ways in which different objects are alike; they are particularly useful as a first step in introducing the uses of figurative language.

Using Pictures

A number of other books, in addition to those mentioned already, can help children become better observers. *Stop, Look, and Write!,* by Leavitt and Sohn[13] leads children to notice and record through a series of structured activities.

Many fine books are available that contain only pictures. Three of them that you may want to look at are *A Taste of Carrot* by Hoest,[14] *A Boy, a Dog, and a Frog* by Mayer,[15] and *Your Face Is a Picture* by the Cliffords.[16] The last of these is a delightful collection of photographs of children. The faces are so expressive of the emotions of all children that they readily convince the "reader" that faces tell a story. You can easily use the photographs in *Your Face Is a Picture* to stimulate discussion as to what must have happened to make each child look the way he/she does.

A good resource while you are focusing attention on pictures is Helen

Borten's *A Picture Has a Special Look,*[17] which has great appeal both because of its appearance and its language. It explains how different tools such as pens, pencils, crayons, and brushes make pictures look different. Borten's illustrations demonstrate the variances she talks about. If you use this book, you may want to have pupils experiment with some of the techniques Borten describes.

Looking at Words

A special kind of observation game with obvious relevance to reading involves noticing similarities and differences in the appearance of words. Here are two that you might want to try. To play "Twins," you need a number of cards on each of which is printed either (1) a pair of identical words (the "twins" of the title of the game), or (2) two look-alike words (such as *quit* and *quite*). The object is to sort out the identical pairs. The next game—"Almost Alike"—has a similar idea. This time, you provide each child with a sheet on which there are pairs of words that are almost alike (e.g., *through* and *though*). As you hold up a card that has one word from each pair on it, the children circle the matching word on their papers.

Pictures in Words

The illustrations in books are one way of developing visual awareness but, of course, you will not want to neglect the power of words to evoke images. You might try reading selections that contain vivid descriptions and having your pupils illustrate what they see. (This activity will work better if you do not announce in advance to your pupils that they will be asked to illustrate the reading.) Some good possibilities for this kind of assignment are:

1. "The Pirate Don Durk of Dowdee" by Mildred Plew Meigs.[18] (You might award a point for every feature of the pirate a pupil remembers. Children who draw a *squizzamaroo* should get a bonus of at least five points!)
2. *Pippi Longstocking* by Lindgren.[19] (The description of Pippi on p. 5 is a good passage to use.)
3. *The Borrowers* by Norton.[20] (Use the description of where the borrowers live that appears on pp. 15–20. For this assignment, you may wish to have your pupils illustrate or construct, bit by bit, the kind of home the borrowers have. Children will think of other examples of minutiae that the borrowers could put to good use.)

Seeing Things Differently

The suggestions and selections in this section are intended to encourage children to use their imaginations and pretend. A good book for reinforcing a child's natural desire to pretend is *I See What I See!* by Selden.[21] This story tells about a group of children who "pretend" in all their ordinary activities. The problem they encounter is with their friend, Jerry, who only sees what he sees, and does not participate in any of their make-believe. How the children scheme to get Jerry to see what is not really there is the plot of the story.

An excellent poem to use to introduce the children to Selden's book is entitled, "One Day We Went Walking," by Valine Hobbs. It can be found in *Language Skills in Elementary Education* by Anderson.[22] This poem describes how a very creative child talks about objects she finds when she goes walking. However, her unimaginative companions each time state that what she calls a "dreadful dragon's tooth" or a "brownie's button shoe" is actually only "a locust thorn" or "a dry pea pod." The persona of the poem wisely decides that when she goes for walks in the future, unless she happens to meet an elf, she will go by herself!

After reading this selection to children, you could name other articles and ask what they could be used for. For example, a rose petal might be a fairy queen's silken mantle, while an acorn cap might be a fitting soup dish for an elf.

A very appropriate poem that picks up a similar idea is found in "If I Were Teeny Tiny" by Beatrice Schenk de Regniers.[23] After presenting the poem to pupils the following questions might be raised. If you were "teeny tiny":

What would you ride on?
What would you sleep on?
What would you wear?
What else might you do?

You might ask the children whether they think it is fun to pretend and then ask them what they would like to pretend. After the children have given their suggestions, you could cast your magic spell and everyone could make-believe as they wish.

Helen Borten, in her book *Do You See What I See?*,[24] explains the effect that lines in drawings as well as colors have on readers. In all her explanations of how the various lines that artists use make her feel, she employs excellent similes. For example, she writes that up and down lines make her "feel as tall as a steeple and as taut as a stretched rubber band."

Children could be encouraged to tell how lines make them feel; how lines make things the way they are. There is a fine poem on "Lines" included in E.E. Smith's dissertation.[25] In the poem a child writes how different lines make such beautiful sights as:

The curve of the horizon at sunset
The little brooks wandering unevenly
Long lines of mountains
Straight lines of tall trees. . . .

Another book that might be used in conjunction with the last two selections is *Let's Imagine Thinking Up Things* by Wolff.[26] The author concentrates on getting children to think of as many things as they can that circles, squares, lines, and triangles can be. Although some of the suggestions that Wolff offers are not that original, the book still could be used as a spur to having children be on the watch for unusual circles, squares, lines and triangles in what they see. It could promote ideational fluency.

It Looked Like Spilt Milk, by Charles Shaw,[27] is an extremely easy book that advances the idea that objects can look different to different persons. The book, which contains many similes, repeats the words "it looked like Spilt Milk, But it wasn't Spilt Milk." Children will become curious to find out what is being discussed. At the conclusion of the book, it is revealed that it is a cloud that is being described. Each picture in the book is white on a deep blue backgroud. Children could be asked to observe the clues given, to see whether they can solve the mystery.

John Farrar[28] has a poem entitled "Watching Clouds," which the teacher could recite at this time. Another excellent poem about clouds has been written by Helen Wing. It can be found in *Language Skills in Elementary Education* by Anderson.[29] The poem describes the different objects the speaker sees as the clouds go by. After hearing such selections, children could be permitted to go out on a warm day and just be allowed to watch the clouds float lazily by the sky. Afterward, they could be encouraged to talk about what they saw.

To follow up the activity of watching clouds, children could be directed to watch the wind at different times and report what they see. A beautifully written book that shows in pictures what the wind does is *I See the Winds* by Mizumura.[30] The words, arranged as a free verse poem, are written on the left side, and directly opposite them is a picture of what the words represent. The picture for the words, "I see the wind on the tree tops tinkling gold spangled leaves against the sky so high," is a splash of gold against blue. Other pictures in *I See the Winds* are somber and quiet and are done in grays and blacks. Many of the pictures resemble water colors. The illustrations are fluid and moving, as befits the title of the book. This book, with its lovely language and pictures, is an excellent tool to help children "see."

A poem to encourage children to envision how things would look from a different stance can be found in *Language Skills in Elementary Education* by

Anderson.[31] The poem tells what the writer would see if he were a star on the top of a Christmas tree.

To encourage children to see things in a fresh way, the poems "Dandelion" by Conkling,[32] "Taxis" by Field,[33] and "Motor Cars" by Bennett[34] could be read. Field compares taxis to spools of colored thread and remarks that they make a most pleasing sight. Conkling, in looking at a dandelion, sees a tiny soldier with a golden helmet guarding her lawn. Bennett, in "Motor Cars," says that the cars look like black burnished beetles. The imagery used throughout the poem centers around the concept of cars looking like beetles.

Other materials that might be used to convince children that objects are different and should be described differently are the poems "Lone Dog," "Sunning," and "City Streets and Country Roads," as well as the book, A Thousand Lights and Fireflies by Tresselt.[35] The first two poems project two completely different "pictures" of dogs. "Lone Dog," by Rutherford,[36] reveals a lean, independent, tough dog; "Sunning,"[37] by Tippett, conjures up an extremely lazy, obviously dependent dog. The words that Tippett chooses for his poem produce a mood of languor. Farjeon,[38] in "City Streets and Country Roads," contrasts the sights and smells of the city as opposed to those of the country. In the poem she reveals her preference for the country. In Tresselt's book the differences between city and country houses, animals, flowers, and birds are pictured.

A tale that could be fitted in and discussed during this period is "The Blind Men and the Elephant." One source for this fable is the Anthology of Children's Literature by Johnson, Sickels, and Sayers.[39]

Joan Walsh Anglund has written a charming book that could be the basis for many "seeing" assignments. In Look Out the Window[40] Anglund directs her readers' attention to the fact that houses are different, as are cats, dogs, and people. She describes houses, cats, dogs, and people and illustrates the points she makes so that children can become aware that words can make one see. After finishing this book and discussing some of the lovely sights that the children enjoy seeing, activities that might be suggested and carried out include having the children:

1. Describe one thing they know or like very well.
2. Describe the wind, snow, rain, or trees as they are at different times.
3. Describe different kinds of hair, hands, eyes, or noses that they either see in their classroom or imagine a fantastic creature might have.
4. Describe the beginning of fear, love, laughter, or tears.

Here is what some youngsters have seen:

WHY I LIKE WINTER
I like winter for many reasons:
The clouds like creamy marshmallows
Snow like soft white feathers
Trees like shivering root-beer lollipops
And the snowflakes like falling shiny diamonds
You can see why I like winter.
   —Susan

SNOW
Snow is a horse galloping down the sky
It's also an apple tree blossoming
It comes pounding
It comes so you can't hear it at all
The sounds of snow are lovely.
   —Lorna

SNOW
What is snow?
Snow is a white blanket
Snow is a rollercoaster
But most of all
Snow is fun!
   —Karen

A QUIET POND
A quiet pond
So cool and solemn.
And everywhere the lilypads blossom.
All the fairies come out of their homes
Which are closed lilypads—shaped like domes.
   —Susan

FRUIT
I love fruit,
Oranges, round and juicy
Blueberries, fat and plump
Apples like big red balls
Cherries, sparkling red and sweet
Bananas, long ski slopes
Melons like big balloons
You can see why I like fruit.
   —Catherine

THE TEAR

At first just a bit of moisture resting on the brink of uncertainty, the beginning of the tear. But it was not to remain so, for it was destined.

The tear grew and reached such voluminous proportions that the liquid brown eye encasing it could no longer keep it within its confines. And so with a silent flickering of the thickly fringed lashes, the tear embarked to its destiny.

It trickled down a pale angular cheek and continued sliding along the slight curve of a diminutive freckled face. The tear went on its way leaving a trace of salt-stained moisture in its wake. Lastly, it reached a trembling chin, whereupon, with a barely perceptible quiver, it tumbled off, and was lost forever.

—Susan

2. TOUCH

The information we get from hearing and seeing may be abstract and generalized, such as when we listen to a lecture or read nonfiction. But the messages we get from our other senses—touch, taste, and smell—are always direct, immediate, and personal. It is through these senses that we form most of our impressions about the physical quality of the world around us. Therefore, if we want our children to read with their senses and to use sense experience in their writing, these senses deserve attention also.

Two books that suggest excellent activities involving touch are *Find Out by Touching* by Paul Showers[41] and *The Touch Me Book* by Pat and Eve Witte.[42]

Find Out by Touching asks its readers a lot of questions—how their faces feel, how the carpet feels, and so on. Showers gives an answer to each of these questions, but children should be encouraged to give their own answers using, as capably as they can, word pictures and precise descriptions. *The Touch Me Book* contains things for children to touch as objects are described. Children who have enjoyed this book may want to make a *Touch Me Book* of their own, including in it a variety of textures and describing each imaginatively.

Myra Gibson has written a book that asks the question *What Is Your Favorite Thing to Touch?*[43] This simple, rhymed book achieves an intimate, personal effect by asking readers questions that draw them into it. It should lead to interesting discussions about the children's favorite things to touch.

You will want to have objects of different sizes and textures in the classroom for children to feel when you are working with the sense of touch. One possibility is to provide a box of varied objects that the children feel without looking. The idea, of course, is for them to guess the object from touch alone. A variant on this idea is to put the various items in paper bags, one bag and object to a pupil. Pupils can then be asked to describe their objects as exactly as they can without using any words that depend on seeing. Thus, children would be asked to describe a stone by telling about how big it was, whether it was heavy or light, smooth or rough, cool or warm, what it could be used for, and so on. They would not mention its color or its exact dimensions. This time, the goal is to have the other pupils try to guess the object described from the given sense data alone.

As youngsters gain some experience in describing the way things feel, you might try providing a variety of textures—sandpaper, silk, velvet, leather, burlap—for children to touch and describe.

Using Literary Selections

To tickle a discussion on physical feeling into being and to arouse an abundance of ideas and to incite each child's associational fluency, the teacher might read the following poems to her group. Two poems by Dorothy Aldis[44] are named "Hands" and "Feet." Each poem enumerates only the things that hands or feet can do. Children might easily be stimulated to try their own creations on what hands and feet can do. Aldis' poems certainly could arouse the children's ideational and associational fluency.

A poem that could be slipped in very easily now is Polly Chase Boyden's[45] "Mud." This poem presents the joy of feeling mud between the toes. Children could tell what other things they like to feel. Teachers should contribute their thoughts, too. Teachers might say, for example, how they like mysterious, lumpy, bumpy packages gloriously wrapped at Christmas time.

A lovely poem that stirs the sense of feeling is E.E. Cummings'[46] "In Just-spring." It calls to mind the time of year when the world is "puddle-wonderful" and "mud-luscious." Teachers might ask their students why Cummings chose to run the children's names together in this selection. They could ask whether this technique is an effective way to show that the children come "running" and "dancing." This poem might foster discussion about what the various seasons offer that are delightful to feel and touch:

Icy-smooth long daggers of icicles
Crunchy, crinkly, wrinkly masses of fallen leaves
Satin ribbons of tender green grass
Silky soft pale rose petals.

Teachers might want to read to their pupils the chapter called "Pippi Goes to a Coffee Party" by Lindgren[47] in the book *Pippi Longstocking*. Pippi declares that nothing is more fun than walking barefoot on a floor that has been sprinkled with sugar.

Aliki[48] has a book called *My Hands*. This simply written book refers to all the wonderful things that hands can do. Some of the ideas and illustrations Aliki includes are quite clever. For example, Aliki says that on all days hands can be used for good manners. Teachers might ask whether hands could indicate that they liked or disliked someone very much, or how else they come in "handy." They might also ask what fun children would miss out on if they did not have hands. Children could be encouraged to illustrate their remarks.

3. TASTE AND SMELL

Because the sense of smell and the sense of taste are closely related as anyone who has tried to enjoy Thanksgiving dinner while suffering from a cold knows, and because there is relatively less material to use in exploring these senses, they are grouped together here.

In "A Matter of Taste,"[49] Eve Merriam asks readers what their tongues like best and gives some suggestions to get them started thinking about tastes. In "A Vote for Vanilla,"[50] the same poet imagines a world made up mostly of vanilla. (Even chairs and mice are vanilla.) Chocolate gets equal time in the title poem from Hooray for Chocolate.[51]

Christopher Morley,[52] in his poem "Animal Crackers," revels in the thoughts of his favorite supper—animal crackers and cocoa.

A book wholly dedicated to the sense of taste is How to Eat a Poem and Other Morsels by Rose Agree.[53] Totally composed of poems about food, this book is bound to make children's mouths water and to get them into the right mood for discussing food.

A poem sung by Komle, the troll, in Hopp's The Magic Chalk[54] lists the items that Komle enjoys eating. For a troll, he has an unbelievable appetite. The amounts he is capable of consuming would almost give the reader a stomach ache just reading about them. After hearing this poem, children might want to compile a list of the favorite foods that they would eat at one sitting if there were no one around to say "no."

After having heard some of the selections mentioned, you might suggest that children talk or write about their most delicious foods. One topic that could be worked on together is "titillating tastes throughout the year." You could ask individuals what some of their favorite foods are in the autumn, winter, spring, and summer, starting the children off by naming delicacies such as:

1. Crispy, crunchy, cold, sweet, red, red apples.
2. Fiery marshmallows, all soft inside, served with steaming cups of delicious hot chocolate, rimmed with cold whipped cream.

3. Huge, plump, red strawberries dripping with cream and sugar.
4. Icy slices of juicy watermelon, all pink and green.

"The Merry Pieman's Song," which is included in Applegate's *Freeing Children to Write,*[55] is a Pieman's love song to his sweetheart in which he compares her to all of the delicious foods he likes best. After reading this poem, children may like the idea of comparing a friend to a food they like a lot. This could make an enjoyable Valentine's Day project.

A hilarious cooking episode can be found in the first chapter of *Pippi Longstocking* by Astrid Lindgren.[56] It gives a picture, a very messy picture, of Pippi preparing pancakes. After reading it, the teacher could then present the poem "Advice to a Young Cook," found in Mauree Applegate's *Easy in English.*[57] Using excellent word pictures, the readers of this poem are told how to bake cookies. You could ask the children whether they thought that Pippi needed some similar advice. The pupils could be encouraged to give Pippi some guidelines for cooking. Some might prefer to imagine what Pippi's advice would be to someone on making cookies.

Up to now, many resources have been described that would help children to talk and write about their favorite tastes. But what about some nauseating tastes? To stimulate such a discussion, teachers could present the story *"Angleworms on Toast"* by MacKinlay Kantor.[58] This story tells what cures a boy of saying "creamed angleworms on toast" whenever he is asked what he will have to eat. Children could think of other items almost as disgusting to eat. They could include real hates such as spinach or liver or imaginary items such as "angleworms on toast."

Another book that could be read at this time is Dr. Seuss's *Green Eggs and Ham.*[59] Although the point the book makes is that, once tried, "green eggs and ham" are truly scrumptious, the title, by itself, presents an unappetizing picture. Incidentally, children could be told that there actually is a kind of chicken, the Araucana chicken, that lays green eggs.

There are several literary selections that teachers can present to their students to help make them aware of the importance of appealing to the sense of smell in speaking and in writing. One book, *What Is Your Favorite Smell, My Dear?* by Myra Gibson,[60] encourages children to respond by naming their own favorite odors. This book presents, in rhyme form, some of the speaker's favorite aromas. Throughout the book there is interspersed the question, "But what is your favorite smell, my dear . . .? What is your favorite smell?" After the book is finished, it would be quite natural for pupils to discuss their favorite smells and, if they wished, write and illustrate a collective piece. Some individuals may want to talk or write separately about the smells they think are irresistible or nauseating.

Four poems that could be considered for introduction at this time are "Smells (Junior)" by Christopher Morley,[61] "The World Is Full of Wonderful Smells" by Zhenya Gay,[62] "Sniff" by Frances Frost,[63] and "Suppose Again" by Merriam.[64] In Morley's piece, the speaker simply mentions what those who are nearest and dearest to him smell like. The one he likes best is Katie, because she always smells just like hot, buttered toast. Gay enumerates some of the wonderful smells the world has to offer and ends her poem by commenting on how terrible it would be if people had no noses to tell themselves of all the luscious smells there are. "Sniff" mentions how much fun it is, when school is out, to follow your nose. Merriam, in "Suppose Again," has the speaker of the poem ask how she could ever smell various things if she held onto her nose. The poem concludes with the speaker citing one thing she would rather not smell anyway. cauliflower!

After presenting some or all of the foregoing materials, you could suggest going on a "Sniffing Tour." This might be done two or three times during the school year during the different seasons. Children could talk and work together and individually on "Smells They Love," "Smells They Hate," "Smells in the Morning," "Smells in the Summer, Fall, Winter, and Spring," and so forth. Do not insist on any one particular oral or written form: just encourage children to express their ideas and try to make an appeal to the senses.

4. AFTERWORD

Young children are uninhibited in their exploration of the world through their senses. Too often, growing up is a process of learning to shut out those sense impressions that are not immediately important or useful. This is regrettable, because all human experience begins with, and remains closely related to, the senses. Encouraging children to make conscious use of their senses in exploring the world around them and entering imaginatively into stories and poems will enrich their lives, as well as their own creative expression.

Literary Suggestions to Use to Bring Children to their Senses

Abisch, Roz, illustrated by Boche Kaplan, *Open Your Eyes*, New York: Parents' Magazine Press, 1964.

Aliki, *My Five Senses*, New York: Thomas Y. Crowell Company, 1962.

Asch, Frank, illustrated by Mark Alan Stamaty, *Yellow Yellow*, New York: McGraw-Hill Book Company, 1971.

Carew, Jan, illustrated by Leo and Diane Dillon, *The Third Gift,* Boston: Little, Brown and Company, 1974. A beautiful book that tells its readers that the best gift is the gift of Fantasy, Imagination, and of Faith.

Charlip, Remy, and Joyner, Jerry, *Thirteen,* New York: Parents' Magazine Press, 1975.

Fisher, Aileen, illustrated by Adrienne Adams, *In the Middle of the Night,* New York: Thomas Y. Crowell Company, 1965.

Françoise, *The Things I Like,* New York: Charles Scribner's Sons, 1960.

Gay, Zhenya, *Look!,* New York: The Viking Press, 1952.

Hawkinson, Lucy, and Hawkinson, John, *Birds in the Sky,* Chicago: Children's Press, 1965.

Hughes, Langston, *Don't You Turn Back,* selected by Lee Bennett Hopkins, woodcuts by Ann Grifalconi, New York: Alfred A. Knopf, 1969.

Ipcar, Dahlov, *The Cat at Night,* New York: Doubleday and Company, Inc., 1969.

Lewis, Shari, and Reinach, Jacquelyn, *The Headstart Book of Looking and Listening,* New York: McGraw-Hill Book Company, 1966. Note in particular "The Little Red Hen," "Nimble B. Bimble," and "The Market Basket," all of which can be used with early primary age children to develop their listening skills.

Lund, Doris Herold, illustrated by Denman Hampson, *Did You Ever?,* New York: Parents' Magazine Press, 1965.

McGovern, Ann, illustrated by Simms Taback, *Too Much Noise,* Boston: Houghton Mifflin Company, 1967.

Martin, Bill, Jr., pictures by Samuel Maitin, *Gentle Gentle Thursday,* Glendale, Cal.: Bowmar, 1970.

Merrill, Jean, and Scott, Frances Gruse, *Here I Come–Ready or Not,* Chicago: Albert Whitman and Company, 1970.

Merrill, Jean, and Scott, Frances Gruse, *How Many Kids Are Hiding on My Block?,* Chicago: Albert Whitman and Company, 1970.

Ness, Evaline, *Exactly Alike,* New York: Charles Scriber's Sons, 1964.

Podendorf, Illa, illustrated by John Hawkinson, *Things Are Alike and Different,* Chicago: Children's Press, 1970.

Raskin, Ellen, *Nothing Ever Happens on My Block,* New York: Atheneum, 1968.

Selsam, Millicent E., *Hidden Animals,* New York: Harper and Row, Publishers, 1969.

Steiner, Charlotte, *My Bunny Feels Soft,* New York: Alfred A. Knopf, 1958.

Thoburn, Tina, pictures by James Caraway, *Discovering Shapes,* New York: Western Publishing Company, Inc., 1970.

Turkle, Brinton, *The Sky Dog,* New York: Viking Press, Inc., 1969.

Ungerer, Tomi, *One, Two, Where's My Shoe?,* New York: Harper and Row, Publishers, 1964.

Vasiliu, Mircea, *What's Happening?,* New York: The John Day Company, 1970.

Wildsmith, Brian, *Puzzles,* New York: Franklin Watts, Inc., 1970.

Yolen, Jane H., illustrated by Kathleen Elgin, *See This Little Line?,* New York: David McKay Company, Inc., 1963.

Zacharias, Thomas, and Zacharias, Wanda, *But Where Is the Green Parrot?,* New York: Delacorte Press, 1968.

5 In the Beginning Is the Word

A word is dead
When it is said,
Some say.

I say it just
Begins to live
That day.
　　　　—Emily Dickinson

Developing in children a love of words and sensitivity to their use is a long-term project, but no other aspect of language arts teaching is more important. Many of the activities suggested elsewhere in this book relate to vocabulary development. This chapter brings together a number of ideas for sparking children's interest in playing, experimenting, and creating with words.

1. INTERESTING WORDS

The word that means the most to children is their name, so talking about names is a good way to begin to kindle an interest in words. (The study of children's names was suggested earlier, in Chapter 2, as one way of building a positive self-image.) You might want to start out with two appropriate poems by Eleanor Farjeon[1]—"Girls' Names" and "Boys' Names." Farjeon mentions a name and then tells what it is like. The poems should stimulate a discussion of associations the children may have with other names. You could then follow up with an investigation into the meaning of each child's given name. An inexpensive resource that your pupils will enjoy using themselves is What Shall We Name the Baby?[2] Webster's New Collegiate Dictionary also provides information as to the origins or meanings of common English given names. You will find a lot of useful background information on names in Our Language: The Story of the Words We Use by Eloise Lambert.[3]

You may wish to continue your discussion of the children's names with some funny or otherwise remarkable names from children's literature. Some possibilities are the poems "Diana Fitzpatrick Mauleverer James" by Milne,[4] and "Godfrey Gordon Gustavus Gore" by Rands.[5] Children may want to play with the sounds of their own names after hearing "Spring Fever" by Eve

Merriam.[6] In this poem, all of the children mentioned are affected by spring fever and do something that begins with the sound of their names:

Al alibis.
Alice amasses.
Barbara boasts.
Frank frets.
John jumps.

Other Kinds of Names

You can extend your investigation of names in a number of different and interesting directions. For instance, children will be intrigued to learn that the names of many foods, drinks, clothes, and other things started out as the names of particular people. A valuable resource for this activity is *People Words* by Bill Severn.[7] Place names offer interesting possibilities, too. Chapter 6 of Lambert's *Our Language: The Story of the Words We Use*[8] provides useful information about place names, as does George Stewart's *Names on the Land.*[9] If you want to make your pupils more aware of the appropriateness of the names given to characters in the selections they read, you might mention the dragon named Custard[10] and the skunk named Aroma.[11] Children might discuss what kind of dragon would have a name like that—its appearance and its behavior—after which you could read the Ogden Nash story. Then, later, you should call attention to characters you encounter in literature that seem particularly well named. Another possibility is making up people and animals with unusual characteristics and asking the children to think of names for them. You can cap your discussion of names with Dorothy Aldis' poem "Names,"[12] in which the poet lists the names of some flowers she finds pleasant to say. Children can then be asked to give some more names that they like the sounds of.

Name Games

There are a number of name games that your children might enjoy playing. One is "What Will They Be?" in which you list some given names and ask your pupils to think of a job that would be appropriate. There are no wrong answers in this game but, of course, some associations will be more apt than others. (Some possibilities are Jimmy—a burglar, Mike—a radio announcer, Bill—a bill collector.) A variant of the game can be played by providing a list of occupations and having the children think of a person's name. For instance, Ray Dio might be the name for a radio announcer and Derek Wells the name for a man who looks for oil.

You can also play a game of making up titles for books, which you then match with a suitable author's name. For example, a book named *People* might be written by someone named I. M. Everywhere and a book entitled *The Strange Reptile* could be written by Liz Ard. A similar game, suggested by Torrance and Myers in *Invitations to Thinking and Doing*,[13] asks children to think up good names for places. For instance, a home for retired cab drivers might be called "The Old Cab Inn." The poem "Stately Verses" suggests an activity that children might want to try.

If Mary goes far out to sea,
By wayward breezes fanned,
I'd like to know—Can you tell me?
Just where would Maryland?

If Tenn went high up in air
And looked o'er land and sea,
Looked here and there and everywhere,
Pray what would Tennessee?

I looked out of the window and
Saw Orry on the lawn;
He's not there now, and who can tell
Just where has Oregon?

Two girls were quarreling one day
With garden tools, and so
I said, "My dears, let Mary rake
And just let Idaho."

A friend of mine lived in a flat
With half a dozen boys;
When he fell ill I asked him why.
He said, "I'm Illinois."

An English lady had a steed
She called him "Ighland Bay"
She rode for exercise, and thus
Rhode Island every day.
    —Anonymous

Of course, the "stately verses" do not really have to be verses. If your children want to play with state names, let them use whatever form suits them best. Some examples written by elementary pupils are:

Arkan sawed a piece of wood. Later someone asked his mother, "What did *Arkansas?*"

The government makes you pay *Texas*.

When there was a fire, we asked, "Did *Tennessee* the fire?

In her poem "Geography"[14] Eve Merriam plays with the names of states and their abbreviations. (For instance, you could say, "Bears in Mass./Are bound to sass.") The poet concludes her poem by saying that she has left out seventeen states so that others can do what she has done. Your pupils may want to take her up on the suggestion. (First, of course, they must find out which states are missing.)

Interesting Word Origins

Interesting as names can be, you will want to move on to other words after a time. Words that have interesting origins make a good subject for investigation after names. If you worked with *People Words*,[15] mentioned earlier, you will be able to make an easy transition into the origins of other words. You should be able to find a number of good books on word origins in your school or local public library. Books such as *Where Did That Word Come From?*[16] and *What's Behind the Word?*[17] by Sam and Beryl Epstein are written on a simple enough level so that children will be able to browse in them. Some other books that you can use for background in word origins are *Comfortable Words*[18] by Bergen Evans, *American Words* by Mitford M. Mathews,[19] and *Heavens to Betsy!* by Charles E. Funk.[20] In addition to learning where words come from, children will be fascinated by the change in meaning of some common words such as *silly*, which originally meant "happy," "holy," or "good," and *brave*, which meant "crooked"—in both the physical and the moral sense.

2. PLAYING WITH WORDS

Word play is fun, but it is also an excellent way of increasing a child's appreciation of language. You will find that one good way of getting into word play is through humorous poems. With this approach in mind, a number of poems are suggested in the following subsections that relate to the various kinds of word play.

Humorous Effects of Words

Certain sounds in words are just funny. Children are already well aware of this fact, and they will respond joyously to the works of authors who use words for comic effect. One good source is the *Arrow Book of Funny Poems* by Clymer.[21] This fine collection of entertaining poems is a good antidote for children who dislike poetry because of their previous exposure to inappropriate selections. One example, a favorite of many children, is the following limerick.

There was once a young lady of Ryde
Who ate a green apple and died;

The apple fermented
Inside the lamented,
And made cider inside her inside.
—Anonymous

After reading that limerick, all you need to do is focus the children's attention on the words "cider inside her inside" and ask why they like these words or find them funny.

Another favorite, in which similar sounding words keep tripping up the tongue is:

A flea and a fly in a flue
Were imprisoned, so what could they do?
Said the fly, "Let us flee,"
Said the flea, "Let us fly,"
So they flew through a flaw in the flue.
—Anonymous

Children might be asked what they think makes this poem funny. Someone is bound to say that the similar sounding words create a hilarious tongue-tripping. Children should be encouraged to compile lists of words that have similar sounds in them. After doing this, a group of children or couples as well as individuals can select a few words or phrases about which they can fashion a humorous verse.

I Met a Man by Ciardi[22] is filled with poems in which the author plays with the sounds of words. One poem that children love is called "When I Went to Get a Drink." It is amusing because of the toying with the letter *s* and the words "sink" and "think." A poem that tempts children to try to create a similar poem is Ciardi's "I Met a Man That Said, 'Just Look!'" After having been exposed to this poem, one second grader wrote the following poem.

I MET A MAN WHO PLAYED A GAME

I met a man who played a game.
I asked, "Does this game have a name?"
He said, "Yes, without a doubt.
It is called, "IN-to-OUT,"
You take the word "IN,"

Then you change it to "PIN,"
You change "PIN" to "POUT,"
Then you change "POUT" to "OUT,"
Or anything like that, without a doubt.
But it must go from "IN" to "OUT."
And that was all he said.
But I'll always keep it in my head.
    —Vicki

A very short Korean tale that children may enjoy hearing is called "Which Was Witch?"[23] It tells a story of a man suddenly plagued by two identical wives—which was witch? Which was which? is his dilemma. In the end he solves his problem. Children will like hearing the phrases—"Which was witch?" and "Which was which?" This story can be found in the *Arrow Book of Ghost Stories,*[24] edited by Nora Kramer.

   A book of poetry that has great appeal to children and allows them to play with words is the book *A Rocket in My Pocket,* compiled by Carl Withers.[25] The book includes the old, loved chants of children such as "I scream, you scream,/We all scream for ice cream." There are chants that children bounce their balls by and jump rope by. There are also tongue twisters, counting out rhymes, and badinage. Four selections that children enjoy are included here. The first selection plays with the sounds of vowels, the second plays with homonyms and words in general, the third deals with "spoonerisms," and the last selection plays with words in general and words that sound like other words.

Did you eever, iver, over
In your leef, life, loaf
See the deevil, divel, dovel,
Kiss his weef, wife, woaf?

No, I neever, niver, nover,
In my leef, life, loaf,
Saw the deevel, divel, dovel,
Kiss his weef, wife, woaf.
    —Anonymous

Do you carrot all for me?
My heart beets for you,
With your turnip nose and your radish face
You are a peach.
If we cantaloupe,
Lettuce marry.
Weed make a swell pear.
    —Anonymous

A great big molicepan saw a bittle lum,
Sitting on the sturbcone
Chewing gubble bum.

"Hi!" said the molicepan.
"Better simmie gome."
"Tot on your nintype!"
Said the bittle lum.
    —Anonymous

Ladles and jelly spoons:
I come before you
To stand behind you
And tell you something
I know nothing about.

Next Thursday,
Which is Good Friday,
There'll be a mothers' meeting
For fathers only.

Wear your best clothes
If you haven't any,
And if you can come
Please stay at home.

Admission free,
Pay at the door.

Take a seat
And sit on the floor.

It makes no difference where you sit,
The man in the gallery is sure to spit.

We thank you for your unkind attention.

The next number will be

The four corners of the round table.
    —Anonymous

An article that may amuse teachers is called "All My Own Work."[26] It can be found in *Time* magazine, May 1964. It tells about John Lennon's book, *In His Own Write* and his playlet called "At the Denis." It describes the fun that Lennon has had in playing with the sounds of words. It is an adult "Ladles and Jelly Spoons."

Alastair Reid's[27] *Ounce Dice Trice* may invite children to start playing with words and may encourage associational fluency. Not only does Reid list words that remind one of other words, but he also lists words that are light, heavy, odd, and so on. He suggests that the reader start compiling words for things such as noises or nightmares. Of course, the children also can list words that they think of as being light, heavy, odd, and so on. Reid gives names that he thinks would be suitable for elephants, cats, whales, nitwits, and houses. He also invents words that he feels are needed in the English language. They are all onomatopoeic words, such as the sound you hear when your shoelace has broken.

Poetic License and Coined Words

A poem entitled "The Panther," written by Ogden Nash,[28] is included in the *Arrow Book of Funny Poems*. In it Nash warns the reader in the final lines that if he/she is ever called by a "panther," not to "anther." The freedom with words that Nash employs in his writings is quite obvious; after hearing a few of Nash's works, children could be led to comment on this trait.

Nash[29] has a story in verse form about the dragon mentioned before —Custard. In this tale, Custard, who previously has always acted cowardly, really does a turnabout when he alone seems to be the one who can protect Belinda, Mustard, and Blink from the fierce pirate who Belinda sees climbing in the "winda." The word play in this short storypoem is sheer fun. Nash uses such words as "realio," "trulio," "pyrate," and "gyrate," and he uses the word "mouseholed" to rhyme with "household." The teacher can ask the children before this is read to them to notice words that they particularly like.

The poems of Laura E. Richards[30] are mirth-provoking, also. Two excellent poems that demonstrate how she plays with words are "Eletelephony" and her poem about "Antonio," who became tired of living "alonio."

Oodles of Noodles by James and Lucia Hymes[31] has many poems that play with words. The title poem is one. Other poems that you may wish to read to your pupils from this book, all of which contain the same kind of word play, include "Enough Is Enough," where the authors rhyme "foursies" with "more-sies," and "Spinach," in which eight words are listed, each in a line, beginning with the letters *sp*. This would also be a fine time to read some Dr. Seuss stories to the children, so that you can enjoy together what can be done with words.

Children should be encouraged to make up their own nonsense verses, "coin" words, and use poetic license, just as the authors they have been listening to have felt free to do.

New Languages

The story "Master of All Masters"[32] is the story of a young girl who goes to work for a strange man who insists on calling himself "Master of All Masters." His bed, trousers, cat, fire, water, and house all must be referred to very strangely with names that he has coined.

The first night that she works at the Master of All Master's house, the servant wakes her master up and, in a most frightened and hurried manner, using all the new words she has learned, advises her master that he had better get out of bed and put on his trousers immediately because his cat has got a spark of fire on its tail and the house may catch on fire if he does not get some water fast. And that is the end of the story. Of course, the fun comes from trying to determine what the message is as the maid rushes through her new vocabulary.

An article that may intrigue many youngsters is entitled, "Did You Ever Make a Framis with a Frankelsnortz?"[33] This article describes the fun that ordinary citizens have had in using nonsense words in advertisements. It goes on to give a stimulus plus some specific helps to those who would like to create a new Moonian language.

A good book for stimulating children to make up their own secret languages is *The Secret Language*[34] by Ursula Nordstrom. You may not want to read the whole book to the class, but the first two chapters will give your pupils a good idea of how to go about creating a language of their own. If your pupils show a strong interest in secret languages, you might read the discussion of them in *Creative Power: The Education of Youth in the Creative Arts*[35] by Hughes Mearns. You might also read the section of *The Abecedarian Book*[36] that describes how Gelett Burgess made up his own dictionary in which he included six hundred words that he thought were absolutely necessary to the English language. One word he made up, "blurb," is now included in regular dictionaries. These revelations should lead to further discussions for the need for new words and the fun of creating a private language.

A poem with great appeal to children is "Mean Song" by Eve Merriam.[37] In it Merriam uses many made-up words that sound mean and that can be used when anyone is in a particularly foul mood. Children could be invited to compose their own "Mean Song."

Other materials that would prove enjoyable to use are the book *Codes and Secret Writing* by Herbert Zim,[38] which tells all about codes and secret writing, and the exercise by Torrance and Myers[39] entitled, "Secret Messages," in which children are invited to break the code—a hard-to-resist offer. After some practice with codes, there probably will be a flurry of secret notes fluttering around the classroom. See if children hate writing when they are busy with their own underground communications.

Two additional resources should be mentioned in connection with secret languages. The first band of the record *Music for Children*[40] by Orff, Keetman, and Jelinek is a selection in which children play rhythmically with made-up words. And, of course, there is "Jabberwocky." In addition to its charming nonsense words, this well-known poem is a good introduction to *portmanteau* words—words that telescope the meaning of two different words into one. (*Smog,* a combination of *fog* and *smoke,* is one example.) Children may enjoy inventing portmanteau words of their own to describe special kinds of weather or for other purposes. (For instance, a hot but breezy day might be described as "heezy.")

Spoonerisms

Spoonerisms are named for an English clergyman, William Archibald Spooner, who habitually transposed letters with hilarious results. For example, he is supposed to have said, "May I sew you to a sheet?" when he meant to say, "May I show you to a seat?" Spoonerisms for pupils to chuckle over may be found in the *Arrow Book of Word Games.*[41] Some more good examples can be found in "The Case of the Sensational Scent" in *Homer Price,*[42] which features a sheriff who shares the Reverend Spooner's affliction. Still other sources for spoonerisms are Eve Merriam's poem "The Sappy Heasons"[43] and "The Spoonerisms"[44] by Joseph Shipley. After some exposure to spoonerisms, your children will be ready to make up some of their own. You might suggest that a group work on a short familiar rhyme together, translating it into spoonerisms.

Tongue Twisters

Children enjoy tongue twisters, and a book that devotes itself completely to this kind of writing is entitled *Peter Piper's Alphabet.*[45] Everyone will be sure to recognize the piece about Peter Piper, but there are others less well known such as "Neldy Noodle nipped his neighbor's nutmegs," which will be sure to set off some child's desire to try some of his/her own tongue twisters. Some children might want to make a tongue twister composed of words that sound just like the first letter of their first names. The day after tongue twisters have been introduced, you might allow the children (e.g., at the morning roll call) to respond with tongue twisters about themselves, their pets, or their friends (real or imaginary).

Another source for working with tongue twisters is Eve Merriam's[46] selection, "Unfinished Knews Item." In this unrhymed piece Merriam presents as many *n* sounds spelled with *kn* as she can. She adds the letter *k,* for consistency's sake as well as for fun, to the words "nobody," "noticed," and "next." Children, after hearing "Unfinished Knews Item," might respond to a suggestion to pick a letter and then, using that letter sound as much as possible, compose a piece around it.

Rebus Riddles

Another activity that pupils might enjoy is working with rebus riddles. The Children's Book Council, 67 Irving Place, New York 10003, at one time put out an inexpensive poster called, "A Rebus of Children's Book Classics." Pictures were included in the poster and, from the clues given in the illustrations, children could figure out the title of the book to which a reference was being made. For instance, clues to the book, *Mary Poppins,* might include pictures of a mare, the letter *e*, a cork coming out of a champagne bottle, an inn, plus the letter *s*, or simply a picture of some pins. The poster gave clues for "Mother Goose," *Wind in the Willows, Hans Brinker, Pinocchio, Robin Hood, Treasure Island, Peter Pan,* and *Rip Van Winkle.* After showing children how to solve rebus riddles using familiar storybook characters, you might ask your pupils how they would go about constructing a rebus for some other book titles. These could be drawn on the board by the children who have ideas for illustrating them. Later, you and the children could write on the board more titles of literary selections, and those who wanted to could work on creating their own rebus puzzles. Another source for this type of exercise may be found in the *Arrow Book of Word Games* by Rockowitz.[47]

3. NAME YOUR "NYM"

Working with homonyms, other "nyms," and homographs is a splendid way to entice your children into composing their own puns and provides excellent possibilities for learning about related word forms. The literary selections suggested in this section give children many opportunities to work with all kinds of "nyms." Just to keep them straight, we can list them.

1. antonym: one or two or more words of opposite meaning. *Dark* and *light* are antonyms.
2. homograph: one of two or more words spelled alike but different in meaning or derivation. *Fair,* as in *county fair* and *fair* meaning "beautiful," are homographs. Homographs may also differ in pronounciation: a *tear* in one's eye; a *tear* in one's dress.
3. heteronym: Like a homograph, except that heteronyms differ in *both* meaning and pronunciation: to *row* a boat or a *row* in a saloon.
4. Homonym: one of two or more words that have the same sound and often the same spelling: a dancing *bear; bear* right at the crossroads. A second meaning is the same as homophone—*bear-bare.*
5. Homophone: one of two or more words having the same sound but

differing in meaning, derivation, and spelling. *Two, too,* and *to,* are homophones.

6. Synonym: one of two or more words with the same or similar meaning: *big, huge, large, great.*

Homonyms and Homophones

An amusing book that concerns itself only with homonyms and homophones is *If You Talked to a Boar* by Michael Sage.[48] Very simply written, this book asks questions such as "If you talked to a boar, would he be a bore?" After reading it, you will probably want to compile lists of homonyms and homophones on the board for discussion. Then you might encourage your pupils to make up their own questions (after Sage's pattern), which you could then have them collect and illustrate as a book of their own. Some questions that children have produced in this activity are:

Would a flea flee if he saw a frog?
If a gnu saw a new hat, would he buy it?

It is important to remember that because of dialect differences what may be a homonym to one person will not be a homonym to another. For instance, *aunt* and *ant* are homonyms in some parts of the country and not in others. Another good source for homonyms is *Rhyming Word Games* by Lael Wertenbaker and Suzanne Gleaves.[49]

Lucia and James Hymes[50] are other authors who play with homonyms. In a poem that they call "Nonsense" they play with the words "cents," "sense," and "scents;" in another verse, "Pane? Pain?," they toy with the homonyms "pane" and "pain."

The *Arrow Book of Word Games*[51] has a page devoted to "double-duty words." Children are to match the pictures that go together. For example, the pictures of a fountain pen and a pig pen would belong together. Children could illustrate other multinyms and then exchange their pictures. They could then see whether they could appropriately pair the other person's set of pictures. The children's contributions could be chosen to appear in a class magazine.

These kinds of assignments can lead children to compose their own humorous writings; for instance:

Oh, you may drive a horse to water
But a pencil must be lead.

Two other books that deal with homonyms are *Word Twins* by Mary White[52] and *Monkeys Have Tails* by Rosalind Van Gelder.[53] *Word Twins* is a very easy book to read. In verse form White tells the difference in meaning between homonyms. For example, the word "beach" is clarified in a four-line, abcb rhyme form; the word "beech" is similarly illustrated. The book ends by asking the readers whether they can name another twin word. Perhaps some pupils will want to try making up their own verses about homonyms. If so, do a few with the children on the board, not stressing any one particular rhyme form. You may find that the children will want to combine the two homonyms, or words that sound alike, in one poem.

In *Monkeys Have Tails*, Van Gelder, in verse form, abcb, asks questions such as "Stores have sales, but can boats use them?" Toward the end of the book, she asks her readers to discover more sound-alike words. After reading this book, children may want to try some riddles using homonyms, or they may decide to construct poems similar to those Van Gelder has done.

In *Playing with Words*,[54] Joseph Shipley provides a group of sentences with blanks in them that students can fill in orally with homonyms. Naturally, you might devise some sentences of your own to use for which children could supply homonyms. Children, after some exposure, might write some sentences themselves that would demand homonyms as answers. Shipley lists some homonyms that some children may elect to use in making up their own sentences. However, once they get the feeling for the idea, it is probable that they will not need either Shipley or you to suggest anything. They can do well using each other as spurs for their own thinking.

Homographs

Wertenbaker and Gleaves also include some games involving homographs ("Look Alikes" and "More Look Alikes") in *Rhyming Word Games*. Homographs lend themselves to riddles and puzzles of this kind.

What kind of painter does not need a brush?
What kind of invalid is never sick?

Children could collect and illustrate their homographs, as was suggested earlier for homonyms. By the way, you may want to follow the lead of *Rhyming Word Games* and refer to homonyms and homographs as "sound alikes" and "look alikes," respectively.

Eve Merriam has written a poem entitled "Nym and Graph,"[55] which cleverly illustrates what homonyms and homographs can do. The same poet's "Associations"[56] and "Beware"[57] both contain plays on homographs and homonyms.

Another source for fun with homonyms and homographs is *Pick-A-Riddle*.[58] On page 44 of this book are two riddles, one rhymed, one unrhymed, that center around "nyms" and "graphs." These may be just the stimuli that will encourage similar oral riddles from many children.

Puns

The foregoing activities should give children a solid background in punning. There are, of course, people who deplore puns and would advise against encouraging anyone to indulge in them. Some of the greatest English poets—from Chaucer to Shakespeare to T. S. Eliot and W. H. Auden—did not share this contempt for puns. And children love them. Working with puns will not only provide amusement, it will also give children useful experience in using homonyms and homographs and sharpen their eyes and ears for recognizing some important phoneme-grapheme relationships.

A good way to begin would be to read to your class "The Hole Story,"[59] a poem about a sock with a hole in it. You could ask children whether they think the title is a good one—be sure to write it on the board for them—and explain how a pun works. Your children will probably know some puns, although they may not know that that is what they are called. Now and throughout your work with puns, encourage them to contribute puns that they have heard or that they have made up themselves.

The paperback *Jest in Pun* by Bil Keane[60] includes hundreds of puns, and you will find some other good examples in Shipley's *Playing with Words*. (Another kind of word play proposed in the Shipley book is called "breakables." Words, such as *deride*, for example, are given unexpected definitions like "put out of the car." Encouraging such divergent responses is really an exercise in originality, the essence of which is simply reacting in an unusual way to given stimuli.) Another way of having fun with puns is in crossword puzzles. *X-Word Fun*[61] by Murray Rockowitz contains a puzzle called "Pun Fun" that your children will enjoy.

Amelia Bedelia

The heroine of the *Amelia Bedelia*[62] books by Peggy Parish deserves a heading of her own for her misadventures with multinyms. Amelia usually knows only one meaning of a word that has several meanings and, alas, the one she knows is never the right one. If her employer, Mrs. Rogers, asks Amelia to *change* towels, Amelia carries out the request by snipping here and there with a scissors until she thinks they have been changed enough. After reading about Amelia's experiences, children may want to write some further adventures of this character on their own.

Synonyms

A repertory of synonyms is an important part of any mature vocabulary and, therefore, deserves an important place in word study in the elementary grades. But, since synonyms rarely have exactly the same meaning, a major emphasis should be on distinguishing among the shades of meaning expressed by the individual words. A game that will focus children's attention on shades of meaning is called "What's the Difference?" You begin by giving some words that can be "acted out," such as the series *amble, shuffle, limp, saunter,* and *bound,* and ask the children to show these different ways of walking. If some of the words are unfamiliar, you can have children look them up in the classroom dictionary or supply the relevant meaning yourself. After pupils understand the idea, you can enlist their help in thinking of other words that can be demonstrated concretely. The visual impact of seeing the differences between synonyms should help pupils to gain and retain an understanding of the nuances of the words.

A somewhat more sophisticated synonym game, appropriate for older children, is "Synonymbles," suggested by Shipley.[63] Each player is given a word and asked to write four synonyms for it. Players then exchange papers and write five sentences illustrating the different meanings of the words. Shipley provides a set of examples to get the players started.

"Would You Rather . . . ?" is a game consisting of questions of this kind.

1. Would you rather be called *slender* or *skinny?*
2. Would you rather be called *curious* or *inquisitive?*
3. Would you rather be called *miserly* or *thrifty?*

Children should be asked to explain their reasons for each choice in their own words. A variation on "Would You Rather . . . ?" involves the construction of a series of synonyms like this:

I am thrifty. You are penny pinching. He is miserly
I am slim. You are slender. She is skinny.

Eve Merriam's poem "Thesaurus"[64] contains a number of synonyms for the poet's "non-Valentines." First, the poem will stimulate children to find out the meaning of some of the synonyms used. Then, they will probably want to try their own hands at a similar kind of comic Valentine. Alternatively, of course, they can choose synonyms with favorable connotations for a regular Valentine.

An activity that is somewhat more demanding, but entertaining, is described in *The Arrow Book of Brain Teasers.*[65] The reader is asked to translate sentences disguised through the use of synonyms into their familiar form. ("A *homo sapiens* who vacillates could become misplaced," for instance, translates to "He who hesitates is lost.") If your pupils are ready for this one, you might provide some short proverbs for them to translate. If you offer enough possibilities, you can have them exchange papers and try to puzzle out the original proverb. A similar kind of puzzle involving proverbs is the crossword puzzle "Wise Old Sayings" in *X-Word Fun*.[66]

Antonyms

Karen's Opposites by the Provensens[67] offers a good way of introducing antonyms. The authors incorporate many antonyms into their simple, rhymed text. You might follow up by giving one word and asking pupils to supply one or more antonyms. Or you could use John Ciardi's[68] poem "I Met a Man That Said, 'Just Look!' ", from his book *I Met a Man*, in which the poet encourages the reader to jump from a word to its opposite through contextual and rhyming clues, to get into the same kind of activity.

Another book that will entertain both you and your pupils is *Word-a-Day* by Mickey Bach.[69] Bach illustrates humorously in cartoon style the meaning of a number of words. Children may want to take up the idea and illustrate their own words. They can then show their drawings and ask others to guess the meanings of the words they have illustrated. (This activity will work better if you list all of the words that have been illustrated to cut down the possibilities.)

Finally, for reviewing your work in word study, you might want to use Mary O'Neill's poem "Antonyms—Synonyms—Homonyms."[70]

4. AFTERWORD

Word games and word play offer entertaining and effective ways of building children's vocabularies and helping them to distinguish between the subtle shades of meaning, which both enrich and complicate English. But these activities have other benefits: they engage children's interest in play and point out the element of play that is present in so much good writing.

Helps

Dale, Edgar, and Razik, Taher, *Bibliography of Vocabulary Studies,* Columbus, Ohio: Bureau of Educational Research and Service, The Ohio State University, 1963. This unannotated bibliography contains 3125 titles of vocabulary studies. The references are divided into twenty-six categories for the reader's convenience. Naturally, some of the titles are included under more than one category.

Davidson, Jessica, *Is That Mother in the Bottle? Where Language Came from and Where It Is Going,* New York: Franklin Watts, Inc., 1972. Fascinating for teachers and older pupils!

Deighton, Lee C., *Vocabulary Development in the Classroom,* New York: Bureau of Publications, Teachers College, Columbia University, 1959. This fine, concise paperback includes some well-chosen remarks about vocabulary development. Among other points, Deighton emphasizes how important it is to make sure that children understand figures of speech. For example, although a child may have met in a different context each of the following words, "Peter was in a pickle," put all together in another context it is the child who winds up being in a pickle! Deighton underscores the importance of reading to children at all age levels, and he indicates two limitations that teachers should be aware of when telling children to use contextual clues in figuring out strange words: (1) there must be an obvious connection between the clue and the new word, and (2) the clue, to be effective, must be near to the word it is trying to clarify.

Hefter, Richard, and Moskof, Martin Stephen, *A Shuffle Book,* New York: Western Publishing Company, 1970. This delightful "book" consists of fifty-three brightly colored and zanily illustrated durable cards, fifty-one of which have a picture and a word or a phrase on each side. The remaining two cards are for children to write in anything they care to. All of the cards wipe clean and the two for the children to write on are lined. As an illustration of what the cards are like, one card has on it the word "died." Underneath is a white tombstone on green grass. On the other side of the card is the phrase "and the grass." The idea is for the children to put the words and phrases together and make up their own crazy stories. Of course, there is no reason why children could not add to the collection that Hefter and Moskof began. Children would enjoy playing with these cards. The authors refer to the book as an "anything" book, since the users can do anything they want to with it.

Petty Walter F., and Mehaffy, Robert, "Basic Annotated Bibliography on the Teaching of Vocabulary," Champaign, Ill.: NCTE/ERIC, 1968. Free five-page briefly annotated pamphlet that contains references and books and articles that deal with teaching vocabulary.

Petty, Walter F., Herold, Curtis P., and Stoll, Earline, *The State of Knowledge about the Teaching of Vocabulary,* Champaign, Ill.: National Council of Teachers of English, 1968. A fine paperback with many important comments in it concerning vocabulary development and vocabulary studies. The authors write that motivation for learning new words should never be overlooked. They also write that most of the vocabulary studies that they have seen are insufferably dull. Additionally, they state that most studies ignore dialectical differences.

O'Rourke, Patrick J., *Toward a Science of Vocabulary Development,* The Hague: Mouton, 1974.

Shuy, Roger W., *Discovering American Dialects,* Champaign, Ill.: National Council of Teachers of English, 1967. A brief paperback that describes dialects, how dialects differ, the reasons for dialectical differences, and American dialects today. It also discusses the influence of foreign languages on dialects.

Literary Suggestions to Use to Build an Appreciation of Language

Adams, Richard, *Watership Down,* New York: Macmillan Publishing Company, Inc., 1972. For mature readers. A novel about rabbits, their adventures, and their language!

Adelson, Leone, illustrated by Lou Myers, *Dandelions Don't Bite,* New York: Pantheon Books, 1972. All about words—their origins and meanings.

Amon, Aline, *Reading, Writing, Chattering Chimps,* New York: Atheneum, 1975. How chimps are learning to communicate with humans.

Babbit, Natalie, *The Search for Delicious,* New York: Farrar, Straus and Giroux, 1969.

Bishop, Ann, pictures by Jerry Warshaw, *Noah Riddle,* Chicago: Albert Whitman and Company, 1970.

Davar, Ashok, *Talking Words: A Unique Alphabet Book,* Indianapolis: The Bobbs-Merrill Company, 1969. Words illustrated concretely.

Eastman, P. D., *The Cat in the Hat Beginner Book Dictionary,* New York: Random House, Inc., 1964.

Emrich, Duncan, collector, illustrated by Ib Ohlsson: *The Whim-Wham Book,* New York: Four Winds Press, 1975.

Evans, Bergen, *Comfortable Words,* New York: Random House, 1962. A fine source for teachers to use to get children excited about the origin of commonly used expressions and words.

Fletcher, Christine, *100 Keys: Names Across the Land,* Nashville: Abingdon Press, 1973.

Funk, Charles E., illustrations by Tom Funk, *Heavens to Betsy! And Other Curious Sayings,* New York: Warner Paperback Library, 1972.

Greet, W. Cabell, Jenkins, William A., and Schiller, Andrew, *In Other Words,* Glenview, Ill.: Scott, Foresman and Company, 1968. A dictionary.

Gwynne, Fred, *The King Who Rained,* New York: Windmill Books and E. P. Dutton, 1970.

Hanson, Joan, *Antonyms,* Minneapolis: Lerner Publications Company, 1972.

Hanson, Joan, *Homographs,* Minneapolis: Lerner Publications Company, 1972.

Hanson, Joan, *Homonyms,* Minneapolis: Lerner Publications Company, 1972.

Hefter, Richard, and Moskof, Martin Stephen, illustrated by Richard Hefter, *Christopher's Parade,* New York: Parents' Magazine Press, 1972.

Hutchins, Pat, *Rosie's Walk,* New York: The Macmillan Company, 1968.

Hunt, Bernice Kohn, illustrations by Jan Pyk, *Your Ant Is a Which: Fun with Homophones,* New York: Harcourt Brace Jovanovich, 1976.

Juster, Norton, illustrations by Jules Feiffer, *The Phantom Tollbooth,* New York: Random House, 1967.

Kaufman, Joe, *Words,* New York: Western Publishing Company, Inc., 1968. A beginner's book that will help a child to identify words.

Keane, Bil, *Pun-Abridged Dictionary,* New York: Scholastic Book Services, 1970.

Levinson, Leonard Louis, *Webster's Unafraid Dictionary,* New York: Collier Books, 1967.

Levinson, Leonard Louis, *The Left Handed Dictionary,* New York: Collier Books, 1968. Levinson's books are *for adults,* but teachers can cull some very funny examples of word play from them to use as charger-starters with their pupils.

Lewis, George Q., *The Dictionary of Bloopers and Boners,* New York: Scholastic Book Services, 1967.

Lionni, Leo, *Frederick,* New York: Pantheon, 1966.

Longman, Harold, illustrated by Abner Graboff, *Would You Put Your Money in a Sand Bank?*, Chicago: Rand McNally and Company, Inc., 1968.

Manniche, Lise, illustrator and commentator, *How Djadja-em-ankh Saved the Day*, New York: Thomas Y. Crowell Co., 1976. Fascinating book that shows readers hieroglyphs and their translations. Two tales told, one from left to right, and one from right to left. The story has been printed on paper that looks like papyrus, and the book is made in the form of a scroll.

Nurnberg, Maxwell, drawings by Ted Schroeder, *Fun with Words*, Englewood Cliffs, N. J.: Prentice-Hall, Inc., 1970.

Pilon, A. Barbara, editor, *Concrete Is Not Always Hard*, Middletown, Conn.: Xerox Education Publications, 1972. A book of concrete poetry that plays with words and invites its readers to play with words too.

Pizer, Vernon, *Ink Ark., and All That: How American Places Got Their Names*, New York: G. P. Putnam's Sons, 1976.

Pop-Up Sound Alikes, New York: Random House, n.d.

Rees, Ennis, illustrated by Quentin Blake, *Pun Fun*, New York: Abelard-Schuman, 1965.

Robbins, Patricia, *Antics*, New York: Simon and Schuster, 1969.

Sackson, Sid, *Beyond Words*, New York: Pantheon, 1977. New word games for bright, mature children and their teachers!

Sarnoff, Jane, and Ruffins, Reynold, *The Monster Riddle Book*, New York: Charles Scribner's Sons, 1975.

Scarry, Richard, *Best Word Book Ever*, New York: Golden Press, 1963.

Scarry, Richard, *Storybook Dictionary*, New York: Golden Press, 1969.

Schwartz, Alvin, collector, illustrated by Glen Rounds, *Kickle Snifters and Other Fearsome Critters*, Philadelphia: J. B. Lippincott Co., 1976.

Shafer, Burr, *The Wonderful World of J. Wesley Smith*, New York: Scholastic Book Services, 1966. A fun book that fools around with words, expressions, and literary allusions.

Shipley, Joseph T., *Word Play*, New York: Hawthorn Books, Inc., 1972.

Thurber, James, illustrated by Marc Simont, *The Wonderful O*, New York: Simon and Schuster/A Fireside Book, 1957.

VIP, *Vip Quips*, New York: Windmill Books, Inc., 1975.

Wilbur, Richard, *Opposites*, New York: Harcourt Brace Jovanovich, Inc., 1973.

Wildsmith, Brian, *Birds*, New York: Franklin Watts, Inc., 1967.

Wildsmith, Brian, *Fishes*, New York: Franklin Watts, Inc., 1968.

Withers, Carl, illustrated by Garry Mackenzie, *A Treasury of Games*, New York: Grosset and Dunlap, Publishers, 1964. See particularly "How Am I Acting?" and "Words, Words, Words," two vocabulary games on p. 160.

6 Keep Them Talking

Invitation

If you are a dreamer, come in;
If you are a dreamer, a wisher, a
liar,
A hope-er, a pray-er, a magic
bean buyer . . .
If you're a pretender, come sit by
my fire
For we have some flax-golden
tales to spin.
Come in!
Come in!

—Shel Silverstein

The development of children's oral language abilities is critically important for several reasons. First, children's reading and writing proficiencies are based on their competencies in oral language. Their knowledge of, and intuitions about, spoken language provide the keys for decoding written language; and although there are differences between written and spoken language, writers, whether they are children or adults, write with the sound of their own voices in their ears. Moreover, oral language provides the chief means by which children satisfy the profound human need to express themselves and to respond to others in cooperative efforts toward common goals. Jerome Bruner[1], in discussing the disadvantages of a wholly self-instructional system, stresses the importance of "reciprocity" as a motive for learning; the give-and-take of talking is the essence of reciprocal learning.

1. GETTING CHILDREN TO TALK

Educators in the sciences say that a laboratory that is clean most of the time is one in which little learning is going on. The same might be said of any classroom in which there is little talk among the pupils themselves and between the pupils and the teacher. Children are innately curious, like the sounds of words, and actively enjoy playing with them. They are stimulated by a changing, bountiful environment, the presence of concrete objects within their immediate surroundings, and verbal interaction with others.

Children need to be able to build up their competencies. They need to be allowed to wrestle with words to attain what they are attempting to perfect. They must not be constantly reproved about their obvious and natural imperfections. Of course, it is imperative that children be reinforced for their successes or their approximations to success. Finally, young children are capable of understanding a great deal and they enjoy hearing stories told to them.

Children Learn Language

A book that provides fascinating insights into language acquisition is *Language in the Crib* by Weir,[2] in which the author describes the tape-recorded monologues of her son, Anthony. The monologues were taped when Anthony was between the ages of twenty-eight and thirty months, with no adult present. The book reveals findings of relevance to teachers of children of all ages, some of which are outlined below.

1. Anthony often would not be able to speak long or relatively complicated sentences without resorting first to what Weir calls "buildups" or "completions." An example of a buildup is "Ball. That's a ball." An illustration of a completion is "Look at that dog. With a bone." Anthony was not able to speak smoothly or perfectly. He struggled, and bit by bit worked at expressing himself. This took time.
2. Anthony spent most of his time playing with words and their sounds. The next longest amount of time he devoted to grammatical practice. He was quite ingenious in structuring his play in order to provide a series of linguistic exercises for himself.
3. It was interesting to note the sparsity of both the topics and the vocabulary Anthony employed in his presleep monologues in comparison to his performance in both of these areas during the day. Weir hypothesized that the child's unchanging environment affected the quality of his output.
4. With the exception of some personalized nouns, the majority of nouns which Anthony used referred to objects within his immediate environment.
5. There were certain words that Anthony favored. These included color words and his own name.
6. The word that received the highest frequency of use was the word "what."
7. Anthony was capable not only of understanding stories told to him but also of appreciating happy endings of stories.

The implications of Weir's study are clear. Children are individuals with individual interests. They are quick to use a word like *what* because it has a big payoff and leads to richer understandings and skills. Indeed, the study would seem to imply that a fruitful experiment might be to explore the results of deliberately teaching young children the words *what* and *why* at an early age with a view to determining the effect on oral expression and listening comprehension.

Chukovsky[3] tells his readers that most children from the ages of two to five are linguistic geniuses in that their use of language is fresh, creative, and spontaneous. This ability begins to fade at about the age of five or six and disappears completely by the age of eight. Could it possibly be that, since this breakdown occurs at approximately the age at which children first go to school, one of the reasons for children's ebb in their language ability is that their opportunities for expressing themselves freely may be more limited than in the past? Might it not also be true that pupils now are rewarded for conformity and are tacitly discouraged from using original, fresh ways of expressing themselves? Bruner[4] thinks that this may be so. He states that perceptive anthropologists have commented that in the early grades a premium seems to be placed on the stereotyped female function in society, that is, on courtesy and refinement. Prudence is favored much more than boldness.

Chukovsky,[5] like Weir, repeatedly tells the reader how children love to play with words and sounds. He says also that children delight in games based on rhymes. Might not teachers make more use of the child's natural joy in playing? Horace long ago insisted that teachers must learn to "instruct with delight." Piaget,[6] in *The Language and Thought of the Child,* emphasizes both the importance that playing with words has for young children and the pleasure that it brings them.

Nonstandard Language

In discussing factors that impede language development, Petty and Starkey[7] observe that of all the environmental factors that cause language retardation, the most important one seems to be the failure of teachers to provide situations that encourage their students to talk. It is interesting to note that, although most educators would say that they believed it important to give children opportunities to talk and, thus, would be appalled by the preceding statement, some, nevertheless, inadvertently fail to maintain the conditions under which children feel free to talk. They accomplish this both by showing disrespect for children's dialects and by being unaware of the importance of the classroom climate in encouraging children to speak.

It goes without saying that to hamper children's language by constant reprimands, corrections, and other indications of disapproval is poor judgment at best. At worst it can cause the child's desire to communicate to shrivel up completely. Once the door is slammed shut on communication, it may never be opened again.

Wilt,[8] Strickland,[9] LeFevre,[10] and a host of others recommend that teachers legalize talking. Lefevre asserts that a child must feel free to make mistakes, to experiment, to dare. He predicts that if teachers insist on immediate correction of every so-called error that children utter, the children will retreat very quickly like clams into their shells. They will learn to hate talking and writing in school. Davies,[11] in discussing the same matter, says that some teachers cause children to feel that opening their mouths means risking a fall into a boobytrap.

Mearns[12] suggests that if teachers want their pupils to express themselves and improve on their oral abilities, the pupils must be able to talk. Teachers must make it clear to their pupils that they are not "on the Sacred Blunder Hunt." Mearns emphasizes in the poem "Grammarian's Child" that teachers cannot expect children to use language that teachers themselves do not use.

GRAMMARIAN'S CHILD

When looking out I see a car
Of friends come calling from afar,
I cry to Mother right away,
"Oh, that is they! Oh, that is they!"

When in my room with girls and boys
I hear, "Who's making all that noise?"
I step outside and cheerfully
Call down, "It's we! It's only we!"

When Teacher asks, "Who has, pray speak
A birthday in the coming week?"
And I have, then I'm mighty spry
To say, "Please, Ma'am, it will be I.'

But pounding on a bolted door
With bears behind me, three or four,
If I should hear, "Who could that be?"
I'd scream, "It's me! It's me! It's me!"

—Hughes Mearns

To the development of oral language, as to so many other aspects of elementary education, the teacher holds the key. The teacher alone can establish a classroom climate in which talk is pleasurable and exciting. The teacher has the responsibility of guiding children's language growth without excessive emphasis on remediation. (A positive approach to the teaching of usage skills is suggested on pp. 130-138.) Finally, the teacher has the obligation to listen to what children are saying since, as Martin[13] points out, our most useful insights into our pupils' world come to us through their language. In this connection, Martin relates the story of a teacher who rejects such a look into a child's real world. He describes a situation in which an inner-city pupil remarks to his teacher, while pointing to a picture of a fire escape, that a fire escape is a good place to go when there is a fight. The teacher wastes no time in "correcting" him. She tells him that he does not mean what he has just said. She translates his comment and tells him that fire escapes are good places to go when there are fires. The reaction signals not only a wide difference in the experience of teacher and child, but also an inability to bridge it.

2. MODELS OF EXCELLENCE

It appears to be true that recognition precedes production in language learning and that repetition aids recognition. Brown[14] describes the three basic processes in the acquisition of syntax as imitation and reduction, imitation and expansion, and inductive understanding of the structure of language. Although it is certainly true that language acquisition is not just a matter of imitation, imitation does play a role in the development of oral language skills. Young children learn to speak by listening to the models available to them, imitating what they hear and generalizing on the data they have collected. (That children make generalizations is evident from the fact that they are able to make statements they have never heard. For instance, children who use *mans* as the plural of *man* may never have heard that form used, they may simply be generalizing from the usual rule for pluralization in English.) The conclusion is obvious: it is impossible to overemphasize the importance of good models of informal, standard spoken English in developing oral language skills.

The foremost model in the classroom is the teacher. Some teachers have inhibitions about reading aloud, being aware that they do not read as professionally as the voices on some of the tapes and records now available. If you have such inhibitions, try to overcome them. A warm, live reading that is responsive to the audience is more enjoyable to most listeners than the most professional canned reading. Remember that what you are striving to develop is a feeling for spoken language, not an appreciation of a dramatic performance. Of course, you will want to speak clearly, with the best enunciation you can manage. In discussing this point, McCullough[15] points out that *goad* and *goat* are very different words. A child, who has much less experience with oral language than an adult, may well be misled by poor articulation. It is a good idea to tape your reading from time to time. The tapes can be used by children who want to hear a favorite story again and by you to check on features of your speech that you might want to work on. And you will want to use professionally recorded tapes and records when they are available. The more samples of spoken language the children hear, the better. Finally, you should not overlook the importance of having children listen to each other. Children should have many chances to speak and should be encouraged to try out new words and experiment with them; they should speak knowing that others are listening with interest to what they have to say.

In addition to providing good models of spoken language, reading aloud can have other benefits. Clegg[16] reports that a teacher in a British infant school says that her pupils write stories modeled on those they hear. This teacher maintains that after a while the children unconsciously begin to use words and phrases they remember from the readings. Piaget[17] makes a similar point. It is important to remember that the children believe that they are creating, not imitating. Such imitation is a natural part of learning and should not be regarded as plagiarism.

3. BUILDING VOCABULARIES

Lloyd and Warfel[18] include a chapter in their *American English in Its Cultural Setting* entitled "Twenty Years to a Larger Vocabulary." The title is an ironic comment on the many books that promise dramatic increases in word power over night, or at least in twenty easy lessons. It is also based on the observation that a person's vocabulary reflects all of his or her interests, his or her experiences in life and in books, everything that has happened to him or her. Real growth in vocabulary is a gradual process, which the teacher can help along by stimulating a love of language in children, encouraging them to use it and play with it, and building confidence in their ability to use it.

Literature and Vocabulary

Cohen,[19] in a study undertaken to determine whether literature selections read aloud to one hundred and fifty-five subjects would result in improved vocabulary and comprehension, discovered that this procedure significantly improved the vocabulary, word knowledge, and reading comprehension of the experimental group. Many other authors agree on the importance of literature in expanding a child's love of language. To interest children in words and in language, teachers may wish to refer to the excellent and briefly annotated book lists compiled by Burns,[20] Delmare,[21] and Tiedt and Tiedt.[22] Book lists are a very helpful first resource but, after introducing children to the right books, activities should be planned so that the learning becomes an active process involving the children as well as the teacher. It must be noted that a teacher must *read* books in order to be able to present the right book to the right child at the right time. Book lists alone can *never* do the job.

Heys[23] relates the advice that a former chief examiner for the College Board's Scholastic Aptitude Test used to give to any friend who wanted to do well on the SAT. The chief examiner said simply to tell the person to read, read, read, and then read some more. Heys says that this is vocabulary study in its rightful place — in context.

Martin[24] suggests that by hearing and reading literature with repetitive phrases, pupils can become familiar with public language. One example of a specific poem that will incidentally expose pupils to the standard past tense form of the word "see" can be found in *Poems and Verses About the City*.[25] It is a poem entitled "A Trip," written by James S. Tippett. There are many other poems that teachers can use for the same purpose. By using Martin's delightful examples of specific literature selections, the teacher would be demonstrating respect and enjoyment of different dialects to pupils. Malmstrom and Ashley[26] suggest that teachers expose their students to writings such as those of James Whitcomb Riley to achieve the same purpose. One of the last statements that Martin makes is that by using literature with children, the exposure to beautiful language becomes impressed on each child's heart and mind, and through these channels the language enters the child's blood stream and remains with him or her forever.

Not Just New Words

Although it is rewarding to hear your pupils using new words they have just acquired from a story, it is important, as Petty, Herold, and Stoll[27] point out, to help your children improve their understanding of commonly used words. *Access to Learning*[28]—a valuable resource that lists hundreds of trade books that can be used with a variety of suggested activities for vocabulary building—stresses the point that overlearning and reinforcement assist language growth.

One problem that teachers need to be aware of in working with children is that a common word can be introduced in one context and that later, when used in a different context the word changes its meaning, there is nothing to indicate to the teacher that perhaps a child, or many children, will not be able to determine the new meaning in the new situation. It seems to be assumed too frequently that the child, having once had a word presented in a particular context, knows all the meanings of that word.

McCullough[29] offers some specific suggestions on how a teacher may help expand a child's understanding of a word. Russell[30] writes that it may be the quality of the associations that a child has concerning a word that is more important than the number of words superficially known. Loree[31] maintains that the more associations one has with a word or concept, the better the information pertaining to that word or concept can be retained.

An amusing cartoon by Charles Schulz, creator of "Peanuts," shows Charlie Brown in a spelling bee after he has just been asked to spell the word, "maze." Charlie says out loud that "maze" is an easy word. Then, he proceeds unwittingly and to his utter dismay and disbelief to spell out "Mays." It is clear that Charlie has more associations with the baseball player than with the story of the Minotaur and its home, the labyrinth, a veritable maze. His teacher must not have supplied enough associations or, as Beekman[32] expresses it, enough "meaningful repetitions" to ensure Charlie's "correct" response when tested.

Dolch,[33] in talking about the way in which vocabulary is taught in schools, says that a pitfall seems to be that teachers are concerned with expanding a child's vocabulary, but are not necessarily concerned with increasing a child's meanings. He refers to this procedure as teaching "synonyms without distinction."

There are many other experts,[34] in addition to those already mentioned, who subscribe to the philosophy of providing many firsthand experiences for children with words. They believe that teachers should make words "live" for children. Apparently, Petty, Herold, and Stoll[35] are not alone in their conviction concerning the influence of expanding a word's meaning by developing many associations with it through concrete experiences and the active involvement of the child in the learning process.

Several remarks in *The State of Knowledge About the Teaching of Vocabulary*[36] are revealing as well as disturbing. The authors state that, although most of the curriculum guides they examined advocated that classroom teachers set aside time for the purpose of enlarging the vocabulary of their pupils, few included methods for reaching the ultimate goal. In many guides in which suggestions for teaching vocabulary were given, the exercises were basically restricted to the type where children learned the meanings of words from looking them up in dictionaries.

Petty, Herold, and Stoll go on to cite the conclusion drawn from Gray and

Holmes' study that indicates that children gain very little from merely being exposed to new words unless they receive some guidance. All in all, modern explorations of language seemed to be disregarded in the experimental materials examined. The authors write that perhaps the studies might enable the students to pass a weekly vocabulary test, if this is indeed the ultimate goal of teachers in presenting vocabulary to their students. However, a very small number, if any of the studies, provided the means that would enable the students to become perceptive of all the elements of language so that they could become literate, cultured members of their society.

It appears clear that there is a definite need for the construction of practical guides for teachers to use when working with their students in developing vocabulary interests and skills. These guides should contain creative, stimulating ideas, be rich in their variety of offerings, and suggest many specific resources for teachers. Another need is for imaginative and psychologically well-founded studies in the area of vocabulary development.

Words and Other Words

One problem with the wordlist approach to vocabulary is the emphasis it puts on isolated words. Obviously, an important part of language growth involves understanding the structure of sentences. Ruddell[37] suggests some interesting activities that lead children to experiment with the movable parts of sentences. Deighton[38] stresses the importance of working with relationship words, definite words, indefinite words, judgment words, and color words.

A few literary selections that can be used with children to accomplish the objectives Deighton talks about include:

1. *Go Dog, Go!*[39] (relation words).
2. *Put Me in the Zoo*[40] (color concepts and relationship words).
3. *Hailstones and Halibut Bones: Adventures in Color*[41] (color concepts).
4. "Streets" by Aileen Fisher[42] (relationship words).

Ashley[43] recommends playing with nonsense words, since many times there are structural clues that will signal a general kind of meaning to the child. Such exercises are fun and delight children. She suggests giving nonsense paragraphs to the children and letting them "translate" them into English stories. An example of such an exercise might be:

The jaddy glab rabbled and rubbled.
Suddenly it wristled.
Do you suppose it might be wristling still?

Perhaps children could be given opportunities to make up their own nonsense stories and then test them out on their friends. The teacher could have available for the children the works of authors such as Dr. Seuss and Ogden Nash, which could be used as models.

Figures of Speech and Idioms

An important comprehension skill for understanding literature is the ability to recognize and appreciate nonliteral uses of words. Deighton[44] suggests that children should work with figures of speech and offers some excellent ideas about how to go about it. Blake and Cohen[45] stress the importance of having children study idioms along with figurative language; they describe entertainingly the fun that their students had in drawing literal illustrations of similes and metaphors. They also suggest playing a game that will help children to recognize the need for precise language. They refer to the game as, "What Do These People Mean When They Say . . .?" The phrase used in their article was "I hate you." Examples of how the activity is to be carried out may be seen by reading the following sentences.

What Did They Mean When They Said, "I hate you!"?

1. A child having to go to bed without seeing his/her favorite television program.
2. A child muttering to himself/herself about his/her teacher after he/she has scored a zero in arithmetic.

Blake and Cohen recommend other games to use to make children aware of the necessity of knowing words that are capable of conveying specific, refined meanings.

Tiedt and Tiedt[46] recommend having pupils try their hand at "word inventions." This activity requires that the children invent words, thus stimulating the thinking of the pupils as well as exciting their imaginations. As mentioned before, the works of people such as Ogden Nash, Dr. Seuss, and Laura E. Richards would help to stimulate children to coin their own words and use poetic license. Tiedt and Tiedt also advocate preparing a series of sheets that involve activities with words. The sheets may be placed in a box labeled "Treasury of Words," and children may select sheets from it. One sheet may have on it, for example, all words to which an o may be added to form a new word. The o may be added anywhere, but the other letters must remain in their original order. Samples of words that may be used are: "slid"-"solid," "ply"-"ploy," and "cat"-"coat." The first word would be the stimulus, and the child would be challenged to respond with the second word.

O'Leary[47] suggests that teachers tell an anecdote about a famous person that would illustrate the meaning of an abstract word. The meaningful association of a word such as "devotion" with Dr. Albert Schweitzer and "versatility" with George Washington Carver or Benjamin Franklin can come through hearing stories about such people, and it is likely to remain with children longer than an isolated abstract definition. O'Leary also advocates using pictures that may suggest adjectives such as "curious" and "downcast." She believes that by displaying pictures and guiding the students in discussion, the desired words may be elicited.

Still another of O'Leary's suggestions is to have the students make their own picture dictionaries. Cutts and Mosely[48] talk about the wit and humor that can be found in children's own dictionaries. For instance, one child defined "Adam" as being a guy who really started something, while "abbey" was described as being a hangout for a monk.

Beggs,[49] like O'Leary, believes in using pictures to develop vocabulary with students. She used pictures as a type of quiz contest. Underneath each picture she placed the part of speech that the picture represented as well as the two beginning letters of the word. Pupils wrote their answers on pieces of paper and, after two days, students exchanged papers. Every student got every word correct. Following this first activity, Beggs passed out a mimeographed copy of a short narrative that she had written. Students were told to fill in the blanks with the words that they had learned. Beggs limited the blanks to four. Later, students wrote their own short themes incorporating the new words. Students soon asked to be allowed to bring in their own pictures that aptly suggested words. They then conducted their own "Guess What Word?" game.

Word Games Again

Some of the activities mentioned in the last few pages will undoubtedly recall the word games described in the previous chapter. And so they should. The reason for grouping the games together is for convenience when you want to look one up. Their main purpose is the development of an interest in, and a feeling for words—the foundation of any good vocabulary program. Since there is always room for more word games, a few more sources are added here.

Dawson, Zollinger, and Elwell[50] offer several lists of suggested activities for vocabulary building, the most useful of which are probably those on pp. 68 and 76. A number of good word games are suggested. Lake[51] believes that making puns and "Tom Swifties" are good ways of getting children to have fun with words. She provides a number of useful suggestions you may wish to try. Swatts[52] suggests guessing games, such as "Twenty Questions" and "What's My Line," to explore the meanings of out-of-the-way words. Well aware of the importance of sustaining children's interest in words, Swatts recommends that the teacher be ready to switch from one activity to another at the first sign that interest is waning—another good argument for having a wide range of word games available.

4. AN APPROACH TO USAGE

No teacher wants to create a situation in which children lose confidence in themselves. In an area as sensitive and personal as usage, however, the teacher always runs such risks. Yet it is the teacher's responsibility to try to do something about forms if the continued use of some might penalize the child in certain situations. A positive attitude and an avoidance of any situation that will humiliate a particular child will help to avoid many problems.

First, it is important that you listen to your pupils in order to determine which oral language problems are really important to work on. If there are many problems, you will have to set your own priorities, always putting those that may stigmatize the child, at least in some situations, high on your list. The suggestions that follow provide examples of positive ways to deal with usage problems. As with the games in the last chapter, these ideas are not exhaustive. They are intended to suggest a general approach that you will find that you can adapt in many ways.

There is, of course, little point in focusing on usage problems unless children have frequent opportunities to hear standard English, use it freely and without fear of making divergencies in speech, and are reinforced positively in the use of standard expressions. At the end of this chapter some literary materials are suggested that will prove useful to teachers who want to be sure that their children have ample opportunity to hear music before they are expected to sing it.

Irregular Verb Forms

There are not very many irregular verb forms in English, but those that exist occur with great frequency. Any devices that will help children remember these forms or help them see patterns that will aid retention are worth trying.

One such strategy is the kind of usage jingle suggested by McKee and McCowen. Here is one example.

ATE-EATEN

I *ate* a green apple;
   That was a mistake,
For now that I've *eaten* it
   My, how I ache!

McKee and McCowen[53] give only one jingle for each pair of troublemakers but, once children get the idea, they enjoy making up usage poems of their own.

For making your pupils more aware of the differences between past and past participle forms of irregular verbs, you might try putting on the board some columns like these.

Gruesome Twosomes

123	1,234
he did	he *has* done
123	1,234
he saw	he *has* seen
1,234	12,345
he took	he *has* taken
123	12,345
it ate	it *has* eaten
1,234	12,345
it gave	it *has* given
1,234	12,345
he knew	he *has* known
1,234	12,345
it grew	it *has* grown
1,234	12,345
it flew	it *has* flown
12,345	123,456
she broke	she *has* broken
12,345	123,456
she chose	she *has* chosen

Other irregular verbs, such as *blow, throw,* and *steal,* can be added as appropriate. Suggest that children think of the numbers above the forms as being the age of the words, thus, *did* is 123 years old, but *done* is 1,234. You

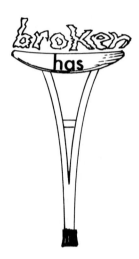
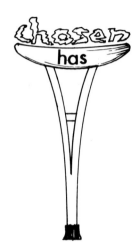

can then tell them that the "old" words need crutches to get around—*have, has,* or *had*. (To emphasize this idea, you could write some of the past participle forms in shaky letters to make them look decrepit and in need of help.) You might also write the crutch words on oaktag crutches and have children choose one to help a word they select from the right column of the Gruesome Twosomes.

A variant that also uses the idea of the "age" of words can be set up as follows. It is important to point out that children are not expected to memorize the "ages" of letters but, if they know their alphabet, they will get the idea quickly which letters are older or younger than others. The numbering is just a device to make the association more real and concrete for children. (The directions that appear at the right of the verb columns can be written on the board or given orally.)

Don't forget to look at the *different* vowel in the last word in the *second* column if the first vowels in the model words are the same length—began begun, for example. Does the second vowel if it is different than the first vowel need a helping word with it—"have," "has," or *had*? Why?

Some youngsters probably will notice right away that the main verbs in each of the tenses are the same length. You can then ask what the students notice about the second vowel in each main verb if the first vowel is the same in both columns, for example, began-begun. Which letter is "older?" Which comes later on in the alphabet? After determining that the letters *o* in "come" and *u* in "begun" are older than both *a* in "came" and *a* in "began," for instance, the teacher could get the answer that the word with

How Old Is Each Letter?

1	2	3	4	5	6	7	8	9	10	11	12	13	14	15	16	17	18	19	20	21	22	23
a	b	c	d	e	f	g	h	i	j	k	l	m	n	o	p	q	r	s	t	u	v	w

24	25	26
x	y	z

1. it c[1:a]me   it has c[15:o]me

2. he b[5:e]gan   he has beg[21:u]n

3. she r[1:a]n   she has r[21:u]n

4. it dr[1:a]nk   it has dr[21:u]nk

5. he sw[1:a]m   he has sw[21:u]m

6. she w[5:e]nt   she has g[15:o]ne

7. it r[1:a]n   it has r[21:u]n

8. he s[1:a]ng   he has s[21:u]ng

9. it r[1:a]ng   it has r[21:u]ng

the older second letter must have a nurse, a helper, a crutch. If there is only one vowel in the words the children are looking at, ask them to observe which vowel is older—"ran"-"run." The word that has the older vowel in it needs assistance. It cannot stand alone.

It seems that for too long we have been teaching "saw"-"seen," "did"-"done," "went"-"gone," and other combinations arbitrarily, in isolation, by rote; usually, the methods employed have failed to produce the results we hoped they would. By inductively studying these groups of words together, children may discover a generalization about them that might help them to decide which of two words such as *ran, run* should be used in a particular context.

Some materials you can use to provide pleasant exposure to the forms of *bring* and *see* are:

1. *May I Bring a Friend?* by Beatrice Schenk de Regniers, illustrated by Beni Montressor (New York: Atheneum, 1970, 1964). The 1970 edition is a hardcover book; the 1964 edition is an Atheneum (Aladdin) paperback edition.
2. *One Bright Monday Morning* by Arline and Joseph Baum (New York: Random House, 1962).
3. *The Golden Apple* by Max Bolliger, pictures by Celestino Piatti (New York: Atheneum, 1970).
4. "Fooba Wooba John" (American Folk Song) in *Oh, What Nonsense,* edited by William Cole, drawings by Tomi Ungerer (New York: The Viking Press, 1969, pp. 64–69).
5. *I Never Saw . . .* by Judson Jerome, illustrated by Helga Aichinger (Chicago: Albert Whitman and Company, 1974).
6. *Who Took the Farmer's Hat?* by Joan L. Nodset, pictures by Fritz Siebel (New York: Harper and Row, Publishers, 1963).
7. *Have You Seen My Brother?* by Elizabeth Guilfoyle, illustrated by Mary Stevens (Chicago: Follett Publishing Company, 1962).

Some oral language exercises that first- and second-grade teachers might find beneficial and fun to use with their pupils can be found in the following sources.

1. *We Talk and Listen, Teacher's Annotated Edition 1,* by Paul McKee and M. Lucile Harrison [Boston: Houghton Mifflin, 1963, pp. 12–17 ("saw," "seen," "done," "come"); pp. 22, 23, 56, 57, 58 ("saw," "came," "did")].
2. *Let's Talk, Teacher's Annotated Edition 2,* by Paul McKee and M. Lucile Harrison, [Boston: Houghton Mifflin, 1961, pp. 65, 66, 142, 153, 144 ("saw," "went," "gone")].

Agreement

To give children experience in distinguishing between singular and plural forms, you might try putting this illustration on the board.

H ←——— He wa⟨s⟩   T ←——— They were

I ⇇ I wa⟨s⟩   W ←——— We were

‌ ⟍ It wa⟨s⟩   Y ←——— You were

S ←——— She wa⟨s⟩

A B C D E F G ⟨H⟩⟨I⟩ J K L M N O P Q R ⟨S⟩⟨T⟩ U V ⟨W⟩ X ⟨Y⟩ Z
‌   H I   S T   W   Y

Tell the children that the word "YOU," because it is so important, takes the plural form of the verb, for example, "You *were*," "You *are*," "You *have*." Also, because "I" is such an important word, it can demand words of its own to go with it—"I am"—in the present tense for the verb "is;" "I have," and so on. After putting the foregoing illustration on the board and suggesting that the children think about what they are seeing for a day, ask the children what they observed and how this helped them. Perhaps just noting the word "HIS" might help them to remember when to use the singular form. In addition, they might notice that *h, i,* and *s* come before *t, w,* and *y* in the alphabet. They could remember that "his," standing for the pronouns *he, she, it,* ends in *s*; this memory trick might help children remember that such words demand a verb with an *s* in it—"was" or "is" or "has." The other letters—*t, w, y*—demand longer, older words, such as "were," "are," and "have," with the exceptions of "YOU" and "I" as previously noted.

To show children which *nouns* take the verb forms of "is," "are"; "was," "were"; "do," "does," a book such as Ruth Krauss's *A Hole Is to Dig,* illustrated by Maurice Sendak, Harper and Brothers, New York, 1952, could be introduced. Sections of Krauss's book, a book of definitions, could be read to pupils. Over and over again, simple sentences using "is" and "are" are given. They are not presented in any order. That is, there is just a series of sentences that use "is" and "are," such as "Rugs are so dogs have napkins;" "A hole is for a mouse to live in;" "A principal is to take out splinters;" and "A lap is so you don't get crumbs on the floor." After hearing many definitions, children could be asked to tell which definitions they liked best. As the children are giving their favorites, you can record them on the board, putting all the "is" sentences on one side and all the "are" sentences opposite them. Then you can tell the children that you have a problem for them to solve. You would like to know how one can tell when to use "is" and when to use "are" in sentences. Read all the sentences on one side and then all the sentences on the other side, asking the children if they noticed anything that was alike about each group. After doing this, tell them you are going to make them all detectives and give them some more clues to help them solve the problem. Then write sentences such as the following on the board.

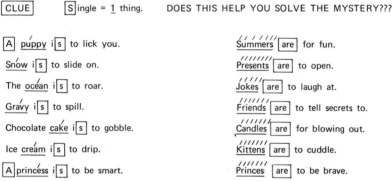

| CLUE | |Single = 1 thing. | DOES THIS HELP YOU SOLVE THE MYSTERY??? |

A púppy i|s| to lick you.   Summers |are| for fun.

Snów i|s| to slide on.   Presents |are| to open.

The océan i|s| to roar.   Jokes |are| to laugh at.

Grávy i|s| to spill.   Friends |are| to tell secrets to.

Chocolate cáke i|s| to gobble.   Candles |are| for blowing out.

Ice creám i|s| to drip.   Kittens |are| to cuddle.

A|princéss i|s| to be smart.   Princes |are| to be brave.

Please note that this generalization applies to nouns that form the plural by adding "s," "es," or "ies" to the base word. For nouns that form their plurals irregularly, for example *men, mice, geese, children,* and so forth, children need to learn to ask themselves whether or not these words mean one thing or person or more than one. The "s" clue contained in regular plural nouns will not help them in words such as these. Obviously, then, children would have to have these words in their aural-oral vocabulary before being asked whether they are plural or not.

After reading each column of sentences separately and stressing the singleness of the nouns in the one column and the plurality of the nouns in the other—perhaps simply by holding up a finger or fingers as you say each noun—children can be helped to discover that when a noun is single it needs an *s* word: "is." Emphasize that the *s* stands for single. You might also help the children realize that the articles "a" and "an" indicate singleness. Other words such as "one" that indicate singleness could be discussed. These associations may help them to remember when to use what verb form. They are seeing and hearing and are actively involved in the learning process.

The procedure that has just been described could be used to let children see that the same principle holds with the verbs "was" and "were," "has" and "have," and "does" and "do," when nouns are used as subjects. Your next step should be to try to get the children to give their own sentences using these words. To reinforce children's seeing and hearing "is" and "are," and so forth, perhaps there could be on a table separate boxes of words containing "is," "are," "was," "were," "has," "have," and "does," "do." A set of nouns (words the children have worked with) could be placed face down in the middle of the table. A child would pick up a card, say the word out loud, and think of a sentence to go with it. He or she then would proceed to pick up from the verb box a word he or she was going to use with the noun. Children watching could be holding three cards—one red, one yellow, and one green. If children thought the youngster who was going to respond was going to answer incorrectly, they would hold up their red card; a yellow if they thought the child needed caution; or a green for a "go-ahead" signal. By flashing these cards, the child about to give the sentence could be helped before saying anything, and the teacher, immediately, could see how many children in the group seemed to be comprehending the concept. This is a game children have enjoyed. As a culminating activity, some children might want to make their own booklets with sentences and illustrations using the forms they have been working with.

Dora V. Smith[54] feels that, if the *teacher* can be creative in teaching grammar, a lot of unnecessary time in teaching isolated grammatical facts can be used in other more beneficial ways. She gives some excellent examples on pp. 53–54 as to how teachers can help children with specific problems. Her first suggestion concerns verb endings. She states that every little child soon comes to realize that *s* at the end of a noun means more than one. Smith says that although the opposite is true for verbs, some people graduate from college without discovering this fact.

In teaching usage, you need to be a diagnostician. You must find out first if there are any significant problems and, if there are, how you can help your pupils. Avoid as much as possible texts and workbooks that present non-standard forms for multiple-choice answers. This kind of exercise often establishes a nonstandard form where a pupil had a standard form before.

For the special problems of teachers of culturally divergent children, the article "Culturally Divergent Children and Creative Language Activities"[55] by Pilon may prove useful. Also helpful may be the NCTE cassette, "Dialects and Reading: Implications for Change"[56] by Pilon and Sims.

I believe that it is so important in working with children not to get "uptight" about their language. If ever you find yourself getting tense about tenses or usage or whatever, try reading these poems that appear in the Hymes's *Hooray for Chocolate*.[57]

AIN'T

You may have heard
There is a word
That sounds like paint
And rhymes with faint.
It is not so. There ain't.

O.K.

Never say "Yeah."
Don't say "o.k."
"Yes" is polite,
And the right word to say
So always remember:
Say "Yes."
   O.K.?

Literary Suggestions to Use in Developing Oral Expression and Punctuation Skills

Armour, Richard, *On Your Marks: A Package of Punctuation*, New York: McGraw-Hill Book Company, 1969. Creative poems that describe and illustrate the uses of various punctuation markers. Every time a particular marker is employed, the author has the marker typed in red so that it is sure to catch the reader's attention.

Borge, Victor, *Caught in the Act*, Columbia Records, New York, 1973. Be sure to listen to Borge's hilarious "Phonetic Punctuation" selection and let children adapt his ingenious idea of punctuating their talk with sounds.

Brown, Marcia, *How Hippo!*, New York: Charles Scribner's Sons, 1969. A "just right" book for proving to children how important it is to differentiate your "how's" in oral expression. How you do it is all important.

Behrens, June, photographs by Ray Ambraziunas, *Who Am I?*, Chicago: Children's Press, 1968. Good book for developing self-concept and for exposing children to the pronoun "I" over and over again. Different pictures of real children are used in this book. Each child tells who he or she is and a little bit about himself or herself. Children of various ethnic backgrounds and races are depicted. The last page states that "WE ARE FIRST GRADERS. WE ARE ALL AMERICANS."

Behrens, June, photographs by Austin Anton, *Where Am I?*, Chicago: Children's Press, 1969. Good exposure to standard forms of "am," "is," and "are" that some black children may not be used to hearing or saying.

Bradbury, Ray, "Switch on the Night" in *Stories and Poems*, edited by Leland B. Jacobs and Jo Jasper Turner, New York: Western Publishing Co., Inc., 1970, pp. 68–70. Children, after listening to this creative story, might be asked to tell what happens when day, happiness, sadness, or fear are switched on. "Switch on the Night" is a short but poetically and imaginatively written tale.

Carlson, Ruth Kearney, *Speaking Aids through the Grades*, New York: Teachers College, Columbia University, 1975. An excellent source book for teachers.

Gardner, Martin, illustrated by Laszlo Kubinyi, *Perplexing Puzzles and Tantalizing Teasers*, New York: Simon and Schuster, 1969. Delightful book filled with puzzles that should be fun for both you and your students to solve. For a good exercise in punctuation, try "Sally's Silly Walk" on p. 34.

Geddes, Barbara Bel, *So Do I*, New York: Grosset and Dunlap, 1972. Good exposure to word "I." Also can be used to stimulate children to talk about what they like. A very simple book to read.

Gordon, Alice Kaplan, *Games for Growth: Educational Games in the Classroom*, Palo Alto, Cal.: Science Research Associates, 1970. See game suggested by Gordon entitled "Stopduts," p. 52. This is a board game that children or their teacher could easily create to get children to pause for commas and stop for periods. Teachers could adapt this game to help children to understand the uses of other punctuation markers. Teachers might also consider using words that the children in their groups have had introduced to them instead of having different-sized and different-colored blank squares for each child. If this adaptation were made, children might reinforce their vocabulary at the same time that they were coming to understand the use of punctuation markers in sentences. If children worked in teams, they could construct meaningful sentences together to make the activity more relevant to language expression.

One suggestion that might be worthwhile trying would be to allow the children to change the positions of the words for the board. This, of course, means that teachers need provide only a track and a suitable number of different words and punctuation markers to fill the track. By doing this, teachers could keep on inserting new words for the children to play with. Additionally, children would have practice in changing sentence patterns and also come to realize which words in sentences were movable. Naturally, teachers could provide different-sized tracks to suit the various abilities of the children in their classes.

Hoetker, James, *Theater Games: One Way Into Drama,* Urbana, Ill.: National Council of Teachers of English, 1975. Some fine ideas for teachers to use with children to help them to communicate their ideas better.

Hurwitz, Abraham B., and Goddard, Arthur, *Games to Improve Your Child's English,* New York: Simon and Schuster, 1969. Section seven of this treasury of games is concerned with grammar and sentence games. Two pages that contain some exercises children might enjoy doing are pp. 270 and 314.

Krahn, Fernando, and Krahn, Maria de la Luz, illustrated by Fernando Krahn, *The Life of Numbers,* New York: Simon and Schuster, 1970. A very creative story that gives fitting personality characteristics to the numbers zero to nine. The illustrations are most imaginative. Perhaps children who have an opportunity to hear as well as see this story might be able to create some stories of their own about numbers or letters.

Krauss, Ruth, "I Can Fly" in *Stories and Poems,* edited by Leland B. Jacobs and Jo Jasper Turner, New York: Western Publishing Co., Inc., 1970, pp. 14–16. A simple story that might be read to get children to tell all the things that they can do. A good selection to use to enhance children's self-concepts.

McPhail, David, *Oh, No, Go,* Boston: Little, Brown and Company, 1973. Only three little words in this book, but it makes a great deal of difference how you say them! Delightful to use for an oral language activity.

Myers, Walter M., pictures by Leo Carty, *Where Does the Day Go?,* New York: Parents' Magazine Press, 1969. A simple story that shows young children trying to answer the title question. The book ends with the father of one of the children answering the question. Teachers reading this book to children might give their children time to think and respond to the question before the father's scientific answer is given. Some teachers may decide just to write their pupils' responses, read them to another group of children, and end the book simply by reasking the question: But where do *you* think the day goes?

Nurnberg, Maxwell, *Punctuation Pointers,* New York: Scholastic Book Services, 1968. An invaluable little paperback crammed with intriguing exercises that are sure to convince children that punctuating can be fun.

Potter, Charles Francis, illustrated by William Wiesner, *More Tongue Tanglers and a Rigmarole,* Cleveland: The World Publishing Company, 1964. For teachers who may want to see what happens when they try presenting some tongue twisters with much of the correct punctuation missing, I would suggest looking at pp. 9, 15, 26, 29, 30, the top tongue twister given on p. 37, and those on pp. 40 and 41. Begin with one tongue tangler. If your children are not driven mad by the whole process, try more.

Platts, Mary E., illustrated by Linda Swanson, *Grammar with Glamour,* Benton Harbor, Mich.: Educational Service, Inc., 1967. A colorful paperback that contains some clever ideas on how to present language concepts to children. Although Platts says on p. 34 that "Every sentence has to have a verb," she elaborates no more on this even though on pp. 15, 16, 51–58 she uses sentences herself such as "How cheery!" "A little here," her book would appeal to most children and teachers. It can be used effectively in helping children express themselves better instead of having them learn parts of speech—Platt's goal. The address of Educational Service, Inc. is P.O. Box 112, Benton Harbor Michigan 49022.

Salisbury, Kent, pictures by Adrina Zanazanian, Tell a Tall Tale, New York: Western Publishing Co., Inc., 1966. Made of heavy cardboard paper each of the six pages in this book is divided into seven movable sections. On each section is a colorful picture and a phrase. Each page by itself makes sense but change one or more sections and a crazy story is the result. The first sentence reads. "Once upon a time a hunter/padded his tippy canoe/down a blue tropical river/to a green palm jungle/where a cranky old crocodile/was catching fish for dinner/and they chased each other in the jungle." By changing a few of the sections, the following nonsense story would result. "Once upon a time a hunter/ran on his giant reptile legs/through the stars in space/to a green palm jungle/where a cranky old crocodile/was attending a grand ball/and they chased each other in the jungle." This is a fine book to use to get children to repeat again and again certain phrases without their getting bored so that they can recognize certain words. The way the phrases are split up should help children who have difficulty in reading smoothly. The book might also prompt children to make their own crazy, mixed-up books as well as encourage them to tell some of their own made-up zany stories.

Wagner, Ken, The One Word Storybook, New York: Western Publishing Co., Inc., 1969. Twelve ideas for stories are presented in this inexpensive book. Each story has a title and three, four, or five rhyming words, each accompanied by a colorful picture. The first story is entitled, "The Boat." The rhyming words are "sail," "gale," "whale," and "tale." The pictures show the adventures of three kittens. Children using the pictures and the rhyming words could be encouraged to tell a story using the words given as stimuli. The idea used by Ken Wagner should help children to develop their language fluency. After doing a few of Wagner's stories, some children might be inspired, with the teacher's stimulation and encouragement, to use rhyming words they know to create their own oral stories that later might be typed by the teacher or a pupil and shared by all.

York, L. Jean, "Basic Bibliography on Handwriting, Capitalization, and Punctuation," Champaign, Ill.: NCTE/ERIC, December 1969. A free, briefly annotated bibliography on the subjects mentioned in the title. The bibliography may be reproduced and distributed without permission from NCTE/ERIC.

Note. Any references made in Chapter 5 would be helpful to use in developing children's language competencies.

7
Spelling
and
Handwriting

Spulling

I reeely ~~like~~ lick
Arithmetic
But spulling
Makes me very sic.
　　　　—Lucia and James L. Hymes

For most teachers as well as their pupils, spelling and handwriting are weari-some although necessary parts of the elementary curriculum. At least part of the reason may be that these skills appear to be taught for their own sake and not in relation to the other language arts and communication skills as a whole. Instruction in both areas can be made more meaningful if it is related to work in reading and writing. And both spelling and handwriting can be made to seem less arbitrary and more interesting when pupils are aware of the accidents of history that have shaped our letters and dictated their ar-rangement into words.

This chapter suggests some ways of relating these skills to language arts instruction generally and presents some sources that cast light on the histori-cal development of the written language. It is assumed that your school has handwriting and spelling books or some comparable organized set of mate-rials for teaching these skills. Therefore, such details as may be involved in presenting a particular system of handwriting or sequencing spelling skills are not treated here. It is hoped that you will be able to adapt and use the ideas in this chapter to supplement and enrich the teaching materials you may have available.

1. CHILDREN'S BOOKS ABOUT LANGUAGE

"Why?" is a natural question for children to ask on being confronted with some of the perplexing inconsistencies in our language. It is a question that deserves a better answer than "Because that's the way it is." A number of good children's books offer interesting answers to many such questions, providing at the same time valuable insights into the growth and develop-ment of English.

An excellent starting point both for your own reading on the subject and for use with your pupils is *The Story of Our Language*[1] by Jo Ann McCormack. In addition to its interesting and highly informative text, this book contains footnotes to professional books that you may wish to investigate for yourself. (Additional references to professional books on the subject are included in the *Helps* section at the end of this chapter.) Some other children's books on communication, word origins, and the beginning and development of our writing system include:

1. *Dandelions Don't Bite* by Leone Adelson (New York: Pantheon Books, 1972). Fascinating etymologies of many of our words used today.
2. *Gifts from the Greeks: Alpha to Omega* by Sophia A. Boyer and Winifred Lubell (Chicago: Rand McNally, 1970).
3. *Is That Mother in the Bottle?* by Jessica Davidson (New York: Franklin Watts, Inc., 1972). Explains why our language may seem so idiosyncratic to us. Good reading for mature pupils in the intermediate grades. Davidson suggests that if you do not understand the title to the book, you should look up the word *mother* in the dictionary to see its derivation and meaning. (It comes from a root that gave the Dutch language the word *modder* which, Davidson tells us, meant "mud, slime, and dregs.")
4. *The Secrets of the ABC's* by Dorothy Dowdell (Mankato, Minn.: Oddo Publishing, 1965). Although easy to read, this book contains fascinating information on how the letters in our alphabet came about. For instance, the reader is told that *J* is the youngest letter and came from *I; G* was formed by the Romans by adding a little line to *C,* and *H* came from a picture word meaning "fence." Can you picture a fence today when you look at a capital "H"? The reader is also told that for a long time

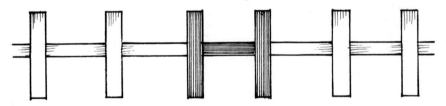

U and *V* were the same letter, had the same name, and sounded like *U*. At approximately the time Columbus discovered America, the letter *U* was written when used as a vowel, as in the word *up,* and *V* was used for the consonant in the word *vowel*. Because *V* was called *U* for so long, the letter *W,* although it is made of two V's, is called *double-U,* not *double-V.* *Z* used to be the seventh letter of the alphabet.

5. *How Our Alphabet Grew: The History of the Alphabet* by William Dugan (Racine, Wisc.: Western Publishing Company, Inc., 1972). Intermediate level reading. Dugan tells how the word *phonogram* derives from two Greek words meaning "voice" and "writing." The book also explains that the word *Bible* came from the name of a Phoenician city named *Byblos,* and the Egyptian word *hieroglyphics* means priest-writing.

6. *The True Book of Communication* by O. Irene Sevrey Miner (Chicago: Children's Press, 1960). Uncomplicated text that many children in the early primary grades can read for themselves.

7. *The Code and Cipher Book* by Jane Sarnoff and Reynold Ruffins (New York: Charles Scribner's Sons, 1975). A delightful book that will be sure to provide you with many exercises that you can use to get children to write legibly in both manuscript and cursive forms: in order to decode any puzzle, legible handwriting is essential. Intrinsically motivational —just plain fun.

8. *Wht's Yr Nm ?* by Margaret C. Taylor (New York: Harcourt, Brace and World, Inc., 1970). An interesting book from which children can learn that the Romans used only capital letters when they wrote and provided nospacebetweentheir wordsnorperiods— imaginehowhard thatmusthave beentoread!

9. *From Scrolls to Satellites! The Story of Communication* by William Wise (New York: Parents' Magazine Press, 1970). Intermediate level.

How Silent Letters Were Silenced

The so-called "silent" letters present problems for children when they read and when they spell. Knowing how these letters were "silenced" may not automatically solve all of the problems involved in their use, but it should make their appearance in modern words more understandable. You will find pp. 21–25 of *The Story of Our Language* particularly useful in explaining to children the disappearance of these missing sounds. Your pupils will be interested in such facts as these:

1. *gh* in "night," "laugh," "thought," and so forth, was originally pronounced with a soft *k* sound, as modern German *ch* is still pronounced in words like *ich* and *nicht.* (Children can easily reproduce this sound if you tell them to make the sound they make when they gargle.)

2. The initial *k* in words like "know," "knight," and "knee" was initially pronounced. (Children can easily produce this old sound of "know" and "knee"—k'no, k'ne. You may want to have them try "knight," also. If so, remind them of the gargling sound for *gh,* mentioned in point 1.)

3. The letter *l*, now silent in words like "calm" and "walk," was originally pronounced.
4. The initial *w* in "write" and "wrap" was originally pronounced.
5. Medieval scholars, in their enthusiasm for giving English words a Latin pedigree, introduced a silent *b* into words like "debt" (originally *det*) because there was one in the assumed Latin original *debitum*. "Doubt" and "receipt" got their silent letters *b* and *p* in the same way.
6. The printing press came to England by way of Holland, and with it came many Dutchmen who were more knowledgeable about printing than they were about English. The Dutch liberally sprinkled *h*'s in English words in places where they would normally appear in Dutch. Most of these, as in the words "ghospel" ("gospel") and "ghossip" ("gossip"), were eventually dropped, but the *h* stuck in modern words such as "ghost" and "ghastly."

Silent -*e*

The unpronounced -*e* at the end of many English words is somewhat more complicated because there are different reasons for its being there in different words. When the final -*e* is a signal for a long vowel preceding it (as in "kite," "hope," and "cake"), it is a relict of a vowel pronounced in English through the fifteenth century. Thus words of this kind had two syllables in Chaucer's day, the first usually having a long vowel and the last a schwa —the sound of *a* in "about." (For further information, consult Mario Pei's *The Story of English,* Greenwich, Conn.: Fawcett Publications, 1962) and Leonard F. Dean's and Kenneth Wilson's *Essays on Language and Usage,* Second Edition, New York: Oxford University Press, 1963.

As every reading teacher knows, there are some silent -*e*'s that are really silent—that is, ones that cannot be regarded as part of a long vowel spelling, as in "love" and "have," for example. In *Understanding Reading*[2] Frank Smith explains the English taboo against allowing words to end with "naked" *v*'s," thus accounting for the final letter in the spellings of these and similar words. He also accounts for the final -*e* in "house" as a signal to show that the word is singular.

Why There Is an *o* Where a *u* Ought to Be

Another change in spelling that affects enough words to make it worth exploring with your pupils is the historical change from spelling English words like "luv" with a *u* to spelling them with an *o*. (The final *e* is explained in the paragraph preceding this one.) In the scribal script introduced into

England after the Norman Conquest, the letters *u, v,* and *n* were produced with two identical downstrokes. Imagine trying to figure out a word such as iiiicoiiiiiiiiiiiicatiiie (uncommunicative)!

To lessen possible ambiguity when two of these letters appeared in sequence, the practice of occasionally substituting an *o* for a *u* arose; thus "luv" became "love," and "tun" became "ton." The problem is they did not change all of the words so today we get words that may mystify pupils and teachers. Some reading authorities advocate that such words be taught as sight words. Many common words were affected as the following incomplete list suggests.

communication	comparison
compare	companion
compass	compartment
command	compile
contain	content as in "He is content with his
complete	life."
confine	confuse
does	love
once	son
come	one
done	some
ton	honey
money	above
none	of
someone	something
sometime	won
among	color
dove	glove
worry	comfort
wonder	Monday
cover	mother
lovely	other
another	front

Instead of suggesting that these words and others be learned as sight words, tell children that if a "long *o*" or "short *o*" sound does not make sense in a word they are trying to decode, they should try a "short *u*" sound. The proper term for the sound that is heard in the words just listed is schwa. The phonetic symbol for the schwa sound is ə.

Borrowed Words

You may wish to follow up the discussion of foreign influences on English suggested earlier in connection with silent letters by telling children that they already know words from many different languages. You could start them out with charts of borrowed words and encourage them to find additional examples to add. Examples of some beginning lists might be as follows.

German	French	Italian	Spanish
kindergarten	robe	piano	patio
sauerkraut	chowder	macaroni	sombrero
hamburger	dessert	maraschino	rodeo
halt	ballet	violin	siesta
poodle	costume	confetti	tapioca
pumpernickel	garage	spaghetti	vanilla
frankfurters	dandelion	ravioli	bananas
pretzels	chauffeur	baloney	barbecue
noodles	infantry	soprano	palomino
strudels	cash	piccolo	corral
seltzer	tailor	quarantine	chili con carne
crullers	mayonnaise	pizza	cafeteria

Interesting Word Origins

Another good way of developing children's growing interest in language is to explore the origins of words and phrases. A good place to start is with the paperbacks by Charles E. Funk suggested in *Helps* at the end of this chapter. The following list of suggestions will provide a good starting point for pupils' investigations. Be sure that you provide them with dictionaries that include word origins (etymologies); some elementary dictionaries do not.

1. goodbye
2. breakfast
3. sneakers
4. sandwich
5. zippers
6. the days of the week
7. the months of the year
8. rubbers
9. sundae
10. sirloin
11. escape
12. alarm
13. Caribbean
14. Europe
15. California
16. museum
17. school
18. companion
19. jeep
20. gymnasium
21. cereal
22. tip
23. disaster
24. beserk
25. denim
26. blimp
27. bonfire
28. Chicago
29. dungaree
30. assassin

Some additional reference books you may find useful for exploring word origins and related aspects of language are:

1. *What's Behind the Word* ? by Sam and Beryl Epstein.[3]
2. *What a Funny Thing to Say* ! by Bernice Kohn.[4]
3. *Names on the Land* by George R. Stewart.[5]

2. THE LETTERS AND HANDWRITING

The handwriting books or comparable materials you have available probably contain useful suggestions for introducing letter shapes and providing practice in their use. The suggestions in this section may be useful in supplementing these resources.

Alphabet Books

Alphabet books usually illustrate each letter and provide pictures of objects that begin with that letter. Such books are useful and attractive, and you can easily adapt their techniques for activities of your own. For example, you may wish to have pupils prepare their own alphabet books, drawing relevant illustrations or cutting pictures of them out of magazines. Pupils will then print the appropriate letter on each page. (You may also ask them to print the name of each object under its picture; if you do, be sure to provide the correct spelling for your youngsters.) Encourage children to share their alphabet books with their friends.

Sonia Delaunay has written a book simply entitled *Sonia Delaunay Alphabet* (Thomas Y. Crowell Company, 1972) that is delightful. She has written each letter of the alphabet in manuscript form (Latin—"manu"—"by hand" plus "script"—"written") with some clever verses all of which have come from the "classic and traditional literature of childhood" (blurb on inside of jacket). The ones that I enjoyed most were these associative rhymes:

M

My story's ended,
My spoon is bended:
If you don't like it,
Get it mended.

V

V and I together meet,
And make the number Six complete.
When I and V do meet once more,
Then 'tis we two can make but Four.
And when that V from I is gone,
Alas! poor I can make but One.

(Roman figures)

X

X shall stand for playmates Ten;
V for Five stout stalwart men;
I for One, as I'm alive;
C for One Hundred, and D for Five;
M for a Thousand soldiers brave,
And L for Fifty who hid in a cave.

(Roman figures)

Children will enjoy copying these traditional rhymes more than the exercises usually provided in handwriting manuals for practicing and reviewing letters learned. Perhaps some may become stimulated to write their own associative poems for other letters as well as for the letters just cited.

For older children there are alphabet books on the market that will tantalize them and excite their curiosity. Two such selections are *Still Another Alphabet Book* by Seymour Chwast and Martin Stephen Moskof (McGraw-Hill Book Company, n.d.) and *Anno's Alphabet* by Mitsumasa Anno (Thomas Y. Crowell Company, n.d.). Chwast and Moskof were overly modest in choosing their title; no one could describe their work as still another anything. Not only would children be practicing the letters of the alphabet if they adapted the authors' creative idea in making books of their own, but they would be motivated to learn to spell and read as well. Chwast and Moskof take a letter of the alphabet and draw something that they associate with that letter. On each two-page spread the letters of the alphabet are printed as capitals *in sequence*. Certain letters stand out because they are printed in a color different from the rest of the letters. The trick is for the reader to figure out the spelling of the word being shown as well as the picture. For example, on the page for *R* the reader's attention is drawn to the letters *D E I N R*. The reader, using the picture as a clue and what he or she knows about the spelling of words, must figure out that the word the authors are thinking about is *REINDEER*. (Note that if a letter is to be used more than once in a word, it is not repeated in the alphabet sequence.) Some of the pictures are very intriguing. For instance, for the letter *D*, a series of *D*'s is shown in a progressive state of deterioration. The letters that stand out in green are *A, D, E, I, P, R,* and *S*. The correct word for this page is

Answers to the riddles are given at the end of the book.

Anno's Alphabet is a highly innovative and imaginative book appropriate for children in the intermediate grades. Anno uses two pages for each letter of the alphabet. On one page is the letter; opposite it is a picture depicting something that begins with the letter. On each of the double page spreads there is a *trompe l'oeil* border in which the author very skillfully hides among the foliage other objects that begin with the letter being worked on. Some children may find they are unable to identify these objects, since many are difficult. For instance, on the pages for *I* there are hidden pictures of iguanas and impalas. Pages similar to this one would be ideal for motivating children to use the dictionary. You could inform children that there are "impalas" and "iguanas" hidden on the page. Then children could be encouraged to look these words up in the dictionary, tell how the words are pronounced and what they mean, and copy the way they are spelled. Anno includes in the back of his book a listing of *some* of the things he has included in his pages. It would be interesting to see how many things children and their teacher can discover. In addition to the puzzlers already mentioned that the author-illustrator provides, there is something "wrong" with each letter that is presented. The reader is not told what is the matter but must figure it out.

Associations with Words and Letters

A wonderful way to get children to learn and practice words and letters is to have them practice depicting them concretely. However, pupils do need warm-ups in order to get the idea as to what is desired in these exercises. In doing these kinds of exercises children will not only have fun in practicing letters and the spelling of the words, but they will be developing their originality, fluency, and senses of humor. Examples of students' words follow.

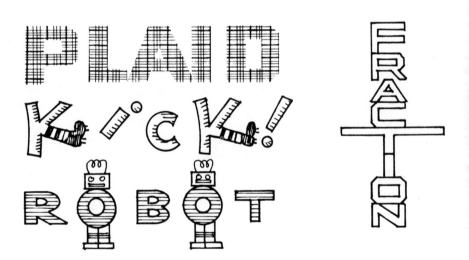

Children practicing letters either in manuscript or cursive form, capital or lowercase, become very creative in developing their own associations for letters. Students I have worked with have thought of many original and appropriate associations for each letter of the alphabet. The following examples were taken from an alphabet letter book written by my students.

Man who speaks with forked tongue.

...and when you get to the fork in the road...

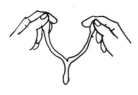

Everything was going along well until you wanted to split up.

How come I look like a tree?

It's good for the circulation.

 Just get out of jail, He'll never go straight

 Don't get mixed up with this guy. He just wants to run around in circles.

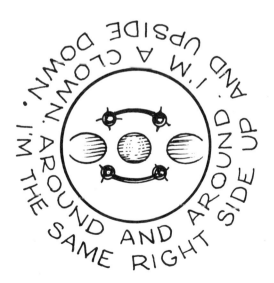 One thing about him.... he'll never be a square.

Some excellent references that may further convince children that learning to spell and write words and letters legibly can be a great deal of fun are:

1. *The Mad Book of Word Power* by Max Brandel (New York: Warner Paperback Library, 1973). Although there are some concrete illustrations included in this inexpensive paperback that would not be at all fitting to show to youngsters in the elementary grades, the book is, nevertheless, a treasure to demonstrate to children the fun that can be had with words. The technique of depicting words concretely is one that teachers should find very helpful in getting children to identify new vocabulary words.
2. *Talking Words* by Ashok Davar (Indianapolis: The Bobbs-Merrill Company, Inc., 1969). From *A* to *Z* the author gives his readers words that look like what they refer to.
3. *Concrete Is Not Always Hard* by A. Barbara Pilon (Middletown, Conn.: Xerox Education Publications, 1972). Concrete poems and illustrations of words along with suggestions to teachers on how the book can be used with pupils.
4. *CDB* by William Steig (New York: Windmill Books, Inc., 1968).

A book that may give children ideas on how to fool around with associations with numbers and thereby may give them creative opportunities to practice writing numbers is Fernando and Maria de la Luz Krahn's ingenious *The Life of Numbers* (New York: Simon and Schuster, 1970).

Some Things to Keep in Mind While Teaching Handwriting

The following suggestions and comments about teaching handwriting may duplicate wholly or in part those given in the guide material to your handwriting books. In any case, they are practical points that deserve at least brief mention.

1. Line a section of your board for handwriting exercises or blackboard assignments. Magic markers will not hurt blackboards, and they save you the trouble of lining your board every day.
2. Use dittos or stencils for children so they will have individual copies of what they are to practice right with them.
3. Do not have children practice needlessly what they already know; this causes boredom and carelessness.
4. Have older children write down and read back the dictated stories and poems of younger children.
5. On the handwriting section of the board, have a space describing the elements that help make handwriting legible: spacing, size, shape, slant, and neatness.
6. Demonstrate to children the monsters of handwriting—the problem letters that can cause their writings to be incomprehensible or misinterpreted. Explain and show concretely how letters can become distorted or look like other letters. If this is done, children will be helped to understand the importance of writing neatly and legibly.

   a. *a's* that look like *o's* or *u's* or *ci's*.
   b. *d's* that resemble *cl's*.
   c. cursive *e's* and *i's* that look like *l's*, and vice versa.
   d. *m's* like *w's; m's* like *n's*.
   e. manuscript *r's* like *n's*.
   f. cursive *r's* like *i's*.
   g. cursive *u's* like *v's;* cursive *u's* like *n's*.

7. When younger children are using lined paper on which a middle line is provided that is either lightly ruled or dotted ‒‒‒‒‒‒‒‒‒ |·········· , advise children to skip one complete line between each line they write on so that letters will not run into other letters on the lower lines.

Your puppy is disturbing my little brother Jimmy. Please bring him in the house.

8. Do not force children into cursive writing if they are having any difficulties at all either with handwriting or reading.
9. Consider discontinuing teaching in the beginning stages of reading the typical manuscript shapes of g and a and, instead, teach the forms that children are going to be seeing and using in printed commercial type—a and g .
10. Be a good example to your pupils.
11. Let children read each others' work—make handwriting exercises meaningful to youngsters.
12. Have an alphabet chart or models of letters prominent in the classroom.

3. SPELLING AND READING

Although both spelling and reading experts properly insist on the differences between encoding and decoding—the processes involved in spelling and reading, respectively—there are some spelling generalizations that have obvious relevance to reading as well. This section suggests ways that you can lead children to form four such generalizations. If you find this approach fruitful, you can easily adapt the method to produce other useful generalizations. You also will find some suggestions for teaching spelling included in this section.

The Hard Sound of c

In working with children to get them to learn inductively a generalization that will be useful to them, it is important to remember that the words used in teaching should be words that are within the children's aural-oral vocabulary—words they have heard and said before. Therefore, the words that are used as samples should be considered just so—as samples only.

Some of the words listed here may not be suitable for use with your particular pupils.

The first step is to put words down on the board that the children are apt to recognize when they hear them. Make sure there is no irrelevant information given that may be given back to you when you ask them what they have noticed about the words. For example, if it is not critical to the generalization that the words be one-syllable words, include multisyllabic words in your lists.

Words used to teach the hard sounds of c might be:

c̲u̲t	c̲o̲lor	c̲a̲ndle
c̲u̲p	c̲o̲unt	c̲a̲mouflage
c̲u̲stard	c̲o̲st	o̲a̲mpaign
c̲u̲pboard	c̲o̲rner	c̲a̲rousel
c̲u̲nning	c̲o̲uch	c̲a̲t
c̲u̲ckoo	c̲o̲okbook	c̲a̲sh
c̲u̲ff	c̲o̲pperplate	c̲a̲pital
c̲u̲ltivation	c̲o̲rrecting	c̲a̲ndy
c̲u̲stomary	c̲o̲smopolitan	C̲a̲lifornia

Note that in each list there are quite a few words. Children should not be expected to form generalizations unless there is enough data from which to generalize. Giving only a few words is usually not sufficient.

Second, you will see that attention has been called to the first and second letters of every word in the lists by means of underlining or squares drawn around letters. Attention might as well be called to the key letters in other ways. These devices are intended to help pupils answer specific questions that will be asked later.

Third, you will observe that the lists are structured with words grouped according to their second letter—*u, o,* or *a.* Even though it is true that all three of these letters have the effect of making the c "hard," that is, having its *k* sound, the generalization will be more easily arrived at through the separate cases.

After listing the words on the board, tell children to *look* at the words in the first column and notice two things that are alike about these words. Pupils will respond that each of the words begins with the letters *cu*. Then *read* the words in the list, pointing to the *cu* in each as you pronounce it. Ask pupils to listen to what sound they *hear* at the beginning of each word. When pupils respond that they all begin with the *k* sound, write a *k* above this column of words. You might then lead pupils to generalize by asking what sound they would expect to hear in a word that begins with *cu*.

Follow the same procedures with the second and third columns. By now, the children will be anticipating the kind of questions you will ask and should answer more rapidly and with assurance. When you have worked through all three columns, ask pupils for a generalization that covers all three cases. They should be able to state in their own words that when a *c* is followed by the letters *u, o,* or *a* it will have its hard (or *k*) sound.

As a reinforcement step, work together with children on other words where *c* can be expected to be "hard." Use examples where the *c* has its "hard" sound in the middle of words as well as in the beginning as in the words *cu* `cu` *mber* and *ca* `co` *phony*. This reinforcement can take many forms—for example, dittos and games.

Last, you may want to give the children some simple associative device to remember what they have just practiced. For example, a sentence such as "Yo<u>u</u> o`k`ay ?" may aid them in remembering that words where *c* is followed by *u, o,* or *a* have the *k* sound.

The Soft Sound of *c*

The same steps taken to show when *c* has the hard sound can be done for *c* followed by *y, i,* and *e*. An associative sentence might be "Wh<u>y</u> *I* `s`ee!"—where *c* is followed by *y, i,* or *e, c* can be expected to have the "soft sound"—*s*.

The Hard Sound of *g*

The same general procedure can be followed for leading children to generalize about words that will have the hard sound of *g*. The lists should be ordered in the same way as the lists for *c*.

gully	golly	garage
gun	gone	gang
gut	gondola	garden
gull	Goldilocks	gasoline

As before, elicit a generalization for each column and then an overall generalization for the three letters following g. In the pupils' own words this may be something like "When the letter *u, o,* or *a* follows g in a word, we expect the g to have its hard sound."

When y Is a Vowel

Your pupils will probably be able to rattle off the names of the vowels, including "sometimes y." But, if asked, they may have difficulty giving an example of a word in which y spells a vowel sound. Suggest that you are going to do an experiment together that will reveal some cases in which y is a vowel, as well as the sounds y can have.

Put on the board lists such as the ones that follow. Use one-syllable words in the first column, words with stress on the last syllable in the second, multisyllabic words in the third, and words in the last column where the y is surrounded by consonants and has the short sound of *i*.

why	reply	lovely	cynic
my	supply	beautifully	syllable
cry	outcry	pretty	system
try	defy	selfishly	mystery
fry	standby	generously	cyst

After working through the first column, try to elicit the generalization that in one-syllable words ending in y, y is a vowel with the sound of long *i.* Build on this generalization in working through the second column, calling attention to the stress on the last syllable. When pupils are ready, have them extend the first generalization: when y appears in a one-syllable word or comes at the end of an accented syllable, it is a vowel with the sound of long *i.*

In working with the third column, try to elicit the observations that the words have more than one syllable and that the accent is never on the syllable with y in it. Help pupils to word their generalization something like this: when y comes at the end of a word of two or more syllables and is not in an accented syllable, it is a vowel with the sound of long *e.*

After working with the words in the last column, children should be able to state something to the effect that when y appears in the middle of consonants, they can try the short sound of *i,* as in "it." It is *imperative* in working with words in this list to be sure that the selections used as examples are within the children's oral-aural vocabulary.

Suggestions for Teaching Spelling

1. Do not hold spelling bees. They tend to provide practice for the best spellers, while the poor spellers who need it find something more interesting to think about.
2. If pupils take spelling lists home, provide them with copies to avoid the possibility of their studying words they have copied incorrectly.
3. Always pretest children on words. If they already know the words, provide other words for them to work on.
4. Correct *with* children. Circle problem areas for them.
5. Help them to develop families of words.
6. Integrate spelling lessons with other language arts areas.
7. Provide meaningful and creative opportunities for pupils to use the new words they learn.
8. Demonstrate to children that you are a word addict.
9. Reinforce children positively for being word addicts—help them spread their addiction.
10. Do not penalize children for spelling mistakes when they are trying to express their ideas creatively or are doing rough drafts.
11. When enunciating spelling words for children in a testing situation, enunciate clearly and distinctly and use the words being tested in context.
12. Try to teach helpful spelling generalizations inductively.
13. Introduce children to familiar patterns of words and have them build and add on to helpful lists that you start with them.
    a. CVC—rat, hop, cap.
    b. CVCe—rate, hope, cape.
    c. CVVC—rain, weed.
    d. Vowels controlled by *r's*—"dark," "far"; "her," "were"; "fur," "turtle"; "bird," "fir"; "word," "worth"; "cork," "fork"—teach words such as these inductively. For an excellent reference concerning the usefulness of such patterns refer to Theodore Clymer's "The Utility of Phonic Generalizations in the Primary Grades," *The Reading Teacher,* XVI, January 1963, pp. 252–258.
14. Encourage children to play word games such as crossword puzzles, letter dominoes, "Ghost," and Scrabble.
15. Avoid putting the notation "sp." on a child's paper to indicate that a word is incorrectly spelled. Simply cross out the letter(s) that are inappropriate and insert the correct one(s). If many letters in the word are

incorrect or if the whole word is wrong, circle the word and above it spell it correctly. Try to note if the child has a pattern of errors. If a pattern is discovered, plan an individual lesson to help the child with the difficulty.

Dictionaries and Different Spelling Books

In the section describing *Anno's Alphabet* the use of dictionaries was mentioned, but it was mentioned in a way that suggested that children look up the words that had already been spelled correctly for them. However, often when children are writing, they are asked to look words up in the dictionary that they do not know how to spell. If children knew how a word were spelled they would not need the dictionary to spell correctly. Therefore, pupils may get very frustrated if they are asked to use the dictionary, since what is being asked is either impossible or too overwhelming a task. There is an amusing little paperback dictionary published by Random House that would provide much help for nonspellers. It is called *The Bad Speller's Dictionary* and is written by Joseph Krensky and Jordon L. Linfield (New York: Random House/Innovation Press, 1967). Because it is so inexpensive, it is feasible to order several of these tiny dictionaries so that children in the intermediate grades would have them accessible when they needed them. On every page there are two columns, one listing the incorrect way to spell a word, the other the correct way. For example, if you wanted to spell *phonics* but did not know how, you might look up *fonics* and you would see printed across from it in dark black letters *phonics*. The book is one hundred and eighty-six pages long and is three inches wide and five and a half inches long. Extremely "handy."

After working with such a book, children can be asked to start compiling words they have found treacherous to spell. In a group they can discuss the correct spellings of their demons and then put them in alphabetical order—a meaningful task to get them to learn this dictionary skill. They may also want to give concrete illustrations for pesky words such as "to," "too," "two"; "its," "it's"; "their," "there"; "your," "you're"; "stationery," "stationary"; "principal," "principle"; "capital," "capitol." Some children may even be stimulated to write simple poems for troublesome word combinations or difficult single words. Warm-ups should be provided for pupils before they are asked if they would like to work on their own contributions. Samples given might be:

STATION⬜E⬜RY — This is the paper on which I write.

STATION⬜A⬜RY — Something I can't move — not with all my might.

CAPIT⬜A⬜L

means

first—rate, super,

A̲, O̲, or D̲

lots of money,

and N̲a̲s̲h̲v̲i̲l̲l̲e̲, Tennessee.

CAPIT⬜O⬜L

is a building in Washington, D.C.

It may also be a help for them to think of some associative devices that will aid them in remembering how to spell tricky words. Paul S. Anderson in *Language Skills in Elementary Education* (New York: Macmillan Publishing Company, 1972) advocates that sentences such as *"All right* is like *all wrong"* be given for "all right," and "A *balloon* is like a *ball"* be used with children to assist them in recalling correctly how to spell words that cause so many children so many headaches.

A book sure to provide many laughs for children is William Steig's *The Bad Speller* (New York: Windmill Books, 1970). Steig has taken advantage of the fact that there are so many ways words can be spelled. The book plays around with the spelling alternatives that can be used in writing down words. The results are hilarious. One example Steig uses in his book is "Poit riting a poim about th mune. He iz yewzing a kwill penn." (The translation should be "Poet writing a poem about the moon. He is using a quill pen.") The pictures aid the reader in decoding the message. It is important for children to know about the alternatives in writing that can produce the same sounds. It is an invaluable skill in deciphering words. We all know that the "long sound" of a, for instance, can be spelled *ea, ei, ey, a(e), ai,* and *ay.* Many other sounds are spelled in a variety of ways, also. The more alternatives children know, the easier it will be to unravel pronunciations of words. *The Bad Speller* should motivate children to think of the many ways words can be spelled. Then, like Steig, they can draw their own pictures, provide amusing captions and, in the back of the book, give the translations; thus, they will be using their spelling abilities. Although Steig uses all capital letters in his book, there is no reason why teachers suggesting the use of this book or any other book mentioned in this chapter, for that matter, cannot recommend that the children use in their handwriting lowercase letters in either manuscript or cursive form, depending on what they want the children to practice.

Steig, of course, is not the only author who fools around with the ways in which our English words can be written. For other literary resources that children may enjoy, refer to:

1. Lucia and James L. Hymes's *Oodles of Noodles* (New York: Young Scott Books, 1964). See poems, "Hide and Seek," "Knot Fair," "What Happened," "No! No!," and "Four Tricky Letters".
2. David McCord's *All Day Long*, specifically the poem "O-U-G-H" (Boston: Little, Brown, 1966).
3. Eve Merriam's *It Doesn't Always Have to Rhyme* (New York: Atheneum, 1964). Note poems, "Unfinished Knews Item,"—good for practicing the letter *k* in handwriting, and "Why I Did Not Reign."

Two interesting books that may cause children to want to search out and compile lists of words that have the same part included somewhere in the words are *Antics* by Patricia Robbins (New York: Simon and Schuster, 1969) and Joel Rothman's *The Antcyclopedia* (New York: Phinmarc Books, 1974). The first book, a paperback, consists of seventy-six pages of words that have "ant" somewhere in them. For "ignorant," there is a picture of an ant with a dunce cap on; for "dormant," an ant is shown lying straight out, eyes closed; "intolerant" is illustrated by an ant in a sheet with a *K* printed on it. Not only would children learn how to spell by seeing this unique book, but they would, because of the simple and humorous illustrations, know what the words meant. There is a lot of word play in this book—"adolescant," "Anttila," "antchovies," "Michaelantgelo," and "presidant." Rothman's book consists of all ant riddles—"How does an ant feel who has fallen in love? —romantic." Each answer is written upside down on the bottom of every page. Children can be encouraged to do some more "ant" riddles after a sufficient warm-up, and then be led to think of some common bases for words that they can play with as Robbins and Rothman have done.

Two adult, innovative paperback dictionaries from which teachers can adapt ideas are Levinson's *The Left Handed Dictionary* (New York: Collier Books, 1963) and his *Webster's Unafraid Dictionary* (New York: Collier Books, 1967). Levinson has included in his dictionaries funny definitions of words that he has collected from many sources.

Glutton—A person who takes the piece of French pastry you wanted.

Anonymous

Goblet —A small sailor.

Judge.

—A small male turkey.

Anonymous, Jr.

Children, after hearing a sufficient number of examples from these books, may be stimulated to write their own "unafraid" dictionaries and read each others' contributions, thus utilizing spelling skills, handwriting skills, and reading skills all at the same time.

George Q. Lewis has published his *Dictionary of Bloopers and Boners* (New York: Scholastic Book Services, 1967) in which there are some most delightful malapropisms that may get children interested in finding out and spelling correctly the words that should have been used instead of the bloopers; "A he-horse is called a mayor; an antidote is a funny story that you have never heard before."

Other books that may induce children to become interested in compiling and illustrating their own words books are:

1. *Antonyms.*
2. *Homographs.*
3. *Homonyms.*
4. *Synonyms.*

These simple books, accompanied by amusing and charming illustrations that make the meanings of the words depicted clear, have been created by Joan Hanson (Minneapolis, Minnesota: Lerner Publications Company, 1972). Be sure to look for her sequels to these books, also.

Other Ideas to Get Children to Practice Writing and to Spell Words Well

1. Use tongue twisters for handwriting practice exercises. As a reference look at Marcia Brown's *Peter Piper's Alphabet* (New York: Charles Scribner's Sons, 1959).
2. Have children become exposed to poems that spell out words.

MI crooked letter, crooked letter I
Crooked letter, crooked letter I,
Humpback, humpback, I, MISSISSIPPI.
—Anonymous

A chicken in the car
And the car won't go,
That's the way
To spell CHICAGO!

A needle and a pin
Spell Cin, Cin, Cin.
A gnat and a fly
Spell CINCINNATI!
　—Anonymous

For other ideas see the poem "Ohio" in *Oodles of Noodles* by Lucia and James L. Hymes (New York: Young Scott Books, 1964) and the poems "Spelling" and "Here Comes the Teacher" in *Jump the Rope Jingles,* a paperback by Emma Vietor Worstell (New York: Collier Books, 1961). Jump rope jingles can be adapted easily to "test" children on any spelling words they may want to use. (Incidentally, do you remember spelling any words out rhythmically as a child in games? If you do, use them with your pupils.)

Have your children write letters! They can be imaginary and humorous (see *Dear Dragon* . . . by Sesyle Joslin and Irene Haas, New York: Harcourt, Brace and World, Inc., 1962). After having fun with the forms of letters in the way Joslin does, introduce children to books such as *1001 Valuable Things You Can Get Free* by Mort Weisinger (New York: Bantam Books, Inc., 1968) and let them compose letters and then let them mail for things that appeal to them. See also the section "Free or Almost

Free" in Peter Cardozo's *The Whole Kids Catalog* (New York: Bantam Books, Inc., 1975).

Naturally, children can also write to pen pals or to children who are their classmates when they are ill or when there are special occasions. The point is for them to realize the meaningfulness and the delight that they can give and receive from the ability to communicate well.

3. Search out books and poems that abound in a number of the letters you want your children to master. Some sources are:

a. *The Mystery of the Missing Red Mitten* by Steven Kellogg (New York: The Dial Press, 1974). Very simple story designed for young children consisting of sentences that are saturated with the letter *m*. Good to use with beginning readers who are being introduced to this letter sound. Children may very well prefer copying a story of this type to take home and read to younger sisters and brothers instead of practicing writing the letter *m* over and over either in isolation or in a meaningless string of words.

b. Poems such as "The Snail's Monologue" by Christian Morgenstern, which has a superfluity of *s*'s and *l*'s:

Shall I dwell in my shell?
Shall I not dwell in my shell?
Dwell in shell?
Rather not dwell?
Shall I not dwell,
shall I dwell,
dwell in shell,
shall I shell,
shallIshellIshallIshellIshallI . . .?

(The snail gets so entangled with his thoughts or, rather, the thoughts
run away with him so that he must postpone the decision.)

> —Christian Morgenstern;
> German poem translated by
> Max Knight

Teaching Other Facts Helpful in Spelling—Affixes and Inflectional Endings

Children should be shown inductively the common affixes (prefixes and
suffixes attached to root words) that appear regularly in so many of our
words. They should be encouraged to compile lists of words containing
affixes. Learning these suffixes and prefixes will be a help to them in spelling
words. Some common ones include:

Prefixes	Suffixes
in-	-en
mis-	-er
non-	-est
re-	-less
pre-	-ful
dis-	-ty
com-	-ly
ex-	-ment
un-	-tion
be-	-able
trans-	-some
	-ness
	-sl ρ

For other references see pp. 26–31 in Lee C. Deighton's paperback *Vocabulary Development in the Classroom* (New York: Teachers College, Columbia University, 1959).

In addition to learning common affixes, children should be taught to add inflectional endings to root words during reading skill lessons in conjunction with spelling skills.

Some common rules are:

1. When a word ends in y and the y is preceded by a vowel —"day" —add the inflectional ending—"day s," "monk e y"-"monkey s."
2. If a word ends in y and the y is preceded by a consonant—"t r y," change the y to i and add the ending—"tr i ed," "tr i es."
3. If a word ends in y and the y is preceded by a consonant but the suffix being added begins with an i, keep the y and add the ending— "t r y"-"t r y ing," "fl y ing."
4. With words that end in "silent" e, drop the e if the suffix to be added starts with a vowel—"hop e "-"hoping," "Flak e "-"flaking," "bak e "-"bak ed."
5. For words that end with *single* consonants that are preceded by single vowels, double the last consonant before adding suffixes that start with vowels—"kn o t"-"kno tt ed," "t a n"-"ta nn ed."
6. With words ending with single consonants preceded by more than one vowel, add the suffix without doubling the consonant "chai n"-"chai n ed," "treat"-"trea t ing."
7. With words ending with more than one consonant keep the consonants when adding suffixes—"rant"-"rant ing ," "rust"-"rust ed ."

4. AFTERWORD

As you work with spelling and handwriting, remind pupils from time to time that both of these skills have one important purpose—to enable us to communicate clearly in writing. You can reinforce the communication value of these skills by relating instruction in them closely to the other language arts. As suggested in this chapter, spelling and handwriting can provide springboards for discovering interesting facts about the history of English, opportunities for sharpening inductive skills, and occasions for entertaining reading and play. If you work on developing positive attitudes toward these skills as well as developing the skills themselves, you may be rewarded by having very few pupils who feel like saying, "spulling makes me very sic."

Helps

Interesting Books on Language for Teachers

Farb, Peter, *Word Play: What Happens When People Talk*, New York: Bantam Books, Inc., 1973, paperback.

Fitzgerald, James A., *A Basic Life Spelling Vocabulary*, Milwaukee, The Bruce Publishing Co., 1951, 161 pp.

Fitzgerald explains that the purpose of the book is to present a review of the research essential to word selection for a spelling curriculum; to set forth a plan for choosing useful words for spelling; to suggest a core of words basic for writing; and to make some suggestions for gradation of words for spelling instruction.

Two thousand six hundred and fifty basic words that comprise, with their repetitions, approximately ninety-five percent of the running writing of normal individuals are presented. They are words that individuals need during development from childhood to adulthood. They should be mastered, Fitzgerald says, by the end of the sixth grade by all but the severely retarded.

The author advises that the most frequently used words of child letter writing in life outside the school, the most frequently used words in well-written language programs in school, and the most frequently used words of adult writing should be combined into one composite, tentative list.

Fitzgerald also implies that any spelling program should be highly individualized. He writes, "The spelling of words should be taught when the child needs them in writing. To say that certain words should be taught formally to all children at a certain grade level is to ignore variation in abilities, needs and interests of groups and individuals."

The author points out that after having analyzed many spelling textbooks it was evident that the great difference among word lists in spelling series was exceeded by the amazing variations in grade placement of words in the textbook. He concludes that more evidence is needed to determine grade placement.

Hall, Edward T., *The Silent Language*, Greenwich, Conn.: Fawcett Publications, Inc., 1959, paperback.

Hanna, Paul, and Hanna, Jean S., "Application of Linguistics and Psychological Cues to the Spelling Course of Study," *Elementary English* 42: 753–759, November 1965.

In this article the authors report five aspects of the spelling program. These include the need for:

1. Selecting important spelling insights and cues from linguistics.

2. Programming a spelling curriculum that encourages pupil discovery of various generalizations.

3. Building teaching-learning strategies that take into consideration individual differences.

4. Selecting words for spelling instruction very carefully while realizing that lists of "important" and "most used" words are no longer sufficient.

5. Mutually reinforcing the skills of spelling and reading.

The Hannas believe in stressing a variety of approaches to use with children stressing sensory motor activities. They mention that children can improve their vocabulary through the knowledge of the structure of American-English orthography.

Hanna, Paul, et al., "Needed Research in Spelling," *Elementary English 42:* 60–66, January 1966.

In this article Hanna describes what is already available through research. He mentions in this context the contributions of descriptive linguistics, computer-based data processing, and structured learning.

He also reports the findings of the Stanford study, which revealed that when the computer was programmed to spell seventeen thousand words, it was able to come out with forty-nine percent of the sample correctly spelled.

Hanna states that research in spelling needs to be done in the areas of content, process, programs, and performance. He mentions things such as expansion of the samples, extension of linguistic generalizations, comparison of methods used, and teacher preparation in the field of linguistics.

Hayakawa, S. I., editor, *The Use and Misuse of Language,* Greenwich, Conn.: Fawcett Publications, Inc., 1962, paperback.

Horn, Ernest, *What Research Says to the Teacher, Teaching Spelling,* Second Edition, AERA, 1954, 32 pp.

This excellent little pamphlet contains many practical suggestions for the teacher of spelling. Among the many worthwhile remarks Horn makes are:

1. It is important that the program in spelling be broadly conceived. The curriculum in spelling includes all experiences that may facilitate or retard the development of spelling ability.

2. Objectives should be realistic in view of what the pupils can be expected to accomplish. One should consider the number of words that *can* be learned by children at different levels of ability in making out time allotments for spelling.

3. There is some evidence that in schools where the spelling words are chosen in connection with various units, many words taught have little or no use in the writing done outside school by either children or adults.

4. After two thousand words are learned, the returns from teaching each additional one thousand diminish rapidly.

5. Help children to learn words they need and use even though they are difficult (e.g., "Halloween").

6. Pupils learn to spell many words by reading. This has been demonstrated repeatedly.

7. There has been too much emphasis on correct spelling, especially in the lower grades. This may discourage children from writing.

8. Removal of mispronunciations and articulation defects will be reflected in better spelling.

9. Research has consistently shown that it is more efficient to study words in lists than in context.

10. When tests are corrected by the pupils and when the results are properly utilized, these activities are the most fruitful (per unit of time) that have yet been devised.

11. Time for the study of words missed on the test should be provided as soon as possible, preferably immediately after the test has been corrected.

12. Enthusiastic, sympathetic classroom teachers often get good results even when they do not otherwise make use of the most efficient learning procedures. The reverse is also true.

13. When a pupil is having difficulty in learning to spell, one of the first things to do is to have him or her explain how he or she proceeds in learning to spell a word.

Horn, Thomas D., "Spelling" in *Encyclopedia of Educational Research,* Robert L. Ebel, editor, New York: The Macmillan Company, 1969, pp. 1282–1299.

Laird, Charlton, *The Miracle of Language,* Greenwich, Conn.: Fawcett Publications, Inc., 1953, paperback.

Lambert, Eloise, *Our Language: The Story of the Words We Use,* New York. Lothrop, Lee and Shepard Company, 1955. Good readers in the intermediate grades who are interested in words and our English language would find this book as fascinating to read as teachers.

Larson, Richard, et al., *A Statement on the Preparation of Teachers of English,* Urbana, Ill.: National Council of Teachers of English Executive Committee, 1976.

Mathews, Mitford M., *American Words,* Cleveland: The World Publishing Company, 1959.

Morris, William, *Your Heritage of Words,* Dell Publishing Company, 1970, paperback. Pages 1–72 and pp. 148–181 are particularly interesting, intriguing, and informative. Chapter titles for pages cited are: "The Wonderful World of Words"; "Names Make Words"; "Foreign Words and Phrases"; "Words and Phrases from the Worlds of Business and Industry"; "Words and Phrases from the Worlds of Art, Literature and Music"; "Words and Phrases from the Language of World Affairs"; "Words to Watch For."

Newman, Edwin, *Strictly Speaking,* Indianapolis: The Bobbs-Merrill Company, Inc., 1974. Newman, in a very readable and delightful way, shows how people have been corrupting our language. Very worthwhile reading. See also his *A Civil Tongue,* New York: The Bobbs-Merrill Company, Inc., 1976.

Pei, Mario, *The Story of Language,* New York: Mentor Books, 1949.

Pei, Mario, *The Story of English,* Greenwich, Conn.: Fawcett Publications, Inc., 1952, paperback.

Robinson, H. Alan, and Burrows, Alvina Treut, *Teacher Effectiveness in Elementary Language Arts: A Progress Report,* Urbana, Ill., ERIC, Clearinghouse on Reading and Communication Skills, 1974, paperback.

Sapir, Edward, *Language*, New York: Harcourt, Brace and World, Inc., 1949.

Winkeljohann, Sr. Rosemary, *English Language Arts Curriculum Guides K-12*, Urbana, Ill.: National Council of Teachers of English, 1975, paperback.

Literary Suggestions to Use to Stimulate Children's Interest in Language

Ames, Winthrop, editor, *What Shall We Name the Baby?*, New York: Pocket Books, 1973, paperback.

Amon, Aline, *Talking Hands*, New York: Doubleday and Company, Inc., 1968.

Asimov, Isaac, *Words from the Myths*, New York: Houghton Mifflin, 1961.

Brewton, Sara, and Blackburn III, G. Meredith, collectors, *My Tang is Tungled and Other Ridiculous Situations*, New York: Thomas Y. Crowell Company, 1973.

Diska, Pat, and Jenkyns, Chris, *Andy Says Bonjour*, New York: The Vanguard Press, 1954.

Duvoisin, Roger, *Periwinkle*, New York: Alfred A. Knopf, 1976. Two lonely animals, a frog and a giraffe, want to be friends and wish to be able to talk to one another, but they must find out the hard way that there are rules for being able to communicate well with any one. A charming book for children in the beginning primary grades.

Emrich, Duncan, collector, *The Whim-Wham Book*, New York: Four Winds Press, 1975. A delightful compilation of all kinds of word games, riddles, and "odds and ends."

Ets, Marie Hall, *Talking Without Words*, New York: The Viking Press, 1968.

Evenson, A. E., *About the History of the Calendar*, Chicago: Children's Press, 1972.

Ferguson, Charles W., *The Abecedarian Book*, Boston: Little, Brown and Company, 1964. Excellent for teachers' use as well as for children who are good readers. Among many other interesting facts Ferguson tells his readers such things as:
　The word "vowel" comes from an old word, *vocalis*, meaning voice (p. vi).
　"Syllables" is a word that is derived from two old words that meant "to hold together" (p. vi).
　"Suffix" means literally to fasten underneath (p. 22).
　The longest word in the *Oxford English Dictionary*, floccinaucinihilipilification, was made up of a series of Latin terms, each of which meant that something amounted to little or nothing (p. 30).
　Gelett Burgess made up his own dictionary which consisted of six hundred words that he thought were needed in the English language. One of his concoctions, the word "blurb," which he said meant to talk like a publisher, now appears in regular dictionaries (p. 31).

Feelings, Muriel, *Jambo Means Hello: Swahili Alphabet Book*, New York: Dial Press, 1974.

Frasconi, Antonio, *See and Say,* New York: Harcourt, Brace and World, Inc., 1955. A picture book in four languages—English, Italian, French, and Spanish.

Gwynne, Fred, *The King Who Rained,* New York: Windmill Paperbacks, 1970. Fooling around with homonyms.

Hautzig, Esther, *In the Park: An Excursion in Four Languages,* New York: The Macmillan Company, 1968.

Hunter, Norman, *Professor Branestawm's Dictionary,* Baltimore: Penguin Books Inc., 1974. Defines words divergently. For example, "quartz—measures of two pints."

Joslin, Sesyle, *There Is a Dragon in My Bed (Il y a un Dragon dans Mon Lit),* New York: Harcourt, Brace and World, 1961.

Joslin, Sesyle, *Spaghetti for Breakfast (Spaghetti per Prima Colazione),* New York: Harcourt, Brace and World, Inc., 1965.

Joslin, Sesyle, *There Is a Bull on My Balcony (Hay un Toro en Mi Balcón),* New York: Harcourt, Brace and World, 1966.

Lambert, Eloise, and Mario Pei, *Our Names: Where They Came from and What They Mean,* New York: Lothrop, Lee and Shepard, Inc., 1960. Good reading for teachers and for students who read well.

Nordstrom, Ursula, *The Secret Language,* New York: Scholastic Book Services, 1960. Novel that tells about how two young girls become friends and invent words of their own to communicate so no one else will be able to understand what they are talking about.

Pitt, Valerie, *Let's Find Out about Names,* New York: Franklin Watts, Inc., 1971. Simple reading about how we came to get our surnames. Tells some meanings for first names. Stimulates children to find out about their own names.

Pop-Up Sound Alikes, New York: Random House, n.d. Easy reading, amusing book on homonyms with simple rhyme.

Provensen, A., and Provensen, M., *Play on Words,* New York: Random House, 1972. Easy reading.

Schwartz, Alvin, *A Twister of Twists, A Tangler of Tongues,* Philadelphia: J. B. Lippincott Company, 1972. A funny book that children will be sure to enjoy. Do not forget to use this book as a source for handwriting exercise!

Severn, Bill, *People Words,* New York: Ives Washburn, Inc., 1966.

Stewart, George R., *Names on the Land,* Boston: Houghton Mifflin Company, 1958. Interesting reading for teachers as well as for pupils of the intermediate grades.

Zim, Herbert S., *Codes and Secret Writing,* New York: Scholastic Book Services, 1948, paperback. Implicit invitations to children to write their own codes and secret writing.

8
Reading
Everybody

Take care of the sense, and
the sounds will take care of
themselves.
—Lewis Carroll

Even though it may not be possible to follow Lewis Carroll's advice to the letter in teaching reading, keeping his words in mind will provide a useful antidote to the mechanical drill on word recognition skills that are all too characteristic of reading programs. One main objective of reading instruction should be to bring the child and the right book together. To do this efficiently, the reading program should be individualized so that each pupil can choose something he or she likes from an array of interesting and appropriate possibilities. Individualizing does not mean necessarily that every child in the classroom will be reading a different book or that needed skills should be taught in a haphazard way. The first two sections that follow suggest approaches and activities intended to develop needed skills, most of which can be used with a particular group. The last section suggests some procedures that you may wish to use in individualizing reading in your classroom.

1. SOUNDS AND LETTERS

It is important that children be taught meaningful ways of helping themselves to decode written symbols into the words they know and to pronounce new words they learn in their reading. In undertaking this task it is useful to know what is relatively easy for the learner and what is hard. Assuming too much knowledge or insisting on generalizations that children do not yet have the power to make can lead only to frustration all around. An analogous situation occurs when the anecdotal Mr. Harrison calls a business associate's home and finds himself talking to a small boy. Since the boy is willing to take a message, Harrison gives his name and then proceeds to spell it out slowly. After a long pause, Mr. Harrison asks, "Did you get all of that?" To which the boy responds, "How do you make an *H* ?"

In general, major phonic elements can be ordered from simple to complex in this fashion:

1. Initial consonant sounds.
2. Ending consonant sounds.
3. Long vowel sounds.
4. Short vowel sounds.
5. Consonant combinations.
6. Vowel combinations.
7. Syllabication rules.

Suggested Steps in Teaching Sounds

The simplest consonant sounds to teach children are those that appear at the beginnings of words and are regularly represented by a single letter and sound. Letters like *d, b,* and *m* are stable, always standing for the same sounds. Letters such as *c, g, x,* or *y,* which can represent more than one sound, should be taught after the other consonant sounds have been mastered. Letters that represent similar sounds or that look alike, such as *b, g, q, p,* and *d,* or *w* and *m,* should not be taught closely together in time. Make sure that the children have mastered one before introducing another letter that they may confuse with the one(s) previously taught.

Another word of caution. To test how well pupils can discriminate between final consonant sounds, you may want to rely on rhymes by asking questions such as, "Does *bib* rhyme with *gag* or with *crib?* If so, avoid distractors that are too close in sound. In the foregoing question, for example, the use of "kid" instead of "gag" might be puzzling to many children, since "kid" actually is a rhyming word—it is called a slant or an approximate rhyme. The following suggested activities may be used first in introducing beginning and final consonant sounds and later for working with vowels and consonant blends.

1. Motivate children by reading a short selection such as *Mary Ann's Mud Day* by Janice May Udry with pictures by Martha Alexander (New York: Harper and Row, Publishers, 1967). This particular story has a preponderance of *m* sounds. Before reading the story to children who need to work on this sound, you could direct them to listen for the "mystery" sound that will be repeated throughout the selection. Pupils could be told that at the end of the story they might be asked to volunteer a word that they think begins with the sound they need to uncover. In reading the story, emphasize the words beginning with the new sound.

2. Put words on the board for the group of children who need to learn the specific sound being introduced. These should be words that the children have in their aural-oral language. Draw attention to the sound being emphasized by underlining or circling appropriate letter(s).
3. When the words are on the board, pronounce each one, emphasizing but not isolating the sound being presented. Ask the children what they notice about the beginning, middle, or ending of the words when they *listen* to them.
4. After you have pronounced them, ask the children to *look* at the words as you say them and notice what is alike in the words at the beginning, middle, or at the end. Repeat the words, pointing to the part of each word you want them to observe. In getting children to listen, look, and learn, you should plan to use numerous examples. It is difficult to generalize about only a few words.

5. The children can be asked what they notice about the sound and the appearance of the words. Children then will use their own language to say what it is that they have observed. Try to avoid selecting words that will elicit irrelevant comments. For instance, if all of the words you use to show the initial *m* sound happen to have short *a* in them, this unimportant fact will distract children from the main point.
6. After a new sound has been presented, have pupils think of other words they know that have that sound. If you are working with simple initial consonant sounds, the children may offer you some words with blends at the beginning as examples. However, the words you offer and put on the

board should not include blends if you are concentrating on single consonant sounds.

Some suggested activities for working with letters, sounds, and words:

1. A bouncing ball game that provides practice in working with initial sounds goes this way.

   S my name is Sally.
   My husband's name is Sam.
   We come from Salem and we sell sailboats.

2. You might also suggest that pupils propose ingredients for a special alphabet soup, requiring that each thing suggested begin with the particular sound being worked on. For the sound b, for instance, pupils could throw into the pot ingredients such as bananas, bologna, bubble gum, berries, butter, and whatever else they think of that begins with this sound.

3. If you obtain a photograph of each child, as suggested in Chapter 2, you can use the pictures to reinforce learning of new sounds. A picture of the child whose name contains the sound being studied can be mounted on oaktag and displayed. [Call attention to the sound-symbol relationship by printing the child's name under the picture with the letter(s) to be noted underlined, circled, or otherwise emphasized.] Other children can then decorate the margins of the poster with pictures of other words containing the same letter and sound. The poster for the initial *b* might look like this:

4. Another idea to use in reinforcing new sounds and letters that have been taught is to group children in teams and let them go on a letter/sound treasure hunt. The objective is to have the children find as many concrete objects in the classroom as they can that begin with the sound being concentrated on.

5. Reading hopscotch. At recess, gym, or whenever the weather permits, teachers could have children in groups reinforce what they have been working on in their skill groups by playing hopscotch. Hopscotch squares could be drawn that might contain blends, short or long vowels, digraphs, initial consonants, ending consonants, prefixes, suffixes, a number that would indicate that they must say a word containing a certain number of syllables, or a combination of elements. Directions would be given and the child jumping in each block would have to say a word that began, ended, or fulfilled the given instruction.

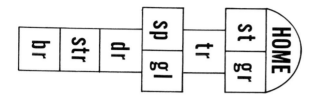

Reading hopscotch could be adapted by including vocabulary words with which the children have been working in the squares. The children might be asked simply to say each word or they might be asked to give a synonym or antonym for every word. They also could be asked to tell how many syllables each word had.

6. Reading musical chairs. Working with a small group, musical chairs could be adapted to a reading game by taping on the backrests of the chairs a word or a letter or letter combination. When the music stopped, the child who scurried to the last chair would have to say a word that contained the appropriate sound taped on the back of the chair. A "standby" child from the group could be waiting to see if the child being asked to respond were able to give an appropriate answer. If he/she could not, a standby child would get the chance to take the seat. All children might have one chance to be a standby child for the day.

7. Jumping rope games. Children could be directed to form two teams. Four children would be selected to swing the ropes initially by a method such as thinking of certain numbers from one to twelve. The remaining children in each team would then line up; when the teacher told them to begin, each child could jump in at his/her turn and then out again, saying a word that contained a certain vowel, consonant, blend, digraph, and so forth. If a child were unable to jump in and out successfully or could not think of an appropriate word, he/she would take the end of a rope until another child missed. A scorekeeper could be appointed for each team by the teacher. Each game should have a time limit so that the scorekeepers would have the chance to jump rope and so that the children would have an opportunity if they still felt like playing to switch to another sound.

Long and Short Vowels

Because vowel sounds are spelled in a variety of ways—long a, for instance, has fourteen different spellings—it is futile to undertake teaching vowel sounds and their spellings once and for all. You may wish to prepare pattern charts illustrating the more consistent spellings of vowel sounds, for instance, *ee, oa,* and *ay.* For long vowels, the pattern, vowel-consonant-final e, also lends itself to this approach. If you are using a basal reader or have one available, you can draw material for your charts from this source. Otherwise a pattern box on this order is easily made.

b	oa	t
g	oa	t
fl	oa	t
	oa	ts

Unfortunately, most rules are not very useful. The familiar one that goes "When two vowels go out walking, the first one does the talking" works for some words but provides no help for many others. (In fact, a child who takes this easy-out generalization to heart may wonder why "out" does not rhyme with "goat" and why the "does" in the "rule" rhymes with "fuzz" instead of with "nose.") Using pattern boxes will help, and many of the activities suggested earlier in this chapter will help pupils to become familiar with common vowel spellings.

To help pupils remember what the short vowels sound like, you might display a chart like this in some prominent place.

A*l* edged *in* on *us*.

In working with the pattern boxes, the words that come up in the suggested activities, and new words that pupils encounter in their reading, you may wish to help pupils recognize certain environmental features that signal whether a vowel has its long or short value. A vowel-cosonant-final e pattern usually provides one such clue to long vowels. Another that you may want to call attention to is a single vowel letter at the end of a word or syllable:

"my," "go," "be," "ma·jor," "ba·by".

For short vowels, you can then point our that a single consonant after the vowel letter makes the vowel in a one-syllable word short ("hat," "bet," "knit") and that in longer words, two consonants after the vowel letter usually create the same effect ("passage," "better," "holly"). It is important, however, that you call attention to three consonant clusters that often follow a long vowel sound: *gh* after *i*, *ld* after *i* and *o*, and *nd* after *i*. Pattern boxes like those below can be used to illustrate these special cases.

f*i*nd	m*i*ld	mold	n*i*ght
b*i*nd	w*i*ld	folding	fight
k*i*ndest	ch*i*ld	bolder	t*i*ghten
h*i*nd		cold	s*i*ght
m*i*nd		golden	
r*i*nd		hold	

Configuration

Although many words have a distinctive look on the page, encouraging pupils to rely on the configuration of a word for recognition is of dubious value. "Hat" and "bat" have the same outline, as do "cabbage" and "cottage." Nor is it helpful to suggest that children will always recognize the word "monkey" if they remember that it has a tail at the end. Many words have "tails" at the end ("cry," "money," "jolly") and so the association mentioned can do nothing for children except to confuse and frustrate them.

Structural Analysis

This important word recognition skill involves recognizing and using prefixes and suffixes and base words. You may wish to focus the pupils' attention on some common affixes as examples appear in their reading. If a word like "unkind" comes up, for example, you might make a pattern box on the board showing some other *un* words and ask pupils to tell in their own words what effect the prefix has on the meaning of the base word.

unkind
unfair
uncertain
unclear

In working with prefixes and suffixes, concentrate on those that are added to free-form bases (i.e., those that are whole words by themselves). Thus, "repay" or "replace" would be good words to work with for the prefix *re*, but "repeat" would not.

You will also want to call the pupils' attention to compound words as they come up in reading or discussion. You can provide additional practice in using compound words by having the children use words such as "ball," "foot," "park," "hand," and "head" to form as many compound words as they can think of.

Frequent incidental work with affixes and compound words will give children the help they need in recognizing structural features of words as an aid to pronunciation and meaning.

Syllabication

Knowing how words divide into syllables can help pupils pronounce some of the new words they encounter. Some knowledge of syllabication is also useful if pupils are to write haiku, tanka, and limericks, activities suggested in Chapter 10.

You can define a syllable as a word part that has a single vowel *sound* in it. Be sure that your pupils do not form the mistaken impression that they can find the number of syllables a word has simply by counting vowel letters. The word "reach," for example, has two vowel letters but only one vowel sound. If you are using pattern boxes for two-letter vowel spellings, this would be a good time to review them.

You may wish to use some or all of the following syllable rules for showing the effect of syllabication on pronunciation.

1. ob·ject
   prac·tice
   bet·ter
   ac·tor

   Point out that the first vowels all have short sounds, calling attention to the consonant that ends, or "closes," the syllable. Note that each first vowel is followed by two consonants and the word is broken up between them, making the first vowel "short." In a word such as "collect" the 'o' would have a schwa sound. See the section entitled "Why There Is an *o* Where a *u* Ought to Be" in Chapter 7.

2. ba·by
   cy·cle
   Bi·ble
   mo·tor
   me·ter

   This time, the first vowels have long sounds because they end the syllable and are not "closed in" by a consonant following in the same syllable.

3. prim·er/pri·mer
   lil·y/li·lac
   sat·in/Sa·tan
   pol·ish/Po·lish

   Use these pairs to show the difference it makes whether the first syllable ends with a consonant or a vowel.

Note. Words of the sort that are listed under numbers 2 and 3 *cannot* be divided into syllables unless the person dividing the words either knows how to pronounce them already (they are within his or her aural-oral vocabulary) or is using a dictionary!

If you have worked with word analysis clues, you can reinforce learning involving affixation and compound words by pointing out that many common prefixes and suffixes are syllables in themselves and that many common compounds divide into syllables between the words that make them up.

Affixes

dis·appear   love·*ly*
re·pay   good·*ness*
un·do   sing·*ing*
mis·take   treat·*ment*

Compound words

fire·man
mail·box
base·ball
snow·man

For creative activities that will strengthen syllabication skills, try some of the limericks, haiku, and tanka suggested in Chapter 10.

And Some Books to Read

Pattern boxes and activities that focus children's attention on meaning and on the relation of sounds and letters have a respectable role in reading instruction, but it should not be forgotten that success in reading is closely related to the pleasure obtained from the experience. With this in mind, you may want to try some of the following books, which combine delight with instruction.

1. *Crictor,* by Tomi Ungerer (New York: Scholastic Book Services, 1970).
2. *Certainly, Carrie, Cut the Cake* by Margaret and John Travers Moore (Indianapolis: Bobbs-Merrill, 1971).
3. *Still Another Alphabet Book* by Seymour Chwast and Stephen Moskof (New York: McGraw Hill, n.d.).

4. *Dr. Seuss's ABC* by Dr. Seuss (New York: Random House, 1963).
5. *Peter Piper's Alphabet* by Marcia Brown (New York: Scribner's, 1959).
6. *The Alphabet Tree* by Leo Lionni (New York: Pantheon, 1968).

The Black ABC's is a resource that contains excellent ideas for letter activities. It consists of a sturdy set of large photographs with upper and lowercase letters on each. Each card features a letter in a one-sentence caption: "A is for afro." "B is for beautiful." "C is for cool."[1] The back of each card contains discussion questions, rhymes, riddles, and other enrichment material.

Finally, you can build a good, entertaining activity by reading *The Hungry Thing*[2] by Jan Slepian and Ann Seidler. After presenting a new sound to your children—initial consonant, long vowel, or whatever—you can encourage them to make up riddles of their own after the pattern in *The Hungry Thing*, each emphasizing the new sound being worked on. You could have each child construct a "hungry thing" and choose words with which to feed it. To be acceptable to the thing, a word must, of course, contain the sound being featured.

2. CONTEXT CLUES

Being able to recognize and use context clues to determine the meaning of new words is an important reading skill, and you will want to be alert to opportunities to develop it throughout all the reading your pupils do. Authors of successful trade books are often adept at finding ways to help their young readers to understand and use new words that come up in their stories. Some of the techniques they use can readily be adapted for use in the classroom. For example:

1. Making the meaning of a new word clear through illustrations.
2. Helping the reader to anticipate the sound of a new word through rhyme.
3. Linking a new word with closely related ideas so that its meaning can be easily guessed.
4. Aiding children to understand the meaning of a new word by giving many examples.
5. Arousing and stimulating children's curiosity so that they are led to anticipate the word an author is going to use.
6. Using reference lines [calling attention to a letter, a word or words by using color, circling, underlining, making a letter or word(s) stand out by making a different size, and so forth].

The following books make particularly effective use of these and similar strategies for helping children to read and understand with delight.

1. *A Very Long Tale* by Eric Carle (New York: Thomas Y. Crowell, 1970).
2. *Arm in Arm* by Remy Charlip (New York: Parents' Magazine Press, 1969).
3. *Where Is Everybody?* by Remy Charlip (New York: Scholastic Book Services, 1957).
4. *Fortunately* by Remy Charlip (New York, Parents' Magazine Press, 1964).
5. *See What I Found* by Myra Cohn Livingston (New York: Harcourt Brace Jovanovich, 1962).
6. *The Touch Me Book* by Pat and Eve Witte (New York: Golden Press, Inc., 1961).
7. *I Met a Man* by John Ciardi (Boston: Houghton Mifflin, 1961).
8. *Go, Dog, Go!* by P. D. Eastman (New York: Random House, 1961).
9. *In, On, Under, and Through* by Joan Elwart (Racine, Wisc.: Whitman, 1965).
10. *Amelia Bedelia and the Surprise Shower* by Peggy Parish (New York: Harper and Row, 1966).
11. *Pop-Up Sound Alikes* (New York: Random House, n.d.).

The best advertised strength of a typical basal reading series is the vocabulary control that provides for practice and reinforcement of new words. Many of the trade books just mentioned contain relatively few words and provide opportunities for children to say words over and over in ways that will not bore, but delight. The language of a good trade book is natural and enriching, not stilted, as the language of many basal readers tends to be. Best of all, children can learn and practice new words in trade books without feeling drilled and grilled.

Developing Awareness of Context Clues

If children are to use context clues to find the meaning of new words, they must be able to recognize a clue when they see one. Illustrations often provide obvious clues to the meaning of words, and children should be encouraged to scan them like detectives.

To acquaint children with verbal context, you might try providing a sentence like

Out on the playground, I like to _____.

and ask pupils to supply a word that will make good sense. In addition to producing some words that the children may not have seen written before, this exercise will demonstrate the importance of the words that come before in figuring out the probable meaning of new words.

Show children how they usually can anticipate the sense of what is coming in a sentence through the understanding of clue-bearing words such as "conversely," "however," "although," "nevertheless," "because," "but," and "consequently."

Substitution sentences can also be used to help children recognize such context clues as related ideas, other words in a series, and contrasting ideas.

Related Ideas

Fire fighters save lives. They *also* save _____.
One comes before two. *In the same way,* three _____.

Series

Foods like apples, oranges, and _____.
Buildings like churches, bus stations, and _____.

Contrasting Ideas

I'm not thinking of something little *but* something _____.
A mountain is high, *but* a valley is _____.

Working with sentences like these will help to make your pupils aware of context clues, but you will also want to take frequent opportunities to lead them to see how they can establish what they do know from a given context. With a sentence like this one, for instance,

Mary got out of bed and stumbled over her *mules*.

you might ask such guiding questions as these: Where was Mary? If she was in bed, what room would she probably be in? If she stumbled over something, how big do you suppose that something might be? What might Mary have beside her bed? Having gleaned all you can from the context, suggest that pupils think of another word that might make sense in this context. Then have them look up "mules" in their dictionaries to see how close they were able to get to the word's meaning. A natural follow-up to this activity might be a discussion of the appropriateness of the names for different kinds of footwear: sneakers, rubbers, pumps, loafers, slippers, Mary Janes, saddle shoes, uglies, and so on.

If you are using a reading program that introduces certain new words in context prior to the reading, you will want to be sure that the context does not give away an important part of the plot, thus lessening excitement and suspense ("Since John was caught trying to sell the jewels, Bill was proved *innocent.*"). It is also a good idea to be sure that words are presented so that they have the same meaning as the words that appear in the selection. Drawing attention to a word by capitalizing it is not helpful for a young child who is still learning letter shapes.

Two resources that you may find helpful to you in the classroom are *Reading Aids through the Grades,* Second Revised Edition by Anne Marie Mueser, Teachers College Press, Columbia University, New York, 1975 and Albert J. Mazurkiewicz's *Teaching About Phonics,* St. Martin's Press, New York, 1976.

Some Additional Suggestions

The following books, like those mentioned earlier in this section, use techniques for helping young readers read successfully that you may want to adapt for your own purpose.

1. *The Very Hungry Caterpillar* by Eric Carle (New York: The World Publishing Company, 1969).
2. *Christopher's Parade* by Richard Hefter and Stephen Moskof (New York: Parents' Magazine Press, 1972).
3. *A & The* by Ellen Raskin (New York: Atheneum, 1970).
4. *One Monday Morning* by Uri Shulevitz (New York: Charles Scribner's Sons, 1967).
5. *Jack Is Glad* by Charlotte Steiner (New York: Alfred A. Knopf, 1962).
6. *The Monster at the End of This Book* by Jon Stone, illustrated by Mike Smollin (n.p., Western Publishing Co., 1971).
7. *Some Frogs Have Their Own Rocks* by Robert and Claire Wiest (Chicago: Children's Press, 1970). Good for phrasing.
8. *Some Things Go Together* by Charlotte Zolotow, pictures by Sylvia Selig (New York: Abelard-Schuman, 1969).

3. PLANNING FOR INDIVIDUALIZED INSTRUCTION

An individualized reading program pays valuable dividends in the interest and pleasure children take from their reading. Such a program can also present the teacher with some challenges, particularly the teacher who is accustomed to the step-by-step suggestions provided by basal reading programs. Since it is likely that you will be conferring with different students about the same book over a period of time, you will find it convenient to begin collecting materials for use with books that are popular with your pupils. For most books, you will find each of the following useful:

1. A synopsis of the plot that includes the names of characters as well as the main events of the book.
2. Notes on motivational techniques for use before and during the reading.
3. Questions for discussion that challenge and stimulate pupils.
4. Dittoed skill sheets for following up the reading.

The guide to *Blue Willow* (New York: Scholastic Book Services, 1958), that follows provides examples of each of these kinds of material. Because the intent is to provide a wide range of examples of questions and activities, the guide is long. Do not feel that you have to prepare so detailed a guide for every book your children choose. And when you have assembled your own guide material, remember that it is not necessary or desirable for every pupil to answer every question or do every activity that you may have noted. Your questions and activities should be resources that you can draw from to achieve these major objectives.

1. Leading pupils to reflect on the ideas and episodes in the work.
2. Helping pupils to relate the work to their own feelings and experiences.
3. Building an awareness of what good writing is.
4. Providing opportunities for creative expression.
5. Helping pupils build needed language skills.

Synopsis

Blue Willow tells the story of a very sensitive ten-year-old girl named Janey Larkin. Janey is the daughter of a migrant worker and his wife. Janey's mother died when she was small, and she has only dim recollections of her life then. She does remember, however, that life at that time was much better for the Larkins. Then, they had a home of their own and cows and a horse. All that is left now of those days is a blue willow plate that Janey treasures. For her it represents beauty, dignity, security, and hope. It is her dream that some day she will have a real home again, and then the plate will be proudly displayed. Until that time, it will be kept hidden safely away in an old suitcase, to be brought out only on infrequent occasions and then packed away once more.

Janey has had so many disappointments and hardships in her life that she is hesitant to make friends in the places where she goes to live. She has learned through experience that just when she comes to like someone a lot, it is time for the Larkin family to move again, and this hurts terribly. The result is that she does not go out of her way to look for friends. Janey always has been forced to accept charity from others. This has made her very sensitive and proud.

At the opening of the story, the Larkins are just getting settled again in an old shack. A young girl, Lupe Romero, who lives across the road, comes over to talk to Janey, and this is the beginning of a wonderful friendship between the two girls.

The Larkins meet the villain of the story, Bounce Reyburn, who comes to collect $5 each month for the use of the shack. Bounce says he is collecting the money for Mr. Anderson, the boss who owns the property. The truth is, however, that Reyburn is pocketing the money for himself. Mr. Anderson has never asked anyone who has occupied the shack to pay for it.

Trouble comes in the form of sickness to Janey's stepmother. The money Mr. Larkin won in a cotton-picking contest is almost gone. Bounce Reyburn comes again and demands to be paid the rental money. To prevent a fight between Reyburn and her father, Janey bravely offers to give Bounce the blue willow plate as payment, and he accepts it.

Finally, the day Janey has been dreading arrives. Her father announces that they must leave. Janey decides she will go to Mr. Anderson and ask him whether she can see her plate for the last time. He does not know what Janey is talking about, so she tells him the whole story. Mr. Anderson is astonished by her tale. He decides to fire Reyburn and to offer Mr. Larkin Reyburn's job.

At the end of the book, Janey, through the kindness of the Romero family, finally gets a home of her own. The blue willow plate is placed proudly on the mantelpiece for everyone to see. Finally, Janey can stay somewhere as long as she wants to. She can even attend "permanent" school where her beloved teacher, Miss Peterson, is, as well as her best friend, Lupe.

Motivation

Motivational techniques like those that follow may be used throughout the story as well as initially.

1. Tell children the blue willow legend. (One version appears in the book
   Blue Willow itself.) The daughter of a wealthy Chinese nobleman elopes
   with one of his servants. When he finds out, the nobleman is furious that
   his daughter would wish to marry someone so far beneath her and pur-
   sues them. As he is about to capture them on a bridge in his garden, the
   gods turn the lovers into birds.

   Explain that the final scene, which shows a willow tree, the bridge, and the birds, is depicted on blue willow dishes. If one of the plates in this pattern is available, you will want to show it to the children. (Paper plates decorated with this pattern are sometimes available if you cannot turn up a china one.)

Explain that to Janey, the heroine of the story, the blue willow plate her family owns is her most cherished possession. You might ask children what their most valued possession is and what object they treasure that might not appear valuable to someone else.

2. Ask pupils who choose to read this book whether they have ever moved. If they have, ask them to tell what it was like. If they have not, ask them to imagine how moving would be. Explain that the heroine of this story moves often, whenever a crop has been harvested. Ask how they would feel about moving often and what problems it might involve.

3. Tell children a little about the author and her book. Doris Gates was working as a children's librarian in Fresno County, California. Because of financial difficulties, the library had to close on Wednesdays. Miss Gates decided to use the day writing children's books. She threw away everything she wrote the first year but, during the second year, she produced a book called *Sarah's Idea,* which was published.

She had met children of migrant workers as a librarian and wanted to write a story about their lives. Her friends tried to discourage her, but she went ahead. The result is this popular and highly successful book.

Information about *Blue Willow* and many other trade juveniles may be found in *The Story Behind Modern Books* by Elizabeth Rider Montgomery.

Questions for Discussion

Many of the questions suggested below are intended to draw out the child's own feelings and experiences. Some demand that the child read between the lines; some require careful thought and should be given to the child beforehand. Some questions require factual answers, and still others call for the use of a dictionary. These different kinds of questions are coded as follows.

1. Own feelings, experiences, ingenuity: I.
2. Possible answers: P.
3. Answers that demand careful reading and occasionally the necessity to do cumulative reading: C.
4. Questions that may be used to stimulate creative writing *after* discussion: W.
5. Questions that demand that a child use a dictionary: D.

Chapter 1, pp. 1–18

1. I, p. 2—If you were living in a one-room shack and it was terribly hot, would you cook inside that room? If not, what would you do? What kinds of food could you have that would demand no cooking?
2. I, W, p. 2—If you were terribly hot, what cool thoughts could you try to think? If you were freezing, what words or thoughts could you imagine to make yourself seem warmer?
3. I, pp. 2–3—What would you do for fun if you had no playmates, toys, or books? What might be the advantage in having no brothers or sisters? The disadvantages?
4. P, I, p. 4—Janey really hated to have someone ask her how long she was going to stay in a new location. What other questions do you think Janey might not like people to ask her? What don't you like people to ask you? Why?
5. P, p. 10—What do you suppose might have been the reason why the Larkins lost their home?
6. C, pp. 12, 15—Does Janey have quite an imagination? How do you know?
7. P, I, p. 17—What is a friend? Does a friend have to be a person?

Chapter II, pp. 19–30

1. I, p. 21—After having read p. 21, what do you suppose one of Janey's dearest wishes might be?
2. P, p. 27—Why do you suppose Janey's father would rather live in a shack than in a cotton camp?

Chapter III, pp. 31–47

1. L, D, p. 33—On p. 33 it says, "At last she grabbed the toes of one foot in her hand and squirmed for all the world like an impatient stork. . . ." Why does she look like a stork? If necessary, look up the word *stork* and see what it says. Look to see whether there is a picture of a stork. This may help you. Draw a picture of Janey looking like a stork.
2. D, p. 38—Look up the word *crane* in the dictionary. See whether you can figure out why it says in the book that Janey "craned" her neck. Can you "crane" your neck? Show me, or draw a picture of it for me.
3. I, P, p. 40—On p. 40 Janey says that she thinks it would be nice if people had glossy coverings like horses that would never wear out and that could not be outgrown. What do you think would be nice if you could wish for something like that and have it come true? Why?

4. C, P, I, p. 47—Why do you think Janey decided to buy a package of gum with her nickel? If you were Janey, what might you have bought to accomplish the same purpose she did?
5. I, C, pp. 45–47—Why did Lupe tell a kindly falsehood to Janey?

Chapter IV, pp. 48–69

1. I, p. 49—Janey "read" her father's voice. Can you say some things in different ways so that I can tell how you are feeling? Try this one sentence and then perhaps later you may think up a sentence of your own and try to do the same type of exercise with it.

   a. If I were you, I would do it right away. (excitement, anticipation)
   b. If I were you, I would do it right away. (anger)
   c. If I were you, I would do it right away. (fear)
   d. If I were you, I would do it right away. (warning)

   Can you imagine what might have been said before the sentence in each different case?
2. I, W, p. 55—Janey loved the words, "Rivers of water in a dry place." What words sound beautiful to you? Are there any words you especially like? What are they?

Chapter V, pp. 70–83

1. I, C, p. 81—Is it true that only in olden days people *had* to be brave? Is Janey brave, do you think? Prove it. What is bravery?
2. D, C, P—Look up the words *blue* and *willow* in your dictionary. See what the meanings are for each word. Then decide for yourself and be able to give your reasons whether or not you believe "Blue Willow" might make a good nickname for Janey.

Chapter VI, pp. 84–99

1. L, p. 85—What were the cash prizes going to be for the first three winners?
2. L, p. 85—What is a "swamper?"
3. I, p. 91—What would you do if you had $1000?
4. L, p. 93—What was the most important possession the Larkins owned? Why was it so important?
5. I, W, p. 95—What smells do you like best? Would you like to prepare "A Dream Meal of My Favorite Foods," complete with illustrations? If so, try it!

Chapter VII, pp. 100–104

1. L, p. 103—Why did Janey like the wild ducks so much?
2. L, p. 108—Why did the eucalyptus wood pile make Janey feel so good?
3. C, P, pp. 108–109—Do you know what season of the year it was when Janey's camp school closed down?
4. P, I, D, pp. 108–109—Why couldn't Janey just say goodbye to Miss Peterson? Try to find out what the origin of the word "goodbye" is.

Chapter VIII, pp. 115–125

1. C, pp. 113–115—Dr. Pierce was a kind man. Prove it.
2. I, p. 120—What did Janey mean when she agreed with Bounce that it was a "dirty night?"
3. L, p. 123—Why did Janey finally decide that it would not be wise for her father to fight Bounce?
4. L, p. 124—Why did Bounce take the plate as payment for the rent?
5. W, I—Can you make up a story that would explain how "Bounce" came to get his name?

Chapter IX, pp. 126–138

1. I, P, p. 126—Why is it good to keep busy when you are unhappy?
2. I, P, p. 127—Have you ever thought what is nice about paper bags? How could they be exciting and mysterious?
3. L, p. 129—Why wasn't it a Merry Christmas even though there were bundles?
4. L, C, pp. 129–138—How did Janey's decision to visit her willow plate for the last time help to make her dream come true?

Chapter X, pp. 139–154

1. I, C, p. 139—Why was it so much fun *now* for Janey to move?
2. L, p. 143—Why wouldn't Mom allow the willow plate to be put out where it could be seen in the tank house?
3. L, C, D, pp. 144–145—Draw a picture proving that spring was coming. In order to draw the picture as well as possible, you may need to look up the words "genista," "China lilies," and "mockingbird" in a large dictionary or in illustrated flower and bird books. (After they have looked up the word mockingbird in a dictionary, the pupils might be asked why a mockingbird could be seen where Janey was living. They could also be asked why it is called a mockingbird.)

4. I, L, pp. 145–147—Are secrets fun to have? Which is more fun—having a secret or telling a secret? State your reason(s) why. What was Lupe's secret?

5. L, I, pp. 153–154—What question did Janey make Lupe ask her? Why did she do this?

More Resources for You

1. After having read *Blue Willow*, children may be anxious to read some more books similar to it. Lois Lenski has written some very good regional books that deal with the problems of migrant workers. One such book is *Cotton in My Sack*, Dell Publishing Company, Inc., Yearling Series, New York, 1959 (paperback). Another book by Lenski available in this series is *Judy's Journey*. In addition, the Yearling Series offers many other paperbacks that the teacher may want to make accessible for the class at this time.

Perhaps to motivate them to read more on the subject of migrant workers you might tell them a little about *Cotton in My Sack*. This is a realistic novel about the Hutley family. They live in Arkansas and are sharecroppers. The story centers around Joanda, called "Nannie," who is about twelve years old. The love of her life is Lally, her baby sister.

The book reflects the terrible poverty and problems of people who are sharecroppers. The language used is the language of these people—"I'm tard of pickin' . . . I ain't never gonna pick no more cotton as long as I live" (p. 4).

Joanda is a bright little girl whose teacher, Miss Fenton, is skillfully indirect and understanding. Because of Miss Fenton, Joanda learns to excel in reading and spelling.

Her parents have very little education and her mother thinks the only purpose of books is to learn lessons from them. Mama is characterized as being a woman who knows how to cook supper, but who does not know the magic of words.

At the conclusion of the story, through the help of Uncle Shine, Nannie's father, Dave, becomes a tenant instead of a sharecropper.

The foreword of this edition is very interesting, because it tells how Lois Lenski came to write *Cotton in My Sack*.

2. *The Legend of the Willow Plate*, by Alvin Tresselt and Nancy Cleaver, pictures by Joseph Low, Parents' Magazine Press, New York, 1968, unpaged.

Sample Worksheets

The following worksheets suggest some possible follow-up activities after reading *Blue Willow*.

I. COMPREHENSION

Do you feel that you know the characters in *Blue Willow* ? Prove it in as many ways as you can.

1. Janey was a proud girl.

2. Lupe was a sensitive, understanding friend.

3. Janey was not a selfish girl.

4. Janey, on many occasions, proved she was brave.

5. Mr. Larkin was a proud man.

II. SIMILES

A *simile* is a kind of comparison that says one thing is like another in some way. When the author of *Blue Willow* wrote that Janey was as "skippy as a grasshopper," she used a simile.

Here are some more examples of similes from *Blue Willow*. Tell what is being compared to what and how the things might be alike.

1. Your face is as red as a cock's comb, (p. 24).
2. Her eyes flashed as cold as blue ice, (p. 45).
3. She could feel joy rising like a swift tide within her, (p. 52).
4. Her voice was as soft as the screech of a peacock, (p. 52).
5. It wouldn't surprise me a bit if you went off, just like a firecracker, (p. 93).
6. The sky was blue, as blue as Janey's eyes, as blue as the willow plate, as blue as the bowl of heaven should be on a day in spring before the sun of summer has had a chance to fade it, (p. 148).

Here are some similes for you to finish for yourself.

1. It was as hot as _____ .
2. Her face was as dirty as _____ .
3. The little boy's clothes were as wrinkled as _____ .
4. He stood like _____ .
5. She worked like _____ .
6. They were as happy as _____ .
7. The puppy's tail was wagging as fast as _____ .

Would you like to make up a few similes of your own now? Try it!

1.

2.

Vocabulary Enrichment: The Difference in Walks

Be ready to *show me* how to walk in the following ways. Then, if you would like to, draw a picture of someone or something doing what the following sentences say. The page numbers indicate on what page you may find the underlined words in *Blue Willow*. Have fun!

1. *Stalk boldly* into the house. (p. 49)
2. The jack rabbit went *bounding stiffly* away. (p. 55)
3. It went *wheeling around* like a small lost shadow searching for its object. (p. 56)
4. She *flew* at Bounce. (p. 63)
5. Danger *slowly* sauntered up to Janey. (p. 66)
6. She was off the schoolhouse steps in *one lunge*. (p. 74)

Can you make up a sentence that would show a person walking in a special way? Try it. Maybe you can even make up two. Think, for instance, how someone might walk to the Christmas tree to open presents, or how someone might walk home after having just broken a neighbor's window after playing baseball!

Sample Worksheets for Other Books

Worksheet Number One

Freddy the Detective, by Walter R. Brooks, Scholastic Book Services, New York, 1962, 153 pp.

I. Finish the following lines and then draw a picture to go with each.

    1. He was as hot as _____ .
    2. The sun looked like _____ .
    3. The rain sounded like _____ .
    4. She was as angry as _____ .
    5. The stars are like _____ .

II. Write or be prepared to tell a short story about what makes you feel funny in your stomach.

III. Be ready to tell what happened when you went to a splash party at the pond mentioned in *Freddy the Detective.* Chapter I, pp. 1–11.

IV. How many words can you write down that would tell about the noises you might hear at the ocean, lake, pond, or pool?

V. Draw a picture of paragraph 6 on p. 4. Then write down or tape what you think the conversation might have been between Uncle Wesley and the big elephant.

VI. Write or tell about one time when you were really scared. Did you let your imagination run away with you? Write down as many scary words as you can.

Worksheet Number Two

The Story of Ferdinand, by Munro Leaf, Scholastic Book Services, New York, 1962, unpaged.

I. You are a lovely flower, a best friend of Ferdinand. What would you say to him when you found out that he was going to the bull ring to fight the matador?

II. Plan a going-away party for Ferdinand. Whom would you invite; what would you do for fun; what would you have for refreshments?

III. You are poor "Barry Bee" that Ferdinand sat on. Write what happened to you on that sad day. Write what Barry said to Ferdinand when Ferdinand sat on him.

IV. You are the proud matador. Write about how you felt on the day you were to fight Ferdinand. Then tell how you felt after the fight was over. What would you tell your friends?

Worksheet Number Three

Mr. Pine's Mixed-Up Signs, by Leonard Kessler, Scholastic Book Services, New York, 1961, 61 pp.

I.   You are Mr. Pine. Draw some other funny signs you might put on the wrong places because you have lost your glasses.
II. Make believe you are Mr. Pine's dog. Tell what kind of a day you had when you wore Mr. Pine's glasses. Tell what your friends thought about you.
III. Pretend you are a boy or girl in this town. When you come to the candy shop, it says "School" over it. The clown in the circus is going to work and the sign on the school says "Circus." Just what do you think might happen if these mix-ups occurred? Suppose, too, that the sign over the jail said, "Police Department," what funny things could happen?

Worksheet Number Four

Curious George Rides a Bike, by H. A. Rey, Scholastic Book Services, New York, 1962, 45 pp.

I.   See how many things you can write down that have made you curious or would make you curious if you saw them.
II. Curious George is coming to your classroom. He has never seen a desk, a lunch box, or a pencil sharpener before. He does not know what a teacher and a principal expect from boys and girls in school. Write or be able to tell what you think might happen.
III. If you were George's mother or father would you do anything about George's curiosity? If you would, tell what it would be and why you would do it.
IV. Pretend you are one of the newspapers that George made into a boat. Tell what happened to you that day and how you felt.

Worksheet Number Five

Homer Price, "The Case of the Sensational Scent," by Robert McCloskey, Scholastic Book Services, New York, 1962, pp. 8–30.

I.   What do you think of the name of Homer's skunk? Rename the skunk and explain your choice of name.
II. Would you like to live in a tourist camp? What do you think you would do in the winter?
III. Try writing an ad for "Dreggs After Shaving Lotion" after Aroma has added his particular gift to it.
IV. What would you do if you almost walked right into a nest of robbers? Do you like the way in which Homer captured the robbers? Would you

have done it in the same way? If not, tell how you would have done it.
Do you think "nest of robbers" is a good description? Why or why not?
V. Pretend you are a mother or father ant preparing to join the robbers for
breakfast. What would you say to your youngsters?

Worksheet Number Six

The Lonesome Bear, by Harrison Kinney, Scholastic Book Services, New
York, 1961, 64 pp.

I. Try to make up another title for this book after having read p. 3. Could
you give another title for the whole first chapter?
II. Write a poem or short story entitled, "Younger Brothers" or "Younger
Sisters." Or, if you happen to be a younger brother or younger sister
yourself, write a story called, "What's Wrong with Being a Kid?"
III. Can you make up a poem or a story called, "Boys' Pockets" or "My
Favorite Food Dream"?
IV. You have just given away a baby bear to one of your friends. Tell him
how to take care of it.
V. Be prepared to act out these things:
P. 5—"Just then a brown bear lumbered down the hill. . . .
He began sniffing at the candy. . . ."
P. 6—Third paragraph.
P. 8—First paragraph and fifth paragraph.
VI. Draw a picture of paragraph 5 on p. 8.

(If you liked this story perhaps you might enjoy the book, *The Biggest
Bear,* by Lynd Ward.)

Worksheet Number Seven

Ripsnorters and Ribticklers, "Kemp Morgan," by Tony Simon, Scholastic
Book Services, New York, 1962, pp. 3–6.

I. If you had a nose like Kemp Morgan, what would you do with it?
Imagine that you had eyes that could see across the country. Make up
an adventure that you could have.
II. Answer the question on p. 4.
III. Find all the tall tales you can that are included right in this one tall tale.
IV. On p. 6 it says, "They began to slip and slide across the sky like eggs
frying in a pan of hot butter." Could you compare the clouds to some-
thing else?

V. Could you make up a fearsome "critter?" Draw him and make up a tall tale about him.

VI. Try to make an illustration for a cover of a book of tall tales that would make the reader know that this was a book of tall tales.

VII. Does this story remind you of any other story you have read? What is it? Why does it remind you of this story?

4. AN AFTERWORD

To achieve the ideal of having every pupil read with pleasure requires not only patience but flexibility on your part. It is important that children be taught meaningful ways of helping themselves to decode the new words they encounter, and it is hoped that the suggestions in the first section of this chapter will assist you toward that end. It is equally important to emphasize the meaning of words; to stress one aspect of learning new words at the expense of the other will usually lead to disappointing results.

Individualizing reading instruction will enable you to diagnose the needs of the particular pupil and to provide the specific kind of help needed at a given time. In addition, this method gives you the opportunity to share with each child the delight and excitement that good books can provide—a very considerable reward for your efforts.

In ending this chapter I would like to share with you an excerpt from a poem called "Riders," by Robert Frost.[4]

The surest thing there is is we are riders,
And though none too successful at it, guiders, . . .

There is our wildest mount—a headless horse.
But though it runs unbridled off its course,
And all our blandishments would seem defied,
We have ideas yet that we haven't tried.

9 Developing Critical and Creative Thinking

Pigeons

Pigeons are city folk
content
to live with concrete
and cement.

They seldom try the sky.

A pigeon never sings of hill
and flowering hedge,
but busily commutes
from sidewalk to his ledge.

Oh pigeon, what a waste
of wings!

—Lilian Moore

In our enthusiasm for developing avid appetites for books in our pupils, it is important that we reflect on and talk about books they have already read. Children should be given frequent opportunities to think and talk about the reading they have done and consider features common to the books they have liked. Besides providing the opportunity of recalling and sharing pleasurable experiences, this kind of stock-taking exercise makes children more aware of literary techniques and sharpens their discrimination. Discussions of literary techniques show children devices they can use effectively and creatively in their own expression. Far too many children think of literature as something wholly different from what they write themselves; children who consciously apply in their own writing techniques what they have noticed and remembered from their reading are less likely to feel this way.

This chapter suggests ways in which children can be encouraged to think about the books and stories they have read and to find common features in them. The sections are headed with questions that all children can explore together, regardless of the specific books each may have read. If the questions succeed in their purpose, they will not only provide lively discussions, but they will suggest ideas that children will want to try in their own writing.

1. WHAT MAKES A BOOK APPEALING?

The physical appearance of books, a notable feature of modern children's books, provides a natural starting point for discussion.

The Shape of Books and Illustrations

Some books for younger children come in intriguing shapes. If possible, have on display some of the Golden Shape Books such as *The Cat Book*[1] (in the shape of a cat curled up for a snooze), *The Fish Book*[2] (in the shape of a fish), and *The Apple Book*.[3] Similar in appeal is Maurice Sendak's *Nutshell Library*,[4] a miniature set about four inches high in a tiny slipcase. Two of the Sendak books in particular may stimulate children to create similar small books of their own: *Alligators All Around,*[5] an alphabet book featuring an alligator family, and *One Was Johnny,*[6] a counting book in rhyme about Johnny, who lived by himself "and liked it like that."

After discussing the "shape books" and the miniature books, you might ask pupils to think about appropriate shapes or sizes for books about a tree, a leaf, a giant, an elf, Easter eggs, the state in which they live, and so on. Encourage them to think about appropriate designs and attractive colors for the covers. You may want to follow through by having them design covers for the book idea they like best. A collection of attractively illustrated trade books is a good starting point for a discussion of the appeal of illustrations. Pass the books around and have children comment on pictures they particularly like (or don't like). Then encourage them to tell about illustrations they liked and remember from books they have read.

Intriguing Titles

The title of a book can contribute as much or more to its initial appeal as format or illustrations. To focus pupils' attention on titles, you might ditto or write on the board a list of titles like these.

1. *Why I Built the Boogle House* by Helen Palmer (New York: Random House, 1964).
2. "The Threap" by Louise Scott and J. J. Thompson (St. Louis: McGraw-Hill Book Company, 1966).
3. *Snow Treasure* by Marie McSwigan (New York: Scholastic Book Services, 1958).
4. *Landslide* by Véronique Day (New York: Dell Publishing Company, Inc., 1961).
5. *Stone Soup* by Marcia Brown (New York: Charles Scribner's Sons, 1947).
6. *Eddie's Pay Dirt* by Carolyn Haywood (New York: Scholastic Book Services, 1953).
7. "The Horse Who Lived Upstairs" by Phyllis McGinley in *Treat Shop,* edited by Eleanor Johnson and Leland Jacobs (Columbus, Ohio: Charles E. Merrill Books, Inc., 1960).

8. *Ripsnorters and Ribticklers* by Tony Simon (New York: Scholastic Book Services, 1954).

Allow children time to familiarize themselves with the titles; then ask which ones sound interesting and why. You may want to note comments as they are made, especially those that involve a question: What's a boogle house? What's a threap? Who got caught in a landslide? You might ask why an author might choose a title that would leave a question in a person's mind.

You might follow up with a short list of titles like these.

1. *Saved in the Nick of Time.*
2. *The Great Escape.*
3. *The Joke Was on Me.*
4. *Too Tricky for His Own Good.*

Children will readily see that although these titles may suggest an interesting story, each gives away the outcome.

One other kind of title you may want to bring up is one that names a character, like *Henry Huggins,* for instance. Some children will object that such titles do not give a reader much idea of what the book will be about. Others will point out that if you have read one book about a character and liked it you will want to read more.

To round off the discussion of what makes a good title, have pupils think of titles for books they would like to read. In addition to making children more aware of titles, this activity may give you some new clues to their interests that will come in handy when you are suggesting new books for them to sample.

Hooking the Reader

Point out that an attractive cover and illustrations and an intriguing title may make a reader pick up a new book, but they are not enough to make a reader finish the book. Suggest that you explore together some of the ways in which writers hook their readers into going to the end of a book.

Skillful Arrangement of Words

The trouble with reading jokes is that your eye may wander to the punch line too quickly. But a joke on one page that has its punch line on an overleaf is different and much more amusing. Many successful children's books use this principle of holding back the answer to a question with great effectiveness. Two good examples that you will want to show your pupils are *What Do You Say, Dear?*[7] and *What Do You Do, Dear?*[8] Both these books by

Sesyle Joslin pose hilarious social situations in which the reader is asked to think of the right thing to say or do. The author gives a solution, but not on the same page with the problem. The reader has to read on to find it, only to be caught up in the next problem.

Other books that use similar devices to lure the reader on are Robert McCloskey's *Burt Dow: Deep-Water Man,*[9] the story of a whaler, and *Please Pass the Grass*[10] by Leone Adelson, which suggests a number of wonderful things that can be done with grass.

Raising Questions in the Reader's Mind

A related stratagem is to suggest a question to readers that they want to have answered. Garth Williams' *The Rabbits' Wedding*[11] provides a fine example of this technique successfully used. One of the two main characters, the black rabbit, looks very sad, and the white rabbit asks what the matter is. The black rabbit replies that he is just thinking. This question, as well as the answer, is repeated again and again, causing the readers to become terribly inquisitive.

To demonstrate the effectiveness of unanswered questions as a stimulus for curiosity, you might read the first chapter of *Henry Huggins*[12] by Beverly Cleary. This chapter tells how Henry gets a dog, Ribsy, and recounts the difficulties he has in getting Ribsy home. When you have finished reading the chapter, you might ask for what questions your listeners would like to have answers. Some questions children may have are:

1. Will Henry's mother let him keep Ribsy?
2. Will Henry get away with bringing Ribsy on the bus in an open box?
3. What idea does Henry get? (p. 7)
4. Will Henry get away with taking Ribsy on the bus in a shopping bag?
5. Will Ribsy be quiet on the bus?
6. What is going to happen when Ribsy gets out of the bag?
7. Is Henry going to be arrested?

Children should be guided to observe that within fourteen pages there appear to be at least seven questions that arise in the reader's mind. The continuous raising of questions leads the reader on and on.

Each chapter in *Henry Huggins* consists of a different adventure. It might be suggested that some pupils read other chapters in *Henry Huggins* and tell the class a little about the chapter they chose and how Cleary succeeded in making the reader read on.

Getting to the Problem Right Away

Another way of getting and holding the reader's attention is to enmesh him/her in the action as soon as possible. Fairy tales are good examples of this technique, for they are usually short and waste little time on preliminaries. You might suggest that pupils sample stories from such collections as those suggested in the following list. When they have finished reading, have them jot down a note about how the writer got into the main part of the story.

1. *Grimms' Fairy Tales,* edited by Nora Kramer (New York: Scholastic Book Services, 1962).
2. *Tales from the Green Fairy Book,* edited by Andrew Lang (New York: Scholastic Book Services, 1960).
3. *The Crimson Fairy Book,* edited by Andrew Lang (New York: Dover Publications, Inc., 1967). (There are eight other paperback fairy tale collections edited by Lang and published by Dover Publications.)
4. *The Twelve Dancing Princesses and Other Fairy Tales,* edited by Alfred and Mary Elizabeth David (New York: The New American Library of World Literature, Inc., 1964).

Good Endings

The object of getting and holding readers' attention is to make them want to read to the end, and the ending should, of course, answer all the readers' questions and tie up the loose ends. Encourage children not to wait passively for the ending to be revealed but to try to think of possible solutions to problems and predict probable outcomes.

As pupils anticipate the solutions to problems, they are exercising their imagination and also developing the ability to make logical inferences from given information. Encourage as many solutions as possible for a particular story, discussing ways in which each might be satisfactory or unsatisfactory. Then, working together, have pupils find out what kind of solution the author chose.

Two books that you will find useful in working with endings are *Invitations to Speaking and Writing Creatively*[13] and *Invitations to Thinking and Doing*[14] by R. E. Myers and E. Paul Torrance. Both books pose interesting problems for readers to solve—in other words, the authors ask the reader to find endings that will resolve a conflict or extricate a person from a predicament. You might try some of these problems at the very beginning of your work with endings and then try some more when pupils have become more adept at finding satisfactory outcomes.

You can use any number of books and stories to give children practice in problem solving. A few good possibilities to start off with are suggested as follows.

1. *Stone Soup*[15] by Marcia Brown. In this familiar story, three tired and hungry soldiers have the problem of using their wits alone to get a good meal and a place to sleep.
2. *The Perfect Pancake*[16] by Virginia Kahl. In this story, quite similar in plot to *Stone Soup,* a woman is famous for her delicious pancakes, which she always gives out one to a customer. A beggar come along and thinks of a way to get all he wants.
3. *The Duchess Bakes a Cake*[17] by Virginia Kahl. A determined duchess puts too much yeast in a cake she is making and, as the cake rises, she is elevated to dangerous heights. The problem is how to get the duchess down safely.
4. *Stories from the Peterkin Papers*[18] by Lucretia Hale. The Peterkin family is confronted with a series of silly problems, which are all neatly and humorously solved.
5. *Twenty and Ten* by Claire Hutchet Bishop.[19] A true story of how twenty French children hide ten Jewish children from the Nazis during World War II. Throughout this book, children can be asked: What would you have done? This is an excellent book to read in its entirety to the class. The children can be asked to contemplate how they would feel if, at the end of the book, there were no indication given of what had happened to Sister Gabriel. (Sister Gabriel was in charge of the twenty French children who came to her while France was occupied by the Germans. The day when the Nazis found the French children's refuge, Sister Gabriel was not there because she had gone to the village for food and letters.)

Children should be able to comment that for a satisfying ending all the pieces must be taken care of. Every important character should be accounted for—there should be no loose ends left dangling. To demonstrate this point further, the class can discuss how Virginia Kahl very neatly winds up all of her characters in *The Duchess Bakes a Cake*. At the end of *The Perfect Pancake,* it is not enough to know that the villagers and the beggar have been able to get all the pancakes they want from the lady who was such a wonderful cook. The reader wants to know both what is going to happen to the beggar, and whether the villagers are going to trick the pancake lady any more. Kahl, knowing this, satisfies all her readers' desires.

2. WHAT MAKES A STORY FUNNY?

Children enjoy humorous stories, and the discussions suggested in this section should afford ample opportunity for children to recall and share amusing episodes from books they have read and to chuckle over new ones. In addition, these discussions should make children more aware of the ways in which writers create humor, some of which the children may be able to use for their own purposes when they set out to write something funny.

As you discuss the various episodes, try to elicit from pupils the reason they find them funny. But do not insist on answers when they come hard and be ready to move on to something else when interest begins to fade.

Rufus M., a book by Eleanor Estes,[20] has a very humorous episode in it that can be read to children quickly because of its brevity. The excerpt recounts the terrible problems Rufus has in getting a library card. Much of the humor results from Rufus' misunderstanding of what the librarian means. In addition, Estes uses the technique of anticipation with her readers. When Rufus perches on the sill of the cellar window, the reader gets ready for what is inevitably going to happen to him—he is going to fall in. Estes uses this same technique in the section where Rufus is asked to write his name on an application form for a library card. The reader already has been clued in to the meagerness of Rufus' experiences with writing and so is ready for what is going to happen.

Another delightful episode, which derives its humor from the reader's anticipating the consequences of an act, can be found in Chapter 4 in Mark Twain's[21] *Tom Sawyer*. Tom has managed by trading with his friends to collect enough tickets (won for mastering two thousand passages of the Scripture) to turn in and get a Bible. Of course, what happens is that the Sunday school superintendent decides to ask "Thomas" to demonstrate what he has learned! Twain uses the same technique in Chapter 21 where a cat lifts off the teacher's wig and there, revealed for all to see, is a gilded, bald head. The teacher's unawareness of what is to happen, coupled with the children's awareness of what is going to occur, makes for a hilarious situation.

"Angleworms on Toast" by Kantor[22] tells how Thomas was cured of saying he wanted to eat "angleworms on toast." The preposterousness of such a dish is funny to begin with. In addition, the reader anticipates both what the household decides to do about Thomas' bad habit and Thomas' reaction to the solution.

Stone Soup by Marcia Brown, discussed before, is funny because it involves the heroes, the good characters, outwitting and tricking the selfish villagers through their cleverness.

The Duchess Bakes a Cake by Virginia Kahl, also mentioned previously, makes the reader chuckle because of the improbability of the whole situation and because of its broad exaggeration.

The title of the book *The Puppy Who Wanted a Boy* by Jane Thayer[23] is amusing because it is so unexpected—it is a reversal of what a reader would anticipate normally. The story describes what a little dog, Petey, does in order to get a boy for Christmas.

Custard the Dragon by Ogden Nash,[24] *The Shy Stegosaurus of Cricket Creek* by Evelyn Lampman,[25] and *The Story of Ferdinand* by Munro Leaf[26] are nonsensically delightful because they are all stories about animals who are out of character. Who would expect that a dragon would be cowardly, a dinosaur devastatingly shy, or a bull peace-loving? The very fact that these animals' characteristics are so unlikely adds to the fun.

"The Horse Who Lived Upstairs" by Phyllis McGinley,[27] included in the volume *Treat Shop,* edited by Eleanor Johnson and Leland Jacobs, makes the reader laugh because the situation is so untenable. The story tells of Joey, a horse who thinks he will prefer country living to city living, but learns how wrong he is.

You might read pupils a tall tale included in the book *Ripsnorters and Ribticklers* by Tony Simon.[28] Then ask the children what the stories had in common. They can be led to discover that all of them use gross exaggeration as a means of tickling the reader's funny bone.

The story of *Mr. Popper's Penguins* by the Atwaters[29] is hilarious because the idea that anyone would keep a penguin in the refrigerator at home is unheard of. The problems that arise from having a penguin provide much laughter, and the laughter increases as the number of penguins in the Popper household multiply.

Stories from the Peterkin Papers by Lucretia Hale gains its share of laughs because of the silliness of the main characters, the Peterkins. Their lack of common sense provides the source for many chuckles.

One of the funniest episodes in any book can be found in the chapter "Laughing Gas" in *Mary Poppins* by Pamela Travers.[30] The notion of having a tea party up in the air is funny enough. In addition, any time a prim and proper person is made to feel or look foolish, the climate is set for gaiety. Children should not miss hearing this delightfully silly chapter, which should make them eager to read the rest of *Mary Poppins.*

Homer Price by Robert McCloskey[31] is filled with humorous situations. The names of the characters are silly—Aroma the skunk, Homer, Uncle Ulysses, and Uncle Telemachus. Perhaps the teacher might tell the children who the original Homer, Ulysses, and Telemachus were and ask them whether they think these names are appropriate or terribly funny for these characters. In addition, the sheriff habitually resorts to talking in spoonerisms, and one chapter, "Nothing New Under the Sun (Hardly)," is a takeoff on the old Pied Piper tale.

Each chapter offers a new adventure. One that could be read to the children is the chapter entitled "The Doughnuts." In this section an extremely wealthy woman comes into Uncle Ulysses' lunchroom and proceeds to make doughnuts. Most children, after hearing one chapter in *Homer Price*, will become Homer Price addicts.

Children love *Pippi Longstocking* by Lindgren[32] for many reasons. One chapter that children think is particularly delectable and funny is the one entitled, "Pippi Goes to School." It is funny because of the way Pippi treats the teachers. She talks to the teacher the way most children dream they could talk to their teachers. It is devilishly daring, incredible, and beyond the attainment of most children, yet they relish the idea of it. Lindgren makes use of improbable situations (Pippi's father is a cannibal king; she lives with her monkey and her horse without the benefits of even one adult to bother her). Lindgren not only gives Pippi the name of Pippilotta Delicatessa Windowshade Mackrelmint Efraim's Daughter Longstocking, but gives her an appearance and qualities to match her inimitable name. Each chapter introduces Pippi to a new adventure. This is another book that teachers easily could lure children into reading. If they enjoy this book, they will also enjoy Lindgren's *Pippi Goes on Board*.

When you have exposed your children to a broad range of humorous writing and have given them plenty of opportunity to discuss it, you may wish to review some of the comic techniques that have been talked about previously. You could put headings such as the following on the board and ask pupils to think of stories that contain good examples of each.

1. Misunderstandings.
2. Unexpected outcomes.
3. Tricking bad or selfish people.
4. Improbable situations.
5. Funny names, words, and titles.
6. The opposite of what is expected (*The Puppy Who Wanted a Boy*).
7. Silly characters.

A natural outcome of your discussion of humorous writing would be to encourage pupils to try their own hands at it. Suggest that they use one or more of the techniques you have reviewed. Pupils could then share and discuss their writing with their classmates.

3. WHAT MAKES A BOOK EXCITING?

The techniques that writers use for creating excitement and suspense are really not very different from those discussed earlier in the chapter as ways of seizing and holding the reader's attention. But mystery, adventure, and ghost stories, all of which trade on suspense, are such favorites of children that this topic deserves a special section of its own. The stories suggested next provide good material with which to work and will lead to lively discussions. Of course, other titles may be substituted. The main thing is to use enough stories to exhibit the means authors use to keep their readers on the edge of their chairs.

Snow Treasure by Marie McSwigan[33] is a true story of how children in the Norwegian village of Riswyk managed to remove $9 million worth of gold from their village under the eyes of occupying Nazi troops. The author does a superb job of sustaining suspense, and her book makes an exciting choice for reading aloud to the class. If you use it in this way, you will also have the opportunity to review techniques such as raising questions and making good endings, both of which are discussed in Section 1. This book provides many opportunities for children to draw inferences about possible outcomes and to relate to the problems and feelings of the characters.

Twenty and Ten, the book about the French children who hide Jewish children from the Nazis, described earlier in this chapter, is filled with suspense. A main source of it is Louis, a four-year-old boy, much younger than the rest. The foremost question in the reader's mind must be whether Louis will let the children's great secret slip.

Call It Courage by Armstrong Sperry[34] and *Robinson Crusoe* are both stories of survival under great difficulties. Their parallels make them interesting books to take up together. In each, the main character is constantly being confronted with new problems that the reader fears he will not be able to handle. A device for producing suspense in *Robinson Crusoe* is well worth calling children's attention to. Crusoe discovers a footprint in the sandy beach of his deserted island, which confirms his suspicion that cannibals from nearby islands visit his island from time to time. The fear of cannibals remains in the reader's mind until the footprint is explained much later.

The Witch of Blackbird Pond by Elizabeth Speare[35] is a beautifully written and fast-moving book that received a Newbery Medal in 1959. Young Kit Tyler travels by herself from Barbados to Wethersfield, Connecticut when her grandfather, with whom she has been living, dies. The time is 1687, and the story explores the attitudes of the people in the New World toward liberty, freedom, religion, and superstition. The episodes in which Kit is accused of being a witch and in which she warns a Quaker woman of a mob coming for her are particularly gripping.

The Arrow Book of Ghost Stories[36] and the *Arrow Book of Spooky Stories,*[37] both paperbacks published by Scholastic Book Services, are collections of stories designed to inspire chills and shivers. Read several of the short stories to your pupils and then ask what they have in common that makes them so terrifying. Specifically, children might be asked who appears in the stories and what kinds of words are used in the tales. Children will quickly sense that there is an abundance of witches, ghosts, and goblins. And there are plenty of words like "gloom," "death," "shiver," "bones," "dark," "shadows," "howling," and "wailing" that conjure up frightening images and sounds.

Children, when they have had the opportunity to read some stories, can work together on compiling words they could use to set an alarming or exciting atmosphere. When a number of words have been written on the blackboard, ask children whether they would like to try composing a beginning sentence or two for a chilling or thrilling story.

Another activity that children could carry out after they have discussed some of these stories would be to create a shadow play. A shadow play is a play that takes place behind raised sheets. With the proper lighting, all that can be seen from the audience are shadows and vague outlines of suggested frightening objects. One of the delights in giving a play of this type is that, if any of the characters in the play are witches or ghosts, they can have a wonderful time trying to speak just the way they think these creatures would. Meanwhile, the audience, because it can see no real faces, can let its imagination run as far as it wants it to go. The children putting on the play might want to invite another class to see it.

Elements from adventure stories and ghost stories are often found together in mystery stories. Events are realistically described, but the suspense is often heightened by a spooky setting. Mystery stories provide good opportunities for children to draw inferences about probable outcomes.

When pupils have read and discussed adventure, ghost, and mystery stories, you may want to return to the original question: What makes a book exciting? Encourage children to draw on their recollections of earlier discussions. For example, raising questions in the reader's minds is obviously a suspense-producing technique. You may also wish to lead them to observe that making the main characters sympathetic is important. The readers care what happens to Robinson Crusoe and to the children in *Twenty and Ten* because they have come to like and understand them. Finally, you might talk about the words the authors use—vivid action words for describing the events in adventure stories, scary words in ghost stories and mystery stories.

4. AFTERWORD

One of the pleasures of reading is being able to recall books you have liked and the delight you have had in others. The activities suggested in this chapter provide the opportunity for children to do both of these things. But the chapter has another purpose. The reading that individuals do is a reservoir of words, phrases, and ways of doing things in writing that they can draw on when they sit down to write themselves. The idea is not that the reader-turned-writer copies what others have done: very few can copy unintentionally. Instead, it is that well-read writers hear not only their own voices but echoes of the voices of the authors they have read. All professional writers, such as those mentioned in this chapter, avail themselves of this advantage. It is hoped that the discussions suggested here will encourage children to follow their example.

Helps

Applegate, Mauree, illustrated by Elizabeth Dauber, *Easy in English,* Evanston, Ill.: Row, Peterson and Company, 1962. Just like Mauree Applegate's other books for teachers, this book, too, is crammed with fresh ideas to make anyone's language arts program sparkle. Anyone who has not had the pleasure of meeting Mauree Applegate through her books is missing a rewarding, pleasurable, and revitalizing encounter.

Braddock, Richard, Lloyd-Jones, Richard, and Schoer, Lowell, *Research in Written Composition,* Champaign, Ill.: National Council of Teachers of English, 1963. The comments made in this paperback contain vast implications for each teacher's language arts program. Three of the comments that need to be reflected on and then acted on are:

1. "Another factor which may rival frequency of writing in importance is extensiveness of reading . . . ." (p. 35)
2. ". . . instruction in formal grammar has little or no effect on the quality of student composition." (p. 37)
3. ". . . written language evolves from oral language . . . ." (p. 51)

Burrows, Alvina Treut, Jackson, Doris C., and Saunders, Dorothy O., *They All Want to Write: Written English in the Elementary School,* New York: Holt, Rinehart and Winston, 1964. An excellent paperback written by teachers for teachers. An invaluable book to read to garner ideas on helping children's inner creative thoughts come out. On p. 222, the authors write that rich expression is aided immeasurably by the students' involvement in literature. They say that "Conversely, the effort of trying to write one's own ideas . . . heightens sensitivity to good literature." On p. 221 the writers state that adults are needed by children "to bring them into effective relationship with new materials. Left to themselves their explorations lead to a thinning of content and a dulling of perception." Burrows, Jackson, and Saunders' book is stocked well with the writings of children.

Carlson, Ruth Kearney, *Sparkling Words: Two Hundred Practical and Creative Writing Ideas,* Berkeley, Cal.: Wagner Printing Company, 1965. Carlson's book fulfills the claim promised in its title. Many of her ideas are incorporated into full lesson plans. The paperback also includes "The Carlson Analytical Scale for Measuring the Originality of Children's Stories."

Clegg, A. B., editor, *The Excitement of Writing,* London: Chatto and Windus, 1965. Excellent advice on how to start children's creative powers and keep them going. This book is filled with the writings of young children who have come in contact with creative teachers.

Cole, Natalie Robinson, photographs by C. K. Eaton, *The Arts in the Classroom,* New York: The John Day Company, 1940. Chapter 5, "Creative Writing," may be of particular interest to teachers. It tells how Natalie Robinson Cole stimulated her urban fourth-grade children to express their own thoughts honestly, simply, and effectively.

Cole, Natalie Robinson, *Children's Arts from Deep Down Inside,* New York: The John Day Company, 1966. Chapter 10, "Home Life," and Chapter 11, "Our Secret Crimes," concentrate on the art of bringing children's writings to life.

Corbin, Richard, *The Teaching of Writing in Our Schools,* New York: The Macmillan Company, 1966. This little paperback is geared mainly toward parents who do not know what is going on in our schools today under the name of "writing," meaning the communication of ideas in written form. The answer that is given is that not much is being done with this subject, and what is being done, for the most part, is not being done well. Remedies and suggestions for improvement are provided. Corbin remarks on p. 50 that inane composition assignments "are handed out by inadequately trained and unimaginative teachers" too frequently.

Evertts, Eldonna L., editor, *Explorations in Children's Writing,* Champaign, Ill.: National Council of Teachers of English, 1970. Evertts, James Britton, Alvina Treut Burrows, and Richard Lewis all contribute thoughts on how to help children express themselves well in writing. A selected bibliography is included at the end of this paperback. Richard Lewis concludes his remarks on p. 95 by telling his readers that the Eskimo word for poetry means "to breathe." That statement should have important implications for any teacher of poetry, any teacher of writing, any language arts teacher!

Karl, Jean, *From Childhood to Childhood: Children's Books and Their Creators,* New York: The John Day Company, 1970. Although this book describes what goes into a book for children that makes that book truly a fine one for children, it also stresses in great detail what those elements are that make a piece of writing fine writing. Karl tells also the steps a book goes through that brings it from its creator to its audience (if it is published by a reputable publishing company, a company that has integrity and pride in its work).

Teachers should gain a great deal of usable knowledge by reading this book. Karl writes on pp. 63–65 that enthusiasm is the essential ingredient of good writing. She also says that "the best writing (to paraphrase Jefferson) is that writing which shows not at all." Karl feels, too, that "good writing reinforces meaning without artificial assistance."

Langdon, Margaret, *Let the Children Write,* London: Longmans, Green and Company, Ltd., 1966. A delightful short book that describes how Margaret Langdon teaches her pupils to express themselves creatively. A joy to read. The book is packed with the writings of children and how those writings came to be.

Petty, Walter F., and Bowen, Mary E., *Slithery Snakes and Other Aids to Children's Writing,* New York: Appleton-Century-Crofts, 1967. Another short book, a paperback, designed to help teachers enrich their stockpile of ideas to use to stimulate children to express themselves creatively. In answer to the question "Can creative writing be taught," Petty and Bowen on pp. 4 and 5 respond that not only can it be taught but that it must be! They write that "While it is true that some painters . . . are innately talented and have received little teaching, the majority of persons engaged in these arts . . ., have received instruction—they have been *taught.*"

Southall, Ivan, *A Journey of Discovery: On Writing for Children,* New York: Macmillan Publishing Co., 1975.

Stewig, John Warren, *Read to Write: Using Children's Literature as a Springboard to Writing,* New York: Hawthorn Books, Inc., 1975. An excellent book to use to help children to write well.

Wolfe, Don M., *Creative Ways to Teach English: Grades 7 to 12,* New York: The Odyssey Press, Inc., 1966. If you want to become the most enriched teacher that you can, forget all about labels. I know that you are concerned about teaching *elementary* school-age children. So am I! But what we are both searching for are good ideas. They can be found anywhere just as long as we are looking. Try this book. You will not be sorry that you did. However, you can skip the sections on teaching grammar very nicely and with no harm whatsoever!

10 Poetry Is When the Words Marry

You will find poetry nowhere
unless you bring some with you.
—Joseph Joubert

Children do bring poetry with them when they come to school; all too often they lose it there and never find it again. They come with a fresh eye and, because they are not yet inhibited by adult notions of what is reasonable or appropriate, they are able to describe the world in fresh new images. They are adept at metaphor. They have made mountains by raising the blanket on their bed with their knees, pushed cars along the road made by the border of a carpet, and bailed out in umbrella parachutes. And they like to play—with words as well as with objects. Partly because children grow up and partly because of their experiences in school, this aptitude for poetic expression is often wasted. This chapter suggests some ways in which children can use the poetry they bring with them to find more poetry everywhere they look.

1. A CLIMATE FOR POETRY

To begin with, you will want to make your classroom a place where poetry can happen and where poetic expression is a natural instead of an extraordinary way of saying things. A number of the books suggested in earlier chapters contain poems or are in verse form; using them along with prose books will help to give the impression that poetry is a normal alternative to a writer. In addition, it is a good idea to take a few minutes from other class activities from time to time to read a poem to children. Some books you might use for this purpose are:

1. *It Doesn't Always Have to Rhyme* by Eve Merriam.[1] In addition to the title poem, which makes a point that you will want to keep reminding pupils of, this book contains some other poems about poetry that children will find interesting. In "How to Eat a Poem," readers are urged not to be polite but to dig in and enjoy themselves; "Mona Lisa" explores an impor-

THE FAMILY CIRCUS   By Bil Keane

"Mommy, this cup and saucer don't rhyme."

THE FAMILY CIRCUS, by Bill Keane, reprinted courtesy The Register and Tribune Syndicate, Inc.

tant difference between poetry and prose; "What Did You Say?" tells readers that a poem speaks only to them and that when "syllables repeat" they do so just for the music.

2. *First Voices* by Geoffrey Summerfield.[2] These four graded paperback volumes (Book One is intended for roughly the third-grade level) contain an excellent selection of poems, both traditional and modern, that children will love. A considerable number of children's poems are also included.

3. *Reflections on a Gift of Watermelon Pickle*[3] by Stephen Dunning, Edward Lueders, and Hugh Smith. A justly famous collection of poetry for young readers, handsomely illustrated.

There are many good collections for classroom use, some others of which are suggested in *Helps* at the end of this chapter.

In your reading of poetry to children, it is important that you do not neglect reading poetry written by other children. Hearing such poems builds confidence in children as to their own ability as poets. In addition to *First Voices*, mentioned previously, the following are good sources for children's poetry.

1. *Miracles,*[4] *Journeys,*[5] and *The Wind and the Rain*[6] by Richard Lewis.
2. *Children Are Poets* by Susan Pulsifer.[7]
3. *Wishes, Lies and Dreams* by Kenneth Koch.[8]

Materials of this kind should be made accessible for children to browse through. Particularly apt phrases or unique or beautiful descriptions should be commented on. Lewis includes in both his *Miracles* and his *The Wind and the Rain* a poem entitled "Raindrops" by Ken Dickinson, age ten. Ken says in his poem that raindrops "measle the window pane." The word *measle* might be remarked on.

To show youngsters that they are truly creative, even at a very early age, they can be read the poems that Pulsifer[9] includes in her little book. Two poems that are included were composed by the same child, one when he was two and then one when he was four. Another lovely poem that should be read to the children is called "Sea Shells." It was thought of by a child who was not yet eight years old.

There are constant references to children's writings sprinkled liberally throughout Applegate's[10] professional textbooks. David Holbrook,[11] Hughes Mearns,[12] and Flora Arnstein[13] pepper their professional books for teachers with children's writings. Such books might be very helpful to teachers, since they provide a clear insight into the capabilities of children.

Memorizing Poems

One question that comes up frequently in talking with teachers about poetry seems to center around memorization. Should children memorize poetry or not? Anyone who has worked with young people of any age soon realizes that they do memorize the things that for one reason or another hold great appeal for them. Therefore, given enough exposure time (think of the time that broadcasters and advertisers devote to repetition), children will learn without conscious effort the things they want to learn.

Robert Frost[14] is quoted on the front inside jacket cover of his *You Come Too* on the subject of poetry memorization. In a four-line verse he reminds the reader that although some people obviously question the virtue of it, it is nice to have pretty things well said in one's head. Pulsifer[15] says that knowing a piece of good writing by heart often serves as a stimulus for creative writing.

The answer, then, to the question: Should children memorize poetry? is: "Yes, they should." But children should not be *made* to memorize poetry. They will memorize some poems that *they* like. And, just like adults, they will know parts of some poems *by heart* (the best way to know a poem).

Occasionally, a group of children working together can memorize a piece they like gradually and then recite it for another class or classes. You can easily make a game out of memorizing. For example, after hearing you recite a short poem twice, the children may be given copies of it. After saying it together twice, you can proceed to write the poem on the board. Looking at the board, the children can say the poem once. Then the teacher can erase the first line of the poem. The children can say the poem again, and this time the teacher erases the second line. Proceed in a similar way until, presto, the board is blank but the poem is on the lips of each child. It would be wise to begin with very short humorous poems of no more than eight lines.

2. SIMPLE BEGINNINGS

The reading of poetry to children should be a continuing feature of your classroom, one of the things that creates a climate for poetry. Reading to pupils will help spark their own thoughts into being, and soon some will be showing you their creations. As children begin to become accustomed to being poets themselves, they will approach the new poets they read more or less as equals and as fellow craftsmen.

In working with poetry, it is a good idea to keep reminding pupils that poems do not have to rhyme. Help pupils to understand that you are much more interested in the beauty and originality of their poems than you are in their ability to find rhyming words. Hughes Mearns[16] properly condemns teachers whose insistence on rhyme leads children to produce inanities such as this:

There was once a cat
Who feared a rat
Who lived in a mat.
They had a spat,
And that was the end of the cat.
Poor cat!

In *Wishes, Lies and Dreams,* Kenneth Koch[17] suggests a number of good ways of getting children started writing poetry liberated from rhyme. The group poems he describes, in which each child writes a line containing an arbitrary collection of things—a color, a city, a comic strip character, and so on—is a good way to demonstrate that the recurrence of similar elements is one way of ordering a poem. You will also want to read or reread some good unrhymed poems. Merriam's book, *It Doesn't Always Have to Rhyme,* is good for this purpose because it makes the point directly. *Reflections on a Gift of Watermelon Pickle* contains some fine unrhymed poems. They include "Arithmetic" by Carl Sandburg, "This Is Just to Say" by William Carlos Williams, and "Unfolded Bud" by Naoshi Koriyama.

Ideas for Poetry

A good idea for a poem should be one that pupils are interested in and one that gives them an opportunity to make fresh observations of their own. In helping pupils recognize a good idea for a poem, you might try rereading John Moffitt's[18] "To Look at Any Thing" (Chapter 4, p. 1), a poem that stresses the importance of looking long and trying to see into the things you observe. Encourage children to get in the habit of carrying a notebook or pad and pencil around with them so that they can jot down a word or idea when it comes to them. (A poem that attests to the value of jotting ideas down as they come to you is "Gone Forever" by Barriss Mills.[19] In the poem the poet, while shaving, suddenly thinks of a word he has been looking for but, because he has nothing with which to write, the word escapes and is never recaptured. The notebooks children keep should be private; you should not have them turn them in from time to time as though they were school assignments. But you will want to mention them to pupils in conferences and on other suitable occasions and encourage them to share their ideas with you if they want to.

Susan Pulsifer[20] suggests that pupils be given uninterrupted time in school for creative expression. This time may be spent in having the students add ideas to their notebooks. It is also important to remember to provide time for them so that they can just think and talk to themselves.

As pupils start writing poems on their own, you may wish to have them try some of the suggestions that Donald Wolfe[21] makes in *Language Arts and Life Patterns*. One such suggestion is that children be asked to write about one moment in time. (An example of such a poem, "Snow Toward Evening,"[22] is included in Wolfe's book.) Wolfe recommends that children do not try for rhyme and that they include in each line color and sound words and, if possible, a comparison. The recommendation requesting specific content in each line is similar to the advice of Koch in *Wishes, Lies and Dreams*, mentioned previously.

Sharing Poetry

Just as children enjoy hearing and reading children's poetry that appears in books such as *Miracles*, they will enjoy the poems written by their classmates. Take as much time as you can for reading and discussing the poetry your children write. Look especially for the word or comparison or the fine-sounding line that you can single out for praise in each poem. Writing a poem in which every line is equally good is too much to expect of children. But every child can produce some beautiful phrases and comparisons. Calling attention to these provides encouragement and helps young poets to form ideas of what they do best.

Incidentally, a common result of having children share their poems is that a word or comparison used successfully by one pupil will be picked up and used by one or two others in later poems. There is no reason to discourage this practice. Borrowing a word or figure of speech is a compliment to the original poet and a sign that the borrower recognizes its effectiveness. You may want to point out that modern poets such as T.S. Eliot and Ezra Pound often borrowed words and phrases from other poets to suit their own purposes.

3. FIGURATIVE LANGUAGE

Because good similes and metaphors provide such a good means for children to express their own view of the world around them and because these figures of speech are of central importance in all poetry, this would be a good time to focus children's attention on them. In addition to working with and composing these figures of speech, you will also want to help them learn to recognize and avoid worn-out figures of speech, or clichés.

Alex Osborn,[23] in talking about writing as a creative exercise, mentions the fact that making up figures of speech is an excellent creative exercise. During this time, children will have many opportunities to create their own figures of speech. Osborn suggests having students define words by figures of speech. For example, Dorothy Parker defined "superficiality" as "running the gamut from a to b." (She used this line to describe a performance given by Katharine Hepburn.)

Children can be made aware that they use figures of speech in their everyday talk. Northrop Frye[24] explains that if someone describes a talk or a piece of writing as dry and dull, he or she is using figures of speech that associate the talk or writing with bread and breadknives.

The following poem, "Comparisons," can be duplicated for children to see and hear. The poem includes many overly familiar similes.

As wet as a fish—as dry as a bone;
As live as a bird—as dead as a stone;
As plump as a partridge—as poor as a rat;
As strong as a horse—as weak as a cat;
As hard as a flint—as soft as a mole;
As white as a lily—as black as a coal;
As plain as a staff—as rough as a bear;

As light as a drum—as free as the air;
As heavy as lead—as light as a feather;
As hot as an oven—as cold as a frog;
As gay as a lark—as sick as a dog;
As savage as tigers—as mild as a dove;
As blind as a bat—as deaf as a post;
As cool as a cucumber—as warm as toast;
As flat as a flounder—as sharp as a ball;
As blunt as a hammer—as sharp as an owl;
As brittle as glass—as tough as gristle;
As neat as a pin—as clean as a whistle;
As red as a rose—as square as a box;
As bold as a thief—as sly as a fox.
    —Anonymous

After hearing this poem, children can be told that when a person uses an expression that has been used time and time again, it is called a cliché. Clichés are worn-out, exhausted comparisons that add little, if anything to a person's speaking or writing. Ask students whether any of the expressions heard in "Comparisons" sound familiar to them. Most pupils will have heard many of them. Suggest that individuals work together on the poem "Comparisons," changing all the tired expressions to bright new ones. You might print the poem on the board, leaving blank spaces to be filled in by the children. Some may want to try to do the whole poem over by themselves after the group venture.

In explaining what a cliché is, you can read Eve Merriam's[25] poem on that very topic. She tells the reader that clichés are what people use when they are too lazy to say what they mean in any other way. She exhorts her readers to think whether toast is the warmest thing that they know and whether a mouse is the quietest thing that they know. Merriam includes excellent examples of fresh similes. After hearing this poem, the children can work with the clichés Merriam refers to and think of different ways of saying something is warm, quiet, slow, and quick. Each child's imagination will be stirred by this activity. You need not stop with the examples Merriam uses, but may continue with other familiar clichés. The teacher should remind the children to jot down on a piece of paper during the day or night any similes that occur to them. Perhaps the children together could compose a quatrain and a couplet, using all fresh similes. The teacher might provide a poem such as the following one as a stimulus:

Round as a yawn,
Warm as a squeeze,
High as a dream,
Loud as a sneeze.

Big as an ink blot on a white dress,
Impossible as your room is when it's a mess.

Marlene Glaus[26] lists some old clichés and suggests discussing with the children what the similes mean. In asking various children the meanings of their expressions, some of the children Glaus worked with responded with lovely new similes. For example, when Patty was asked what it meant to feel as happy as a lark, she responded that it meant that she felt like a new penny.

Children can listen to the selection "Stones" on Side 4, Band 1 of the record, *Music for Children*.[27] This is a recording of one of Christina Rossetti's[28] poems in which she compares different gems to different things. Both similes and metaphors are used. Another selection from this record, which uses and plays with the sounds of four figures of speech, is "Ensembles" (Exercise 2 on Band 3). After being exposed to many figures of speech in poems, children might enjoy choosing some to say rhythmically on a tape recorder, as the children on the *Music for Children* record did.

A book similar to Merriam's poem, "A Cliché," is Karla Kuskin's[29] *Square as a House*. It is excellent because it involves children greatly when they read it. Kuskin continually asks questions of the reader such as "If you could be square would you be a . . .?" All of her questions stimulate children to think what they would be as soft as, as loud as, as red as, as small as, and so forth. Kuskin gives fine suggested answers but, of course, pupils can come up with their own. They might even write their own "Square as a House" book, giving one or more original similes for each of the stimulus words Kuskin provides.

Similes

Write some of the similes you have been working with on the board and ask pupils what is the same about them. Elicit the response that similes compare one thing to another and that they use the words "like" or "as." You may wish to point out in discussing similes (and again in discussing metaphors) that the things compared do not have to be alike in all respects. These comparisons focus on one feature that the writer or speaker wants to emphasize. Thus, saying a car sped "as fast as a bullet" compares the car and the bullet in only one respect—speed. If you want to provide additional practice in using similes, you might try with your class the activity Koch[30] describes in *Wishes, Lies and Dreams*.

R. E. Myers and E. Paul Torrance[31] in their workbooks, *Invitations to Speaking and Writing Creatively* and *Invitations to Thinking and Doing*, offer some exercises for working with similes that you might want to try. Nina Willis Walter,[32] in her book *Let Them Write Poetry*, also includes some fine exercises for working with similes. In addition, Walter presents many fine writings of children that have resulted from working with similes. These could be read to the class.

Metaphors

Metaphors are a little harder for children to understand than similes, although after they have the idea they will make very effective use of them. The best way to introduce metaphors is probably to put a simile on the board that can readily be turned into a metaphor. For instance, you might write, "a star is like a hole in the sky," and then, crossing out "like," ask pupils to imagine that a star "is" a hole in the sky. Point out that one of the good things about a metaphor is that you can keep it going. For example, if you think of a star as being a hole in the sky, what makes it so bright? What might fall or pass through it? How did the sky get holes? Repeat this process several times until children get the idea.

Later, you will want to explain that a metaphor doesn't always say that one thing is another. Sometimes the comparison is implied. For instance, in "the ship plowed the sea," the ship is being compared to a plow and the sea to a field. You might follow this discussion up by reading "Metaphor" by Eve Merriam,[33] where the poet compares morning to a sheet of fresh paper.

Children may be asked to look for similes and metaphors in their reading, or you may wish to read one or more selections that provide good examples. One good possibility is *A Bear Before Breakfast* by Eth Clifford,[34] which demonstrates to children how commonly figures of speech are used in the everyday world. Another story that makes imaginative use of common figures of speech is Shan Ellentuck's[35] *Did You See What I Said?* One more possibility that you might try is Bernice Kohn's[36] *One Day It Rained Cats and Dogs*. This is a very easy book to read. Kohn presents a figure of speech on every page and then supplies a literal illustration for each. Needless to say, the pictures are bound to provide chuckles for everyone. The picture for "The choir sang off key" shows a maestro standing on the end of a key conducting a choir. Discuss with your pupils what each figure of speech really means. Children can decide whether their explanations of the figures of speech are more picturesque than the actual figures of speech themselves.

Modern Monsters

A good follow-up for the discussion of similes and metaphors might involve thinking of "modern monsters." Begin by reading some poems in which a modern object is compared to a monster. For example, in the poetry section of *The Arbuthnot Anthology of Children's Literature*, Rowena Bennett[37] compares a train to a dragon in a poem called "A Modern Dragon." The entire poem is a metaphor. In the same source, William Jay Smith[38] in his poem "The Toaster," compares a toaster to a dragon. Once more the figure of speech that is used is a metaphor.

In *Reflections on a Gift of Watermelon Pickle,* compiled by Stephen Dunning, Edward Lueders, and Hugh Smith, there is a poem called "The Garden Hose" by Beatrice Janosco,[39] in which the author compares a garden hose to a serpent. Also, there is a poem by Charles Malam[40] in which a steam shovel is compared to a dinosaur. Another modern monster, "Radiator Lions," was created by Dorothy Aldis.[41]

After reading enough selections to get the children thinking about modern monsters, have them imagine some new ones of their own. If some children have problems thinking of any, you might suggest a vacuum cleaner, garbage disposal unit, automatic carwash, derrick, or some other familiar machine that has monster possibilities. Suggest that pupils write about their modern monster.

4. WORKING WITH VERSE FORMS

Your main objective in working with poetry should be that children enjoy writing poems and that they are able to express themselves freely and naturally in verse. Unless there is some content, form matters little. However, you will not want to neglect form altogether, particularly since the strictures of a given form, if not insisted on too rigorously, can be a valuable discipline for the young poet. Several forms that your children may enjoy experimenting with are suggested in this section.

Haiku

Haiku are unrhymed poems that follow a strict syllabic pattern. You will want to begin by reading enough examples to give pupils the feeling for this new form. Two good sources are *Cricket Songs,* translated by Harry Behn[42] and *The Moment of Wonder,* edited by Richard Lewis.[43] In another source, *Cavalcade of Poems,* edited by George Bennett and Paul Molloy,[44] the section devoted to haiku is subtitled "Poems of Observation." Haiku can help teach children to be observant and to notice and react to beauty in everyday things. In talking about them, you might remind pupils of Moffitt's "To Look at Any Thing" again.

When pupils have been exposed to a number of examples of haiku, encourage them to generalize about the content and form of these poems. They will readily see that haiku typically deal with an image from nature that causes the poet to reflect for a moment. Each involves a season of the year.

Each embodies a delicate, beautiful thought. As for the form, pupils can discover for themselves that the first line regularly has five syllables, the second seven, and the third five.

It is a good idea to work with children as a class in composing the first few haiku. Together you can agree on a beautiful thought concerning things such as trees, leaves, fog, frost, the sun, the moon, a bird, or a flower. Call the pupils' attention to the total number of seventeen syllables available and their distribution by lines—five, seven, five. Some pupils may be a little hazy about what syllables are; if so, you can review briefly here. (Suggestions about teaching syllabication are included in Chapter 8.) After you have worked through several haiku together, let your pupils try their hands at individual poems. Encourage children to try for the right number of syllables in each line, but allow them to be a little irregular if necessary in expressing their thought. Richard Lewis[45] remarks in his foreward to *The Moment of Wonder* that in translating haiku from Japanese to English, it is sometimes impossible to do it in seventeen syllables. The problem of translating an existing poem adds greatly to the problem of observing the syllable count. But Lewis' observation indicates that slightly irregular haiku are acceptable even to an expert. So you need not worry if your pupils come up with an occasional long or short line.

A related form with which your pupils may enjoy experimenting is the tanka, a variant on haiku with two extra lines of seven syllables each. That makes five, seven, five, seven, seven—or thirty-one syllables. Because there is more room in it, a tanka allows more of a story to be told and does not require as much delicacy as a haiku.

Couplets

Even though you have convinced your pupils that a poem does not have to rhyme, they will have read and heard a lot of rhymed poetry and will enjoy trying some rhymes of their own. Couplets offer a simple and undemanding starting point.

A good poem for introducing couplets is Eve Merriam's[46] "Couplet Countdown," in which the poet shows what a couplet is and how it works.

As with the haiku, a good way of getting children started on couplets is by doing some together, with you recording them on the board. There are several approaches you can use to get their ideas flowing. You could try the advertising jingle device of giving a line and having children come up with a rhyming line:

A lovely way to spend a day

You could start both lines in a way that suggests comparison or contrast.

Grownups _____

Children _____

Or you could provide the rhyming words and have children complete the rest of the lines.

_____day

_____play

Another good way of getting children started on writing couplets is to read poems that will determine the content of the couplets. One such possibility is "Choosing," by Eleanor Farjeon,[47] which simply asks four times whether the reader would rather have one thing or another. Children can use the same format to ask other choosing questions. David McCord's[48] poem "Crows" is also composed of couplets and uses repetition as an organizing device. After reading this poem, you might ask pupils to volunteer second lines for beginnings such as:

I like to see

_____

I like to touch

_____

I like to hear

_____

I like to pretend

_____

Quatrains

The quatrain is a familiar form, and examples for use in introducing it are easy to find. Eve Merriam's[49] "Quatrain" is a convenient one because it explains what a quatrain is. Since the poet makes the point that all four lines do not have to rhyme, this poem makes a good model for children.

Some other good poems to use for this purpose are "The Hippopotamus" by Georgia Durston,[50] which makes entertaining use of made-up words like *squdgy* and *oozely*, Gelett Burgess'[51] "The Purple Cow," and Vachel Lindsay's[52] "The Little Turtle," all of which may be found in *The Arbuthnot Anthology of Children's Literature*. [Since "The Purple Cow" is a parody of

Emily Dickinson's "I Never Saw a Moor" (also included in Arbuthnot), you may want to read this poem first. Shel Silverstein, you may recall from reading Chapter 3, has written an amusing parody of "The Little Turtle" called "Not Me," which can be found in Geoffrey Summerfield's *Voices, The Second Book*, Rand McNally and Company, 1969.]

If you have read some or all of the animal poems described for children, you might suggest that they try a quatrain about a pet, a zoo animal, or an imaginary animal. You might remind them of their discussions about modern monsters (suggested in Section 3 of this chapter), one of which could make a good subject for a quatrain.

Limericks

Limericks are fun for children and, after gaining some experience with simpler poetic forms, this familiar one should present no great difficulties. Once again, the best way to introduce the form is to read some examples. The *Arrow Book of Funny Poems*[53] devotes ten pages to limericks. This section is introduced by a poem that explains what a limerick is, but you may wish to postpone reading it until children have had an opportunity to discover for themselves how a limerick is put together.

To help pupils discover the elements of limerick form, put some examples on the board or make copies for pupils to read. Here are three that you might use in this way.

There was a young man of Devizes
Whose ears were of different sizes:
    The one that was small
    Was of no use at all,
But the other won several prizes.

—Anonymous

There was a young fellow named Hall,
Who fell in the spring in the fall:
    'Twould have been a sad thing
    If he had died in the spring,
But he didn't—he did in the fall.

—Anonymous

A sleeper from the Amazon
Put on nighties of his gra'mazon—
    The reason that
    He was too fat
To get his own pajamazon.

—Anonymous

After children have heard and read a number of limericks, you should be able to elicit observations such as:

1. Limericks have funny subjects.
2. The first, second, and fifth lines have one rhyme and the third and fourth lines have a different rhyme.
3. The long lines (one, two, and five) have three strong beats and the short lines have two.

You may want to point out that here it is strong beats that matter, not the number of syllables, as was the case with haiku. A few limericks will be enough to familiarize the class with the characteristic lilt of a limerick, and then even the counting of accented syllables will be unnecessary. After your discussion of what makes a limerick, read the limerick poem from the *Arrow Book of Funny Poems,* which sums up the features nicely.

As with the other forms, you may want to try a limerick in class together before letting pupils write their own.

A good follow-up to limerick writing—or an accompaniment to it—is a reading of Scott Corbett's *The Limerick Trick,*[54] the story of Kerby Marshall, who wants very badly to win a bicycle that is the first prize in a poetry contest. He seeks help from his strange friend Mrs. Graymalkin, who tells him what to do. He follows her advice and succeeds in writing a good poem, but he finds that there are times when he can speak only in limericks. Later, he gets over speaking in limericks only to start speaking in couplets. Corbett's book contains another description of limerick form and gives some good examples of internal rhyme, a common feature of this form. Since Corbett does not always put Kerby's poems in conventional limerick or couplet form, you may want to have pupils write some of them out in the usual way.

5. PUBLISHING THE POETRY

Eve Merriam's[55] point in "Mona Lisa," that a poem needs a reader, applies to the poems your children produce. You may suggest that pupils make booklets of their own poems, that the class compile an anthology, or that they combine these projects. Whichever activity you decide on will provide a good reason for having pupils make clean, neat copies of the poems to be included. It is better not to worry children about capitalizing first lines, spelling, and punctuation while they are writing their poems, but these matters become important when they set out to make their poems readable and presentable to other readers.

You can handle the capitalization of first lines inductively by copying some poems on the board (or passing out ditto copies) and asking what is alike about the beginning of each line. To call attention to punctuation at the end of a line, you might also ask if each line is capitalized because it begins a new sentence. Pupils will readily see that this is not always the case.

To illustrate the possibilities for punctuation at the end of a line, you can put some examples on the board in which a comma, period (or other end mark), or no mark at all is appropriate. Lead pupils to associate the idea of a short pause, long pause, or no pause with the various choices. To make the point, you will have to give the line that follows the one you want to talk about.

6. AFTERWORD

One reason for starting to work with poetry early was suggested at the beginning of this chapter: children are good at it and enjoy it. Mauree Applegate and others have offered abundant proof that children are natural and spontaneous poets; and Applegate[56] goes on to say that all too often adults "allow children to forget a language so natural to them."

One last thought from John Ciardi's[57] How Does a Poem Mean? is that the way for anyone to develop a poetic sense is to use it. The implications to teachers are clear enough.

Helps

Arnstein, Flora J., *Children Write Poetry: A Creative Approach,* New York: Dover Publications, Inc., 1967. Mrs. Arnstein describes the approaches she has used with children to get them to put down their poetic thoughts. The paperback is filled with helpful ideas and abounds with the fine writings of children.

Brooks, Cleanth, and Warren, Robert Penn, *Understanding Poetry,* New York: Holt, Rinehart and Winston, 1960. This is an adult book meant to help individuals who want a deeper insight into the workings of a poem. Poems, explanations, and exercises intermingle throughout the entire book. The last part of the book contains a glossary of poetic terms.

Carlson, Ruth Kearney, *Writing Aids through the Grades,* New York: Teachers College Press, Teachers College, Columbia University, 1970.

Ciardi, John, *How Does a Poem Mean?,* Boston: Houghton Mifflin Company, 1959. Another professional book for adults that can help to give them a richer understanding of the inner workings of a poem.

Haviland, Virginia, and Smith, William Jay, compilers, *Children and Poetry: A Selective, Annotated Bibliography,* Washington, D. C.: Superintendent of Documents, U. S. Government Printing Office, 1969. This inexpensive paperback is well worth looking at. The annotations are not one line say-nothings, but give a lot of information about the sources listed. In many cases, tasty chunks of poems are included that come from the various books that are discussed. Because it is a small volume, naturally, there are many fine volumes of poetry that are not cited in this book. Nevertheless, *Children and Poetry* is a fine resource tool for teachers.

Hawley, Robert C., Simon, Sidney B., and Britton, James, *Composition for Personal Growth: Values Clarification through Writing,* New York: Hart Publishing Company, Inc., 1973.

Henderson, Harold G., *An Introduction to Haiku,* New York: Doubleday and Company, Inc., 1958.

Hopkins, Lee Bennett, *Pass the Poetry, Please!,* New York: Citation Press, 1972. Mr. Hopkins includes in this paperback many fine ideas that should serve as battery chargers for the ideas of budding young poets and their teachers. There is a wealth of information given about the lives of contemporary poets who write for today's children. Countless poetry sources are referred to and discussed.

Lewis, Richard, editor, pictures by Ezra Jack Keats, produced by Morton Schindel, *In a Spring Garden,* Weston, Conn.: Weston Woods. "A six minute iconographic motion picture. Price: color, $90." *In a Spring Garden* can be rented from Weston Woods for $5. A filmstrip and recording are also available.

McCord, David, drawings by Henry B. Kane, *Take Sky,* Boston: Little, Brown and Company, 1962. McCord plays around with words continually in this volume. Additionally, a section that might intrigue and amuse both pupils and their teachers is the section entitled *"Write Me a Verse,"* pp. 49–64. On these pages, McCord explains, in verse form, how to write couplets, quatrains, limericks, and triolets. McCord, in the guise of "Professor Brown," invites his listeners to try some of these rhyme schemes after he has given several examples of each. Children should enjoy listening and working with his exercises.

McCord, David, drawings by Henry B. Kane, *For Me to Say,* Boston: Little, Brown and Company, 1970. Like *Take Sky,* McCord continues in this book to instruct his audience on how to create verse forms. In the last segment of this book, "Write Me Another Verse," he proceeds in verse form to give examples of tercets, villanelles, ballades, clerihews, cinquains, and haiku. Again, he issues invitations to his readers or listeners to try to attempt some of these forms for themselves.

MacKinlay, Eileen, *The Shared Experience,* London: Methuen and Company, Ltd., 1972. The writings of college students training to be teachers in "infant and junior schools" and the writings of pupils are shared in this paperback. Many fine suggestions for teachers and their pupils to try.

Mearns, Hughes, *Creative Power: The Education of Youth in the Creative Arts,* New York: Dover Publications, Inc., 1958. Although this book was first published in 1929, one would have to look at the copyright date to believe it. It is as fresh as tomorrow. Mearns's sensitivity and original ideas should inspire all teachers. I would put it on a *must* list for reading. It is a beautiful book filled with the thoughts of a creative teacher and the thoughts of the pupils and teachers whose lives he has touched.

Norris, Ruby Lee, and Sange, Sally Harris, editors, *A Borrower Be: An Interchange of Culture in the Classroom,* Richmond, Va.: Humanities Center, 1975. See particularly pp. 25–85.

Purves, Alan C., editor, *How Porcupines Make Love: Notes on a Response-Centered Curriculum,* Lexington, Mass.: Xerox Corporation, 1972.

Rubin, Peter, *The Day Is Two Feet Long,* Weston, Conn.: Weston Woods. "An eight minute live action color film, $120 in color." This film can be rented for $5.

Society for Visual Education, Inc., *Poetry by and for Kids,* Chicago, Ill., 1976. A kit that contains seven copies of four separate paperbacks, a filmstrip, a cassette, blank cards for children to write their own ideas on (erasable), and a box of special crayons. Highly recommended to spur children's thoughts into action.

Simpson, Louis, *An Introduction to Poetry,* New York: St. Martin's Press, 1967. For those teachers who might want a deeper understanding of what goes into making a poem, pp. 1–58 of this paperback delve deeply into poetic techniques and devices. The middle section of the book consists of an anthology (not for children, for adults). The last part of the paperback is a glossary of poetic terms.

Wilson, Smokey, *Struggles with Bears: Experience in Writing,* San Francisco: Canfield Press, 1973.

Wolsch, Robert A., *Poetic Composition through the Grades: A Language Sensitivity Program,* New York: Teachers College Press, Teachers College, Columbia University, 1970.

Literary Suggestions to Encourage Children to Become Poets

Baron, Virginia Olsen, editor, illustrated by Yasuhide Kobashi, *The Seasons of Time,* New York: The Dial Press, Inc., 1968.

Cassedy, Sylvia, and Kunihiro, Svetake, translators, illustrated by Vo-Dinh, *Birds, Frogs, and Moonlight,* New York: Doubleday and Company, Inc., 1967.

Caudill, Rebecca, illustrated by Ellen Raskin, *Come Along!,* New York: Holt, Rinehart and Winston, 1969.

Fukuda, Hanako, illustrated by Lydia Cooley, *Wind in My Hand,* California: Golden Gate Junior Books, 1970.

Issa, Yayu, Kikaku, pictures by Talivaldis Stubis, *Don't Tell the Scarecrow,* New York: Scholastic Book Services, 1969.

Lewis, Richard, editor, pictures by Ezra Jack Keats, *In a Spring Garden,* New York: The Dial Press, 1965.

Lewis, Richard, editor, photographs by Helen Buttfield, *The Way of Silence: The Prose and Poetry of Basho,* New York: The Dial Press, 1970.

11 More to Grow On: An Olio of Ideas for Speaking, Writing and Imagining

"I'm seven and a half, exactly."

"You needn't say 'exactly,' the Queen remarked. "I can believe it without that. Now I'll give *you* something to believe. I'm just one hundred and one, five months and a day."'

"I ca'n't believe *that* !

"Ca'n't" you?" the Queen said in a pitying tone. "Try again: draw a long breath, and shut your eyes."

Alice laughed. "There's no use trying," she said: "one *ca'n't* believe impossible things."

"I daresay you haven't had much practice," said the queen. "When I was your age, I always did it for half-an-hour a day. Why, sometimes I've believed as many as six impossible things before breakfast."

—Lewis Carroll

The suggestions in this chapter are intended to develop each child's imagination and to provide springboards into speaking and writing. The general approach will be familiar by now; stories or poems to which children can respond creatively are suggested. Some of the ideas are new ones, while others develop suggestions made in earlier chapters. Unlike the suggestions made in earlier chapters, however, those made here are not related to a particular aspect of language arts instruction; instead, they are grouped according to a particular kind of stimulus for engaging the child's imagination. Although a specific kind of outcome is usually suggested—a poem or a story, for instance—it will be clear that most of the suggestions made can equally well stimulate other kinds of creative activity. Use the ideas in this chapter in the way that seems best for your class on a particular day.

1. MYTHS

Northrop Frye[1] recommends that children be introduced early to classical myths because they are beautiful and imaginative and because they are alluded to in so many other literary works. (Children who have read some of the Greek myths will gain insights into the names of characters in *Homer Price* books, to mention only one instance.) A good book for introducing pupils to Greek myths is *Hercules and Other Tales from the Greek Myths* by Olivia Coolidge.[2] Another excellent resource is the paperback collection *Gods and Heroes: Myths and Epics of Ancient Greece* compiled by Gustav Schwab.[3] You will find the Schwab book a good one for reading (or, in some cases, retelling) myths to your children. A third possibility, which is suitable for older children, is Nathaniel Hawthorne's[4] *Tanglewood Tales*.

Stories as rich in human interest as the Greek myths can stimulate your pupils to many different kinds of creative activity. They may wish to write new myths of their own involving some of the characters they have been reading about, or they may follow the ancient Greek dramatists' example by making plays out of the stories. *The Wonderful World of J. Wesley Smith*[5] includes cartoons about Ulysses and Procrustes that may induce some of your pupils to try creating their own cartoons on mythological subjects. A related idea is to put such captions as the following ones on the board after children have been exposed to a number of myths:

Ariadne, you know I don't like it when there are strings attached to things.

It's been a long, hard trip. Surely Father will understand why our sails are so dirty.

I've always loved opening boxes.

Ask children who might have made each of these remarks; then suggest that they draw illustrations to go with each.

You might also explore the influence of Greek myths on our language by listing words and expressions like those below on the board and asking pupils to investigate their origins. Since the children may be unacquainted with some, it will be a good idea to use each item in a sentence.

tantalize	Achilles' heel
like a Trojan	ambrosia

Children might also investigate the symbolic use to which the names and images of the following gods and goddesses are put in the modern world:

Mercury, Pegasus, Apollo, and Athena. The following books will provide useful references for such activities and will suggest other interesting words and names to explore:

1. *Words from the Myths* by Isaac Asimov.[6]
2. *People Words* by Bill Severn.[7]

A good follow-up activity to your reading of Greek myths would be a display of advertisements clipped from newspapers and magazines, each of which associates a modern product with a god or goddess: Mercury cars, Venus pencils, Ajax cleaning powder, and so on.

Ann T. White's *The Golden Treasury of Myths and Legends*[8] is another good source for Greek myths, and it includes Norse myths as well. If you wish to encourage your pupils to investigate Norse myths further, you might try *Norse Gods and Giants* by the D'Aulaires.[9] If you work with Norse as well as Greek myths, a good topic for writing or discussion would be to have children compare a Greek god and the Norse counterpart. If pupils select a variety of figures, the resulting discussion should provide some insights into the differing attitudes and beliefs of these peoples.

2. POURQUOI STORIES

Pourquoi (why) stories bring to mind Kipling and animal stories such as "Why the Bear Is Stumpy-Tailed." But it is useful to include in this category many other myths and legends that purport to explain how something got to be the way it is. Children will readily see how the curiosity of primitive people led them to create these explanations, and they are quite likely to be inspired to write or tell their own "why" and "how" stories. Some pourquoi and origin stories you may want to try out on your class are:

1. *The Moon Is a Crystal Ball* by Natalia Belting.[10] A collection of legends, most of which will be unfamiliar to pupils, about the moon, stars, and sun gathered from all corners of the earth.
2. *Just So Stories* by Rudyard Kipling.[11] You might read a few of the stories, such as "How the Whale Got His Throat," and "How the Leopard Got His Spots."
3. *Popular Tales from the Norse* by George W. Dasent.[12] Includes "Why the Bear Is Stumpy-Tailed" and other pourquoi stories.

In addition to the sources for Greek myths mentioned in the previous section, you will find Sally Benson's *Stories of the Gods and Heroes*[13] a good source for creation myths. Children will be fascinated also by stories told by American Indians to explain the origins of things. One good source for such stories is *Tales of the North American Indians*[14] by Stith Thompson.

A contemporary pourquoi story is William Du Bois' book, *Lion.*[15] This story tells how all animals came to be and how they got their names and sounds. In particular this book tells how the lion came to be exactly as he is in the "Planets of the Universe." It turns out that an artist named Foreman invented the lion in the drawing room of The Animal Factory, a palace that existed long, long ago way up in the sky.

Le Grand has written some modern pourquoi stories that are bound to get children writing their own "why" stories. Among the tales Le Grand has written are *The Amazing Adventures of Archie and the First Hot Dog,*[16] *Cap'n Dow and the Hole in the Doughnut.*[17] "Why Cowboys Sing in Texas,"[18] and *How Baseball Began in Brooklyn.*[19] All of these stories have the characteristics of tall tales in them, and all are written with a light touch. *The Amazing Adventures of Archie and the First Hot Dog* not only tells the origin of the hot dog but also the beginning of the hot dog roll, and the reason why people put mustard and relish on their hot dogs. The explanation for the holes in doughnuts is that Cap'n Dow found that they were much more manageable that way for sailors, especially when they needed two hands to steer with during a storm.

After hearing so many origin stories, children might try writing stories such as "The First Stove," "The First Permanent," "The First Frown," "The First Smile," "The First Laugh," "The First Rainbow," "The First Pet," "Why the Sky Is Blue," "Why Dogs Chase Cats," or "Why Cats Chase Mice." One sixth-grade boy's story was inspired by the chapter "The Doughnuts" in *Homer Price.*

The Discovery of Doughnuts

The most interesting thing about the discovery of doughnuts is that they were never discovered at all! This is how it happened:

Once upon a time, there was a "hole" manufacturer whose name was Angelo Apice. Angelo manufactured holes of every size, shape, and depth. He manufactured gopher holes and sold them three for $1. He also sold bullet holes, shell holes, moth holes, and well holes. He even manufactured cavities for people's teeth!

After a while business got bad and Angelo found himself in a big hole! Things got worse and Apice had no money. Soon, Angelo's clothes were full of . . . (You guessed it! Holes).

One day Angelo got an idea. He thought that he could sell holes if he wrapped something around them! Meanwhile, back at the house, Mrs. Apice was busy making Italian breadsticks when Angelo rushed in and grabbed the breadsticks. An hour later after finally getting the breadsticks around the holes, "Eureka!" screamed Angelo. "I have just created a doughnut!"

Angelo's product was very successful. People came from far and wide to test the doughnuts. Angelo also sold coffee so that they would have something to dunk their doughnuts in.

Today, doughnuts are used for such things as ringtoss games and for toy automobiles, but most of all doughnuts are used to keep us happy.

    —Gary

In reading other literary materials, children could be inspired to write their own stories for origins of creatures, objects, or phenomena. As one other example, children might read J.M. Barrie's play *Peter Pan*,[20] and become intrigued by Barrie's explanation in Act I of how fairies are born and why they die. From reading this section they could be led to tell or write their own stories about why magical creatures such as fairies exist.

In Le Grand's story, "Why Cowboys Sing in Texas," an explanation is offered for the expression, "Yippee yi, yippee yay—yippie." In *How Baseball Began in Brooklyn,* Le Grand traces the beginning of baseball to the time when the Indians and some pioneers, the Denboom family, lived in Cow Cove—where Brooklyn is today. What started out looking very much like a battle between the Denboom boys and some young Indians evolved into the game of baseball.

A wonderfully imaginative book that tells how man first may have come to conquer horses is Pers Crowell's[21] *First to Ride.* It is suggested that this book be read in its entirety to intermediate-grade children because it is so well written and exciting. After reading it, you and your pupils might discuss what other first happenings you have wondered about. Perhaps some may wonder how man first came to use fire, tools, arms, or to build a shelter for himself. They might be stimulated to tell or write an imaginative story of how one of these things came to be. A good way of following up would be to read the book *The First Men in the World* by Anne White[22] to your children. This is a beautifully written book that traces man's progress from the very earliest beginnings. After reading it, you and your pupils will marvel at man's imagination, ingenuity, and perseverance. The book is inspiring, one that will make the reader proud to be human. The book ends with the great beginning for man—agriculture.

3. FOLK TALES

Folk tales are as old as language. Most of them were passed down from one generation of storytellers to the next in continuous oral tradition and were not recorded until late in the eighteenth century. The survival of a story over centuries is a good indication of its enduring interest; and children today find folk tales just as fresh and intriguing as did children hundreds of years ago.

Inexpensive collections of folk tales are in abundant supply. Some good possibilities for starting out are:

1. *Grimms' Fairy Tales* by Kramer.[23]
2. *Tales from the Red Fairy Book* by Lang.[24]
3. *The Crimson Fairy Book* by Lang.[25]
4. *Tales from the Green Fairy Book* by Lang.[26]

5. *The Twelve Dancing Princesses and Other Fairy Tales* by David and David[27] (includes some contemporary fairy tales as well as traditional ones).

Just as pourquoi stories provide insights into the ways that primitive peoples tried to understand the world around them, folk tales provide insights into the way people thought life should be lived. Because the attitudes toward life vary in interesting ways from one country to another, folk tales from other places provide fascinating glimpses into other cultures. Children will also be interested to see the recurrence in one nation's folklore after another of common themes such as the Cinderella story, spells and magic sleep, and reward for kindness to animals. An additional resource that you may find useful are the book lists and teaching units available through the Information Center on Children's Cultures, a service of the United States Committee for UNICEF (321 East 38th Street, New York, N. Y. 10016).

Encouraging children to read independently in collections is a natural way of getting children to become storytellers, as they share tales they have discovered with their classmates. An idea you might try is suggested in Ruth French's article "Working the Vineyard," which is included in *Children, Books, and Reading*.[28] She describes a storyteller in West Africa who wears a story hat, from the brim of which dangle many interesting objects. A person who wants to hear a story chooses one of the objects and the storyteller tells a tale about it. Your pupils could be encouraged to make story hats or to bring to class objects or pictures of objects featured in the stories they have to tell.

In the discussions following the storytelling, you will want to lead pupils to generalize about some of the elements common to folk tales. Besides the recurring themes mentioned earlier, you might talk about such characteristics as these:

1. Magical characters.
2. Three wishes (and the use of three generally—tasks, brothers, sisters, etc.).
3. A necessary journey.
4. Tests to win a princess.
5. The hero who is thought to be foolish.
6. The use of disguises.
7. The use of repetition.
8. The use of riddles.

Children will be interested in using one or more of these common elements to write folk tales of their own.

Modern Tales of Magic and Fantasy

Working with folk tales can lead children into reading modern tales of magic and fantasy. Three excellent books that can be introduced to children for this purpose are C.S. Lewis' *The Lion, the Witch, and the Wardrobe*,[29] Edward Eager's *Half-Magic*,[30] and Mary Norton's *The Magic Bed-Knob*.[31] Of course, there are many wonderful modern stories of fantasy, but these three are mentioned because they are very apt to stimulate children to write more adventures about the main characters.

Perhaps your might decide to read Lewis' book in its entirety to your students. The story tells about four children who go to live in a professor's house during the period that London was being bombarded with air raids. In the spare room of the professor's house the children discover a magical wardrobe that, when entered, takes them into the world of Narnia, where they have marvelous adventures. The other two books might be introduced to the children through tantalizing excerpts. Eager's selection appears in the *Anthology of Children's Literature* by Edna Johnson, Evelyn Sickels, and Frances Sayers. The excerpt presented tells how four children find a magical charm that can grant only half of every wish. The children quickly solve the problem by wishing twice for everything they want. Each child takes a turn for his wish. After reading this excerpt, which tells about the children's adventures when they enter the world of King Arthur, you could suggest to the children that they pretend that they own the magical charm and write what they would wish for. *The Magic Bed-Knob* by Mary Norton, who is also the author of the books about the *Borrowers,* describes the deal that three children make with Miss Price. It seems that the children suspect Miss Price of being a witch and, indeed, she is studying to be one. The children bargain with her and swear that they will not tell anyone her secret if she gives them something magical. If they tell the truth about her, then they will have to forfeit the magical object. She cooperates by casting a spell on the brass bed-knob that Paul has with him. The brass bed-knob, when twisted about half-way on the bed post, will grant a wish. The bed will then take the children any place they want to go. After hearing this provocative selection, children can tell what would be the first wish they would make if they had such a wonderful bed-knob in their possession.

Riddles

Because solving a riddle is a characteristic task in so many folk tales, working with riddles makes a natural kind of follow-up activity for a folk tale unit. (Riddle activities are also suggested in Chapter 5.) Besides being entertaining in their own right, riddles call for the ability to recognize ways in which otherwise different things can be related and thus provide a good way of developing associational fluency. Some resources you can use to stimulate children to create their own riddles are:

1. *Would You Put Your Money in a Sand Bank?* by Harold Longman (n.p., Rand McNally and Company, 1968).
2. *The Monster Riddle Book* by Jane Sarnoff and Reynold Ruffins (New York: Charles Scribner & Sons, 1975).
3. "Rhyming Riddles," a poem by Mary Austin, and Mother Goose riddles—*The Arbuthnot Anthology of Children's Literature: Time for Poetry,* Fourth Edition (Glenview, Ill.: Scott, Foresman and Company, 1976, pp. 59–60).
4. "Winter Rune," a riddle poem by Elizabeth Coatsworth that offers no answer. (The answer is snow.) This selection can be found in *Sung Under the Silver Umbrella,* Literature Committee of the Association for Childhood Education International (New York: The Macmillan Company, 1935, p. 161).
5. The excerpt from Tolkien's book, *The Hobbit,* entitled, "Riddles in the Dark," appears in the *Anthology of Childrens's Literature* by Edna Johnson, Evelyn Sickels, and Frances Sayers (Boston: Houghton Mifflin and Company, 1959, pp. 645-652). (Eight riddles are posed. Perhaps different children could be called on who could, in turn, pretend to be the hero, Bilbo. If, after an arbitrary period of time, the child chosen cannot answer the riddle, then, as the story suggests, the Gollum will eat him or her. Horrors!)
6. *Pick-A-Riddle,* a paperback by Ennis Rees (New York: Scholastic Book Services, 1966).
7. *The Arrow Book of Jokes and Riddles,* a paperback illustrated by William Hogarth (New York: Scholastic Book Services, 1962).

Don Wolfe[32] created seven story riddles to be used with fourth graders, for which he includes no answers. Wolfe's personifying questions can produce results such as the following:

Q. What did the flag say to the wind?
A. If I weren't fifty, you wouldn't be blowing me around.
A. Stop it, you're making me see stars.

—Steven

Q. One day Sammy Apple fell to the ground. What did he say to the ground?
A. You're lucky I'm not a crab.

—Lorna

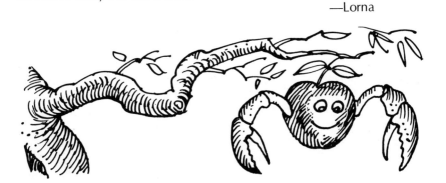

Q. What did the worm say to the robin as the robin was pulling him out of the ground?
A. Only a worm could squirm out of this.

Q. What did the refrigerator say to the ice cream inside?
A. You're full of the raspberry.
A. You're really cool.

Q. What did Sputnik say to a star?
A. How come I get stuck with these dizzy jobs?

—Donna

4. EXPANDING STORIES

The Lion, the Witch, and the Wardrobe, Half-Magic, and *The Magic Bed-Knob* suggest the possibility of having children write sequels or continuations that tell about the further adventures of the characters in these stories. Two other books that lend themselves to this kind of expansion are *The Saturdays* by Elizabeth Enright[33] and *Paddle-to-the-Sea* by C. H. Holling.[34]

The Saturdays explains how the Melendy children pool their allowances so that each Saturday one of them can use all of the accumulated money in a way that is enjoyable and worthwhile. Eight different Saturdays are included in the book. You might decide to present "Saturday One" to the children and then let those interested read about the other Saturdays. Later, children can imagine new Saturdays of their own.

Paddle-to-the-Sea tells how a little Indian boy's carving started out in the Nipigon country north of the Great Lakes and made its way to the Atlantic Ocean. Read this book to your class and ask the children to think of other adventures that Paddle-to-the-Sea might have encountered. The National Film Board of Canada distributes a beautiful film version of *Paddle-to-the-Sea*. The photography, music, and narration are all superb. From the first moment the film starts, everything is action. It is filled with suspense. The film adds some adventures of *Paddle-to-the-Sea* not mentioned in the book. The film will give children other ideas for experiences that Paddle-to-the-Sea might have had.

5. POEMS THAT LEAD TO WRITING

Poems, like stories, can excite children's own creative thoughts. For example, Marlene Glaus[35] obtained good results when she read Leland Jacobs' poem "First Things First"[36] to primary-grade children. In this brief poem, Jacobs mentions three things that come first and then tells what follows naturally. One of Glaus's pupils wrote "First a smile and then a friend."

Le Galliene's poem "I Meant to Do My Work Today"[37] will strike a responsive chord in most children, who may be interested in writing about things they should do but do not want to do. You might join in this activity yourself. Mauree Applegate includes in *Helping Children Write*[38] a delightful poem by a teacher who does not "want to teach today." Applegate points out that teachers cannot expect children to share their thoughts with them if they never share theirs.

Another poem that might lead to a flurry of writings is John Drinkwater's[39] "I Want to Know." This poem presents some of the puzzling questions children have. Some of the lines suggest the seeming irrationality of parents to their children.

After reading *Mary Poppins*[40] by Travers to children, you might read Ivy Eastwick's poem, "Where's Mary?".[41] Children could be asked whether the character being referred to in this poem might be Mary Poppins. They could then tell where Mary is. Of course, their answers might be in prose form instead of in verse.

Rosemary Carr and Stephen Vincent Benét's[42] poem "Nancy Hanks," like "Where's Mary?," stimulates answers to the question it raises. In this poem it is said that if Nancy Hanks came back as a ghost, she probably would inquire about her son Abraham Lincoln. Then questions are presented that she might ask if she did come back. One answer to the Benét poem "Nancy Hanks" appears on the same page in *The Arbuthnot Anthology of Children's Literature* as "Nancy Hanks." It is called "A Reply to Nancy Hanks" and is written by Julius Silberger.[43] After hearing these selections, children might be encouraged to write a reply to "Nancy Hanks" or to make up a poem about another famous person. For instance, they might write about questions the Wright Brothers or Alexander Graham Bell or Martin Luther King might have if they came back.

Two other question poems that are likely to stimulate children to write are "The New Neighbor" by Rose Fyleman[44] and "Bundles" by John Farrar.[45] "The New Neighbor" poses a series of questions that might be asked of a new acquaintance. Farrar's poem tells how wrapped packages pique a person's curiosity. He wonders whether it would not be more fun to carry packages undone. Children can respond with similar questions of their own or an account of what makes them curious.

6. WHAT IF . . . ?

What if questions are natural spurs to the imagination, and there are plenty of selections that pose such questions in intriguing ways. Four short books that children enjoy working with are *If Apples Had Teeth* by Milton and Shirley Glaser,[46] *If Everybody Did*[47] and *Why . . . ? Because* by Jo Ann Stover,[48] and *Supposing* by Alastair Reid.[49] *If Apples Had Teeth* by the Glasers is a book of sheer delight. You might read the first part of each problem and then let the children offer answers before giving the one the Glasers offer. The answer to the question suggested by the title is that "If apples had teeth, they would bite back." Encourage more than one answer to each question. Another "if" situation that the Glasers present is, "If a zebra wore striped pajamas you would never know." Of course, the goal, after you finish reading this book to the pupils, is for the pupils to come up with their own "if" questions, answers, and illustrations. Children should see the colorful and imaginative illustrations in this book.

If Everybody Did by Stover is an uproariously funny book that depicts what would happen if everybody squeezed the cat, stepped on Daddy's feet, and did other such things. The illustrations are highly imaginative. Through discussion children can be led to compose their own "if" predicaments.

Stover's *Why . . . ? Because* is another book that should start children wondering and conjuring up imaginative answers to "whys" such as those that Stover presents—"Why is a ball round?" or "Why are shoes where they are?"

You may want to select only a few situations from Reid's book *Supposing*. Some that might work well can be found on pp. 5, 11–12, 24–25, 40, 45, and 48. An example of the kind of problem that Reid offers on these pages is the one that he uses to begin the book. A child paints the view from his window, making the river yellow; the next morning when he goes out he finds the river really is yellow. What the child should be asked to do in any of the "supposing" cases presented to him/her is to tell what might happen. After hearing the "supposing" situations suggested, children can make up some "what if" questions of their own, which might later start a writing avalanche. Two the teacher could use as starters with her pupils are as follows.

What would happen if a dragon came into the library during a story hour?

What would happen if your pet did everything that you did?

Mauree Applegate[50] includes two "supposing" poems in her book *Free-ing Children to Write* that were written by children. These two poems could be read to pupils.

In "What Would You Do If . . . ?"[51] Leonore Klein asks questions such as "What would you do if you saw a rhinoceros coming down the street?" Very short answers are given by the children in the story. Then Klein usually addresses the question to the reader ("What would *you* do . . . ?" "What would *you* wish for?"). Children can be encouraged to give their own creative responses to some of the "what if" propositions offered in this brief tale.

A poem that has a "what if" motif is Beatrice Schenk de Regniers' "If We Walked on Our Hands." This poem is included in her book *Something Special.*[52] It suggests that under certain conditions—if "we all ate paper instead of meat"—there certainly would be a mixed-up world. Different "ifs" are presented—"If we walked on our hands . . ."— and then a refrain is given. Children can easily be encouraged to present new "if" situations, and then everyone can chant the refrain.

Because of their former experiences with riddles, children may enjoy working with "what if" riddles. Thirteen riddles of this type may be found in

The Arrow Book of Jokes and Riddles, illustrated by William Hogarth.[53] Hopefully, after hearing these, some children may start composing their own humorous "what if" riddles.

Three resources that may prompt children to think of various answers to problems are R.E. Myers' and E. Paul Torrance's workbooks *Can You Imagine?*[54] and *Invitations to Speaking and Writing Creatively,*[55] and Marksberry's *Foundation of Creativity.*[56] In *Can You Imagine?* five "what would happen" type questions are introduced. Since very little space is provided for answers, you may wish to use the questions Myers and Torrance offer and give blank sheets of paper to the children, allowing them to choose questions that appeal to them and to make their responses as long or as short as they want. Marksberry, in her *Foundation of Creativity,* provides a series of questions that would help to stimulate each child's imagination. She gives "what would happen" questions, poses problems for the reader to solve, and includes exercises that should enhance the growth of ideational fluency. An example of this latter type of exercise that she offers is her question, taken from a series of questions, "What uses can you think of for nut hulls?"

7. NEW COMBINATIONS

One characteristic of creative people is their ability to find new and imaginative uses for familiar things or to recombine features of things in a new way. Problems like the one cited from *Foundation of Creativity* can lead children to exercise their faculties for invention. Some other books that will provide this kind of stimulation are described briefly in the following paragraphs.

The Happy Birthday Umbrella by De Jong[57] is a very easy book to read. What it tells is how an umbrella undergoes changes for the better. You might, as you read the book, ask the children what they would do so that the umbrella could have a handle, be prettier, and be seen through. After hearing this story, children might be asked to think of other objects and how they could be improved. The objects might include toys, articles of clothing, kitchen implements, and vehicles such as bicycles, wagons, scooters, and cars. After discussing how some of these things might be improved, children could be encouraged to write stories such as "The Perfect _____ ." A discussion of this kind can lead children to talk about inventions that every mother, father, or child dreams about. (One idea you might suggest for mothers would be children who are processed to resist stains, spills, and bruises.)

Kenyon Cox,[58] in a series of poems, makes good use of the feature of recombination. Three of his poems are "The Bumblebeaver," "The Kangarooster," and "The Octopussycat." The poems describe animals that combine the characteristics of more than one creature. After hearing these three short poems, a discussion could follow in which the children could try to think of what benefits might follow from other similar combinations.

An easy book that might follow the introduction of Cox's poems is Helen Palmer's[59] *Why I Built the Boogle House*. The story tells how a pet house keeps on changing to adapt to the specific needs of its different inhabitants, each one of whom, for various reasons, is ousted. Finally, the hero of the book decides he will fix up his pet house for a pet that will never cause any trouble. He builds a "Boogle" house. The book ends with the builder saying he does not know what a Boogle is, but hopes to find one some day. The story provides an excellent beginning for another story. Children who are interested can write a story explaining what a Boogle is, where it comes from, and what it does. Some might want to describe the kind of creature that could live in a house originally designed for pets such as turtles, ducks, rabbits, dogs, goats, and horses. They might also want to design a strange pet house of their own and then tell a story about its inhabitant.

Seuss's books, *If I Ran the Zoo*[60] and *On Beyond Zebra*,[61] are both highly imaginative. In *If I Ran the Zoo*, the hero, Gerald McGrew, tells how he would first get rid of all of the run-of-the-mill creatures and replace them with the most exotic wild animals in the world if he ran the zoo. This nonsense book should excite children to imagine, talk about, and finally write about exotic animals that they would have if they ran the zoo. In Seuss's *On Beyond Zebra* the hero, Conrad Cornelius o'Donald o'Dell, creates his own alphabet using strange symbols and depicting what strange purposes the symbols are used for. On one page Seuss says that a person cannot write the word "Humpf," without using its own special symbol (but then he does!). Perhaps children, after being exposed to this book, could make up their own strange symbols beyond the letter Z. Beside the symbols, they might show phonetically what the symbols sound like and then use the symbols in their new words. They should be encouraged to give the meanings for their new words and to refer to occasions when the words might come in handy.

One last resource that could arouse some creative thinking, discussion, and writing is Winifred Welles's short question-poem, "Curious Something."[62] Welles wonders what kind of curious "something" persons would have instead of faces if they smelled with their ears, received sounds through their noses, and so forth. Perhaps some children might write an answer to the inquiry.

8. WORKING WITH TITLES

Some titles like "Curious Something" are so thought-provoking or intriguing that they should not be overlooked as a means of getting children to write. Many of the titles referred to elsewhere in this chapter could be used to promote some excellent writing after discussion periods. Some other titles that teachers could use to initiate discussions and then writings are:

1. *What Color Is Love?* by Joan Walsh Anglund.
2. *The Enormous Egg*—by Oliver Butterworth.
3. *Call It Courage*—by Armstrong Sperry.

The book, *What Color Is Love?*[63] could be used to provoke discussions and writings describing the color of happiness, the color of pain, and the color of sadness. Children might be asked to illustrate how happiness, pain, and sadness look. Children could combine their ideas in a book of their own.

The Enormous Egg[64] describes what happens when one of Nate Twitchell's hens appears to lay a peculiarly large egg that hatches into a dinosaur! Just hearing a title such as *The Enormous Egg* can provoke all kinds of discussions as to what kind of creature could be in it and what the creature would be capable of doing once it was hatched. After discussing this title, children might tell or write fairy tales, tall tales, or science fiction stories using this title.

The title of the book, *Call It Courage,*[65] discussed earlier, could start children talking about what they thought courage was. Children may have been introduced already to Elizabeth Speare's[66] *The Witch of Blackbird Pond* or Scott O'Dell's[67] *Island of the Blue Dolphins,* both of which deal explicitly with courage. The pupils, after discussing what they think courage is, could be asked to write a story that would demonstrate someone's courage. Of course, other concepts, such as honesty and loyalty, could be handled in the same way.

9. WORKING WITH DEFINITIONS

Definitions like those included in Ruth Krauss's *A Hole Is to Dig*[68] can provide a good stimulus for expression. After reading the Krauss book to children, you can have them try their own definitions for these and other words. A few definitions written by children in the intermediate grades are:

1. Teeth are to lose.
2. Candy is to get fat on.
3. Skirts are to spill on.
4. Stars are to wink at.
5. Grass is to chew.
6. Puddles are to jump in.
7. Cookies are to sneak.
8. Spaghetti is to splash you.

Pupils might compile their definitions with illustrations in their own dictionary.

Marlene Glaus,[69] in her book *From Thoughts to Words,* suggests that children, after hearing *A Hole Is to Dig,* be given a piece of paper that has a hole cut in it. Each child is to decide what summer picture the hole brings to mind. They then are to draw that picture. Glaus includes as examples in her book illustrations of a ship with portholes in it and a shoe with a hole in its sole. Perhaps children might be told to draw as many pictures as they can instead of suggesting that they draw one picture or limiting them to a summer picture.

Mommies Are for Loving by Penn[70] tells the many things that Daddies, Mommies, and children are for. Although some of the statements are rather stereotyped, the idea of giving definitions of mothers, fathers, children, and so forth is a fine one. One page of Penn's book lists some favorite sayings of children such as "How come?" "Me, too!" and "I don't want to!" You can use this section to inspire the children to tell and write some other favorite sayings of children as well as the favorite expressions of mothers, fathers, and teachers. These could be put together in a book entitled, *They Say.* Some poems that are sure to bring to mind some all too familiar expressions, especially of parents, are:

1. "Washing" by John Drinkwater, p. 1042 in Edna Johnson, Evelyn Sickels, and Frances Clarke Sayer's *Anthology of Children's Literature* (Boston: Houghton Mifflin Company, 1959).
2. "My Job," pp. 17–18; "What a Waste," p. 19; "This Is Killing Me," pp. 22–23; "TV," p. 29; "I Don't Like Don't—I Don't, I Don't," pp. 36–39; "Bubble Gum," p. 39; "It's Not Fair," p. 44 in Lucia and James L. Hymes's *Hooray for Chocolate.*[71]
3. "I Woke Up This Morning" by Karla Kuskin, pp. 14–15 in *The Arrow Book of Poetry,* edited by Ann McGovern.[72]
4. "Independence" by A.A. Milne, p. 17 in *When We Were Very Young* (New York: E.P. Dutton and Company, Inc., 1961).
5. "Bedtime" by Eleanor Farjeon, p. 108 in the poetry section of *The Arbuthnot Anthology of Children's Literature* (Chicago: Scott, Foresman and Company, 1961).

A Boy Is a Boy, by Ogden Nash,[73] is a rollicking, frolicking, thoroughly enjoyable verse tale. After hearing this story, children might want to tell or write their own ideas on what boys are like. On the first page of this book Nash explains that Tim and Spot went together as naturally as a sock and a shoe. (Some children might respond to the suggestion that they explain why things like hands and mittens go together so naturally. An excellent poem to use to stimulate an interest in this idea is John Drinkwater's poem "Twos."[74] In this poem the speaker wants to know why so many things come in twos.)

Ogden Nash wrote a book about girls entitled *Girls Are Silly*.[75] In response, Phyllis McGinley wrote *Boys Are Awful*.[76] These two books could be read one after the other, and then children could write their reactions. This activity can prove to be quite a bit of fun for all of the children involved as they share their works. Battle lines will be drawn very quickly in all probability.

Charles Schulz has written several definition books. One of the most popular is *Happiness Is a Warm Puppy*.[77] The goal, after hearing Schulz's various definitions of happiness, is to have the children create their own. After *Happiness Is a Warm Puppy* was presented, two definitions of happiness given by children were:

Happiness is a cat going in and out between your legs.
Happiness is the shine on your new shoes.

Naturally, you need not stop at having the children make up their own "happiness" definitions. You can also have them tell what "misery" or "security" means to them. (One child's definition of security was, "Security is knowing your television set works.")

Joan Walsh Anglund has written a series of short definition books. Among them are *A Friend Is Someone Who Likes You, Love Is a Special Way of Feeling,* and *Spring Is a New Beginning.* Before starting *A Friend Is Someone Who Likes You,*[78] you might ask your students who and what they think a friend is. The book may very well give children new ideas as to who their friends are—"a tree that lets you climb it easily," or "a dog that wags its tail extra hard." The book ends by saying that everyone has at least *one* friend. It then asks, "Where did you find yours?" The end can serve as a beginning for children to tell where they found their friend.

Love Is a Special Way of Feeling[79] is a sensitively written book that, like Anglund's other books, is for "all ages." The book explains how love starts, how it feels, and where it can be found. Like *A Friend Is Someone Who Likes You* the book should give children fresh ideas about love that they later may want to write about. *Spring Is a New Beginning,*[80] another of Anglund's books, can inspire children to write not only about spring but about other seasons as well. The illustrations in all of Anglund's books contribute a great deal to their charm.

10. WISHES AND DREAMS

Wishes and dreams can provide fruitful topics for creative thinking and writing. The titles mentioned in this section offer good ways to begin exploring this area of experience.

Bruno Munari's *The Elephant's Wish*[81] is a creative book that must be seen to be appreciated. The idea portrayed in the book is that each creature, starting with an elephant, is discontent with what he is and wishes to be something else. In the portion of the picture of each creature where the creature's mind would be, Munari has inserted an extra bit of paper that, when opened, reveals what the creature wants to be. The last animal, an ox, comes back full circle and wishes that he were an elephant. This very brief book may remind children of the poem "Raccoon" by William Jay Smith,[82] which they may have encountered previously. This poem might be reviewed now. These works could easily nudge children into discussing what they would like to be if they could be anything they wanted to be in the world. In their writings they could tell why they chose what they did.

(This would be a good time to review Annette Wynne's poem "I Keep Three Wishes Ready."[83] After hearing this poem, children can be asked what three wishes they would keep ready.)

I Often Wish by Babette Deutsch[84] is a book of poems that tells all the creatures that the speaker of the poem wishes he were. He tells why he wishes to be a giraffe, a snake, a pig, and a traffic cop, and then he also tells why he is just as glad he is not what he temporarily wishes to be. Children, after being exposed to these poems, might pick some persons or animals they think they might like to be and then think of what disadvantages there might be if they really became these other beings. They could also tell of the advantages of being themselves. Naturally, their writing need not be in verse form.

A poem that might set children thinking, talking, and writing is Rose Fyleman's "If Only . . . ."[85] The poem tells what the speaker of the piece would do if he had some money. The children might want to write what they would do "if only," after reading this selection.

Someday by Charlotte Zolotow[86] expresses a series of "someday" wishes that almost everyone, young and old, dreams about. For example, Zolotow offers this "someday" wish of a child: "Someday my mother and father are going to say, 'Why are you going to bed so early?' " Another example Zolotow gives is: "Someday I'm going to catch a high, high ball and my team will win because I did it." Although this book is written from a girl's point of view, boys, after reading it, could be coaxed into discussing their special "someday" wishes. After discussing them, children could write down their own private wishes that later could be collected and put into a class "someday" book. (Children might be most interested in hearing some of your "someday" wishes as well.)

One ten-year-old girl, a former pupil of Alice F. Cummings, wrote the following wish poem after being exposed to Dorothy Baruch's *I Would Like to Be a Pony and Other Wishes* (Harper and Row, 1959).

FOR THAT ONE MOMENT

As I sit under a flowing willow tree
I let whatever the world has in store happen to me.
My life is blank,
My thoughts are blind,
I sit motionless and uninclined.
For what I feel this poem has to say,
The world is too busy, too rushy for me.
There are so many things,
More valuable than the human eye can see.
I wish this world would come to a stop.
Just for a moment,
Then I'd turn back your clock!
Then you can continue with your rush, rush about.
But for that moment!
I'd want to touch the feeling,
Of a still, motionless, unbusy world.
Ah!
If people could only clear their minds,
Then the world might better face,
A day of life.
    —Lisa Fontes

Marguerite Dorian's simply written and beautifully illustrated book *When the Snow Is Blue*[87] begins with the question "What would you like to do on a day like this when heavy snow is falling and there is not much to do indoors? The speaker of the story, a girl, tells that she would like to go to her friends, the Bears, to invite them to tea. This is a story for young girls who have vivid imaginations and who love to pretend. Perhaps all some children might need to hear to set them thinking about what they would like to do is the opening question.

A Child's Book of Dreams by Beatrice Schenk de Regniers[88] is a book for everyone. (You can refer to it simply as *A Book of Dreams* if you think that the term *child* will put off some of your pupils.) This book is highly imaginative and should send children off scribbling about their dreams, real and imaginary. De Regniers' book talks about wonderful dreams such as "The Flying Dream," "The Spaghetti Dream," and "The Dream of Seeds and Flowers." The first two dreams float right into each other, one ending and one beginning just as easily as real dreams do.

A poem that is about dreams and that is steeped in questions is Eve Merriam's "My Dream."[89] What children might want to talk or write about after reading this selection is what they would like to do on a day of their very own.

A very interesting book that succeeds in producing a pervasive dreamy mood throughout the entire book is Sandol Stoddard Warburg's *The Thinking Book*.[90] The book is about a little boy who is in a half-waking, half-sleeping state. Warburg presents in capitalized letters the words that the little boy's mother says to her son. Following this are the ideas that are set off in the child's mind when the mother speaks. For example, the mother tells her son to put on a yellow shirt, and the child immediately starts thinking first of yellow things such as "all the pieces of dust that float and shine in the sunshine." (The words themselves seem to be floating because of the way Warburg has arranged them.) Then the color yellow brings to mind yellow fruits, and he starts thinking of lemons. Next his attention turns to limes, oranges, and watermelons. This very imaginative book should be read to the pupils. The language is lovely. Moreover, it would be helpful if the children could see the excellent pictures in the book and be made aware of the fine handling of the arrangement of the words. The entire format of the book is very appropriate for the mood of this story.

After hearing this selection perhaps the children, with the teacher's guidance, could make some free association responses to certain phrases such as:

Put on the dress with the blue ruffles.
Wear your new white shirt.
Shine your brown shoes.

You might then suggest that some children attempt their own "thinking book."

Just as reading about pleasant dreams can stir a child's imagination so, too, can reading about nightmares. A book that could start a discussion about nightmares is the 1964 Caldecott award-winning book *Where the Wild Things Are* by Maurice Sendak.[91] The pictures look as though they came right out of one's most frightening nightmare. The book is about Max, who is sent to bed without his supper because he shouts at his mother, "I'll eat you up!" Although Sendak does not say so, Max falls asleep, and he sails "to the place where the wild things are." He becomes the king of all the wild things and initiates a "wild rumpus." The book ends very satisfactorily with Max sailing back into his own room where he finds his supper waiting for him, still hot.

11. AFTERWORD

The word *olio* can mean "a rich, highly seasoned stew," "a miscellaneous collection," or "a medley." As is generally true with words like that, the reader's associations determine the shade of meaning. It is hoped that you have found this particular olio sufficiently rich in suggestions to justify the first association. Although these suggestions conclude this book, they are meant to be a starting point for you as you search for materials and ideas that will stimulate children to speak, read, and write creatively. Try to be constantly on the watch for poems and stories that will help to give every child an inexhaustible reservoir of ideas—a magic pitcher like Baucis and Philemon's that never empties. To the extent that you realize this goal, you can be confident that your children will continue to read and write independently and with pleasure long after they have left your classroom.

References

Preface

[1] Lewis, C. S., "On Three Ways of Writing for Children." In *Only Connect: Readings on Children's Literature,* edited by Sheila Egoff, G. T. Stubbs, and L. F. Ashley, Oxford University Press, Toronto, 1969, p. 213.

Chapter 1

[1] Karl, Jean, *From Childhood to Childhood: Children's Books and Their Creators,* The John Day Company, New York, 1970, p. 6.

[2] Larrick, Nancy, *A Teacher's Guide to Children's Books,* Charles E. Merrill Books, Columbus, Ohio, 1960, pp. 85–86.

[3] Piper, Watty, *The Little Engine that Could,* Platt and Munk Publishers, New York, 1961, unpaged.

[4] Sawyer, Ruth, *The Way of the Storyteller,* The Viking Press, New York, 1942.

[5] Larrick, Nancy, *A Parent's Guide to Children's Reading,* Doubleday and Company, Inc., New York, 1975.

[6] Huck, Charlotte S., *Children's Literature in the Elementary School,* Third Edition, Holt, Rinehart and Winston, New York, 1976.

[7] Yensen, Amy Elizabeth, "Attracting Children to Books," *Elementary English,* 33: 332–339, October 1956.

[8] Egoff, Sheila, Stubbs, G. T., and Ashley, L. F., editors, *Only Connect: Readings on Children's Literature,* Oxford University Press, Toronto, 1969.

[9] Hopkins, Lee Bennett, *Books Are by People,* Citation Press, New York, 1969.

[10] Siks, G. B., *Creative Dramatics: An Art for Children,* Harper and Row, Publishers, New York, 1958.

[11] Conger, Lesley, *Tops and Bottoms,* Four Winds Press, New York, 1970.

Chapter 2

[1] Joseph, S. M., editor, *The Me Nobody Knows: Children's Voices from the Ghetto,* Avon Books, New York, 1969, p. 20.

[2] Bowman, P. H., "Improving the Pupil Self-Concept." In R. D. Strom (Ed.), *The Inner-City Classroom: Teacher Behaviors,* Charles E. Merrill Publishing Company, Columbus, Ohio, 1966, p. 77.

[3] Maslow, A. H., "A Theory of Human Motivation." In W. R. Baller (Ed.), *Readings in the Psychology of Human Growth and Development,* Holt, Rinehart and Winston, Inc., New York, 1964, p. 256.

[4] Ibid., pp. 265–266.

[5] Ibid., p. 266.

[6] Ibid.

[7] Silberman, C. E., *Crisis in the Classroom,* Random House, New York, 1970, pp. 101–102.

[8] Carey, Josie, "I Like You As You Are." In H. B. Dowdy and M. E. Lichtenwalner, *Wondering About Us,* Perspective 1, Semester 2, American Baptist Board of Education and Publication, Judson Press, Valley Forge, Pa., 1969, p. 140.

[9] Rollins, Charlmae, *We Build Together,* National Council of Teachers of English, Champaign, Ill., 1967.

[10] Torrance, E. R., "Fostering Creative Behavior." In R. D. Strom (Ed.), *The Inner-City Classroom: Teacher Behaviors,* Charles E. Merrill Publishing Company, Columbus, Ohio, 1966, pp. 59, 60, 61–62, 64–65.

[11] Silberman, C. E., *Crisis in the Classroom,* Random House, New York, 1970, p. 8.

[12] Hanauer, Joan, "New Rich in America Live Like Rest of Us," *The Indianapolis Star,* August 3, 1969, Section 1, p. 28.

[13] Hentoff, Nat, *Our Children Are Dying,* The Viking Press, New York, 1967, p. 104.

[14] McKee, Paul, *A Primer for Parents,* Houghton Mifflin, Boston, 1971.

[15] Schulz, C. M., "Peanuts," United Features Syndicate, New York, September 5, 1970.

Chapter 3

[1] Taylor, Stanford E., *Listening,* National Education Association of the United States, Washington, D.C., 1973.

[2] Lundsteen, S. W., *Listening: Its Impact on Reading and the Other Language Arts,* National Council of Teachers of English, Urbana, Ill., 1971, p. 4.

[3] Bereiter, Carl, and Engelmann, Siegfried, *Language Learning Activities for the Disadvantaged Child,* Anti-Defamation League of B'nai B'rith, New York, n.d., pp. 18–19.

[4] Arbuthnot, M. H., et al., compilers, *The Arbuthnot Anthology of Children's Literature,* Fourth Edition, Scott, Foresman and Company, Glenview, Ill., 1976, p. 42.

[5] Summerfield, Geoffrey, editor, *Voices: An Anthology of Poems and Pictures,* the Second Book, Rand McNally and Company, Chicago, 1969, p. 63.

[6] Merriam, Eve, *Catch a Little Rhyme,* Atheneum, New York, 1966, p. 30.

[7] Frye, Northrop, *The Educated Imagination,* Indiana University Press, Bloomington, 1964, p. 116.

[8] Arbuthnot et al., op cit., p. 61.

[9] Arbuthnot, M. H., et al., compilers, *The Arbuthnot Anthology of Children's Literature,* Third Edition, Scott, Foresman and Company, Glenview, Ill., 1971, p. 115.

[10] Ibid., p. 127.

[11] Ibid., p. 61

[12] Ibid., p. 111

[13] Ibid., p. 136.

[14] Ibid., p. 149.

[15] Brown, Marcia, *Peter Piper's Alphabet,* Charles Scribner's Sons, New York, 1959.

[16] Merriam, Eve, *It Doesn't Always Have to Rhyme,* Atheneum, New York, 1966, pp. 56–57.

[17] Arbuthnot, M. H., et al., compilers, *The Arbuthnot Anthology of Children's Literature,* Fourth Edition, Scott, Foresman and Company, Glenview, Ill., 1976, p. 113.

[18] Ibid., p. 113.

[19] Ibid., p. 124.

[20] Arbuthnot, M. H., et al., compilers, *The Arbuthnot Anthology of Children's Literature,* Third Edition, Scott, Foresman and Company, Glenview, Ill., 1971, p. 152.

[21] Arbuthnot, M. H., *The Arbuthnot Anthology of Children's Literature: Time for Poetry,* Revised Edition, Scott, Foresman and Company, Glenview, Ill., 1961, p. 127.

[22] Arbuthnot, M. H., et al., compilers, *The Arbuthnot Anthology of Children's Literature,* Fourth Edition, Scott, Foresman and Company, Glenview, Ill., 1976, p. 86.

[23] Ibid., p. 124.

[24] Ibid., p. 99.

[25] Ibid., p. 142.

[26] Ibid., p. 113.

[27] Ibid., p. 137.

[28] Ibid., p. 113.

[29] Ciardi, John, *How Does a Poem Mean?,* Houghton Mifflin, Boston, 1959, pp. 663–664, 669.

Chapter 4

[1] Linderman, E. W., and Herberholz, D. W., *Developing Artistic and Perceptual Awareness,* William C. Brown Company, Publishers, Dubuque, Iowa, 1964, p. vii.

[2] Burton, D. L., "Teaching Students to Read Literature." In *Perspectives in Reading No. 2: Reading Instruction in Secondary Schools,* edited by Robert Karlin, Margaret Early, and Gwen Horsman, International Reading Association, Newark, Del., 1964, pp. 90–91.

[3] Aliki, *My Five Senses,* Thomas Y. Crowell Company, New York, 1962.

[4] Radlauer, R. S., *About Four Seasons and Five Senses,* Melmont Publishers, Inc., Chicago, 1963.

[5] Fuller, E. M., and Ellis, M. J., *Learning How to Use the Five Senses,* T. S. Denison and Company, Inc., Minneapolis, 1961.

[6] Ungerer, Tomi, *Snail, Where Are You?,* Harper and Brothers, New York, 1962.

[7] Emberley, Ed, *The Wing on a Flea: A Book About Shapes,* Little, Brown and Company, Boston, 1961.

[8] Myers, R. E., and Torrance, E. P., *Invitations to Speaking and Writing Creatively,* Ginn and Company, Boston, 1965, pp. 5, 53–55, 73–74.

[9] Gardner, Martin, *The Arrow Book of Brain Teasers,* Scholastic Book Services, New York, 1959, pp. 28–29.

[10] Tresselt, Alvin, *Rain Drop Splash,* Lothrop, Lee and Shepard Company, Inc., New York, 1946.

[11] Tresselt, Alvin, *White Snow, Bright Snow,* Lothrop, Lee and Shepard Company, Inc., New York, 1947.

[12] Myers, R. E., and Torrance, E. P., *Can You Imagine?,* Ginn and Company, Boston, 1965, pp. 10–11, 30–31.

[13] Leavitt, H. D., and Sohn, D. A., *Stop, Look, and Write!* Bantam Books, New York, 1964.

[14] Hoest, Bill, *A Taste of Carrot,* Atheneum, New York, 1967.

[15] Mayer, Mercer, *A Boy, a Dog and a Frog,* The Dial Press, New York, 1967.

[16] Clifford, Eth, and Clifford, David, *Your Face Is a Picture,* E. C. Seale and Company, Inc., Indianapolis, 1963.

[17] Borten, Helen, *A Picture Has a Special Look,* Abelard-Schuman, London, 1961.

[18] Arbuthnot, M. H., et al., compilers, *The Arbuthnot Anthology of Children's Literature,* Fourth Edition, Scott, Foresman and Company, Glenview, Ill., 1976, p. 83.

[19] Lindgren, Astrid, *Pippi Longstocking,* Scholastic Book Services, New York, 1959.

[20] Norton, Mary, *The Borrowers,* Harcourt, Brace and Company, New York, 1952.

[21] Selden, George, *I See What I See!,* Ariel Books, New York, 1962.

[22] Anderson, P. S., *Language Skills in Elementary Education,* The Macmillan Company, New York, 1964.

[23] De Regniers, B. S., *Something Special,* Harcourt, Brace and Company, New York, 1958.

[24] Borten, Helen, *Do You See What I See?* Abelard-Schuman, London, 1959.

[25] Smith, E. E., *Procedures for Encouraging Creative Writing in the Elementary*

School, Unpublished doctoral dissertation, Northwestern University, Evanston, Ill., 1943, p. 206.

[26] Wolff, Janet, *Let's Imagine Thinking Up Things,* E. P. Dutton and Company, Inc., New York, 1961.

[27] Shaw, C. G., *It Looked Like Spilt Milk,* Harper and Row, Publishers, New York, 1947.

[28] Huber, M. B., compiler, *Story and Verse for Children,* The Macmillan Company, New York, 1965, p. 115.

[29] Anderson, op. cit., pp. 305–306.

[30] Mizumura, Kazue, *I See the Winds,* Thomas Y. Crowell Company, New York, 1966.

[31] Anderson, op. cit., p. 353.

[32] Arbuthnot et al., op. cit., p. 130.

[33] Ibid., p. 55.

[34] Ibid., p. 55.

[35] Tresselt, Alvin, *A Thousand Lights and Fireflies,* Parents' Magazine Press, New York, 1965.

[36] Arbuthnot, M. H., compiler, *Arbuthnot Anthology of Children's Literature,* Revised Edition, Scott, Foresman and Company, Chicago, 1961, p. 47.

[37] Ibid., p. 47.

[38] Ibid., p. 87.

[39] Johnson, Edna, Sickels, E. R., and Sayers, F. C., editors, *Anthology of Children's Literature,* Houghton Mifflin Company, Boston, 1959, p. 126.

[40] Anglund, J. W., *Look Out the Window,* Harcourt, Brace and Company, New York, 1959.

[41] Showers, Paul, *Find Out by Touching,* Thomas Y. Crowell Company, New York, 1961.

[42] Witte, Pat, and Witte, Eve, *The Touch Me Book,* Capitol Publishing Company, New York, 1961.

[43] Gibson, M. T., *What Is Your Favorite Thing to Touch?,* Grosset and Dunlap, Publishers, New York, 1964.

[44] Literature Committee of the Association for Childhood Education International, compilers, *Sung Under the Silver Umbrella,* The Macmillan Company, New York, 1935, pp. 46–47.

[45] Arbuthnot, M. H., op. cit., p. 157.

[46] Johnson, Sickels, and Sayers, op. cit., p. 1011.

[47] Lindgren, op. cit., pp. 83–94.

[48] Aliki, *My Hands,* Thomas Y. Crowell Company, New York, 1962.

[49] Merriam, Eve, *There Is No Rhyme for Silver,* Atheneum, New York, 1962, p. 16.

[50] Merriam, Eve, *It Doesn't Always Have to Rhyme,* Atheneum, New York, 1966, p. 14.

[51] Hymes, Lucia, and Hymes, J. L., Jr., *Hooray for Chocolate,* William R. Scott, Inc., Publisher, New York, 1960, pp. 8–9, 26, 34–35, 27.

[52] Arbuthnot, M. H., compiler, *The Arbuthnot Anthology of Children's Literature: Time for Poetry,* Scott, Foresman and Company, Chicago, 1961, p. 166.

[53] Agree, R. H., *How to Eat a Poem and Other Morsels,* Pantheon Books, New York, 1967.

[54] Hopp, Zinken, *The Magic Chalk,* translated by Susanne H. Bergendahl, David McKay Company, Inc., New York, 1959, pp. 98–100.

[55] Applegate, Mauree, *Freeing Children to Write,* Harper and Row Publishers, New York, 1963, pp. 9–10.

[56] Lindgren, op. cit., pp. 1–10.

[57] Applegate, Mauree, *Easy in English,* Row, Peterson and Company, Evanston, Ill., 1962, p. 105.

[58] Johnson, E. M., and Jacobs, L. B., editors, *Treat Shop,* Charles E. Merrill Books, Inc., Columbus, Ohio, 1960, pp. 237–241.

[59] Seuss, Dr., *Green Eggs and Ham,* Beginner Books, Inc., New York, 1960.

[60] Gibson, M. T., *What Is Your Favorite Smell, My Dear?,* Grosset and Dunlap, Publishers, New York, 1964.

[61] Arbuthnot, M. H., op. cit., p. 3.

[62] Ibid., p. 105.

[63] Ibid., p. 107.

[64] Merriam, Eve, *There Is No Rhyme for Silver,* Atheneum, New York, 1962, p. 19.

Chapter 5

[1] Arbuthnot, M. H., et al., compiler, *The Arbuthnot Anthology of Children's Literature,* Fourth Edition, Scott, Foresman and Company, Chicago, 1976, p. 5.

[2] Ames, Winthrop, editor, *What Shall We Name the Baby?,* Simon and Schuster, Inc., New York, 1973.

[3] Lambert, Eloise, *Our Language: The Story of the Words We Use,* Lothrop, Lee, and Shepard Company, Inc., New York, 1955, pp. 94, 96.

[4] Arbuthnot, M. H., et al., compilers, *The Arbuthnot Anthology of Children's Literature,* Third Edition, Scott, Foresman and Company, Glenview, Ill., 1971, p. 11.

[5] Ibid., p. 136.

[6] Merriam, Eve, *It Doesn't Always Have to Rhyme,* Atheneum, New York, 1966, p. 5.

[7] Severn, Bill, *People Words,* Ives Washburn, Inc., New York, 1966.

[8] Lambert, op. cit.

[9] Stewart, G. R., *Names on the Land,* Houghton Mifflin Company, Boston, 1958.

[10] Nash, Ogden, *Custard the Dragon and the Wicked Knight,* Little, Brown and Company, Boston, 1961; "The Tale of Custard the Dragon." In *The Golden Treas-*

ury of Poetry, edited by Louis Untermeyer, Golden Press, New York, 1967, pp. 166–167.

[11] McCloskey, Robert, Homer Price, Scholastic Book Services, New York, 1962, pp. 8–30.

[12] Hollowell, Lillian, editor, A Book of Children's Literature, Holt, Rinehart and Winston, New York, 1964, p. 550.

[13] Myers, R. E., and Torrance, E. P., Invitations to Thinking and Doing, Ginn and Company, Boston, 1964, pp. 37–39.

[14] Merriam, Eve, There Is No Rhyme for Silver, Atheneum, New York, 1962, pp. 21–23.

[15] Severn, Bill, People Words, Ives Washburn, Inc., New York, 1966, pp. 23, 143, 29–30, 39, 9, 107–111, 112–113, 6–12, 35.

[16] Miller, Albert G., Where Did That Word Come From?, Bowmar, Glendale, Calif., 1974.

[17] Epstein, Sam, and Epstein, Beryl, What's Behind the Word?, Scholastic Book Services, New York, 1964, pp. 55–59, 54, 35.

[18] Evans, Bergen, Comfortable Words, Random House, New York, 1962, pp. 167, 172, 33, 40, 41, 182, 188, 216, 197, 203.

[19] Mathews, Mitford M., American Words, The World Publishing Company, Cleveland, 1959.

[20] Funk, Charles E., Heavens to Betsy!, Warner Paperback Library, New York, 1972.

[21] Clymer, Eleanor, compiler, Arrow Book of Funny Poems, Scholastic Book Services, New York, 1961, p. 36.

[22] Ciardi, John, I Met a Man, Houghton Mifflin Company, Boston, 1961, pp. 10, 68–74.

[23] Arbuthnot, M. H., et al., compilers, The Arbuthnot Anthology of Children's Literature, Fourth Edition, Scott, Foresman and Company, Glenview, Ill., 1976, p. 343.

[24] Kramer, Nora, editor, Arrow Book of Ghost Stories, Scholastic Book Services, New York, 1960.

[25] Withers, Carl, compiler, A Rocket in My Pocket, Henry Holt and Company, n.p., 1948, pp. 3, 183, 193, 196, 199.

[26] "All My Own Work," Time, 83: E7, 100, May 1, 1964.

[27] Reid, Alastair, Ounce Dice Trice, Little, Brown and Company, Boston, 1958, p. 18.

[28] Clymer, op. cit., p. 26.

[29] Nash, "The Tale of Custard the Dragon," op. cit., pp. 166–167.

[30] Arbuthnot, op. cit., p. 75.

[31] Hymes, Lucia, and Hymes, J. L., Jr., Oodles of Noodles, Young Scott Books, New York, 1964, pp. 7, 48, 20.

[32] Arbuthnot, op. cit., p. 157.

[33] "Did You Ever Make a Framis with a Frankelsnortz?", Read, 13: 22–23, January 1, 1964.

[34] Nordstrom, Ursula, *The Secret Language,* Scholastic Book Services, New York, 1960.

[35] Mearns, Hughes, *Creative Power: The Education of Youth in the Creative Arts,* Dover Publications, Inc., New York, 1958, pp. 57–62.

[36] Ferguson, C. W., *The Abecedarian Book,* Little, Brown and Company, Boston, 1964, p. 31.

[37] Merriam, *There Is No Rhyme for Silver,* op. cit., p. 12.

[38] Zim, H. S., *Codes and Secret Writing,* Scholastic Book Services, New York, 1962.

[39] Myers and Torrance, op. cit., pp. 81–83.

[40] Orff, Carl, Keetman, Gunild, and Jelinek, Walter, *Music for Children,* Angel Records, New York, 1958, 2 records, 33⅓ rpm, Side 1, Band 1; Side 1, Band 2; Side 4, Band 2.

[41] Rockowitz, Murray, *Arrow Book of Word Games,* Scholastic Book Services, New York, 1964, p. 25.

[42] McCloskey, Robert, *Homer Price,* Scholastic Book Services, New York, 1962, pp. 8–30.

[43] Merriam, *There Is No Rhyme for Silver,* op. cit., pp. 56–57.

[44] Shipley, J. T., *Playing with Words,* Cornerstone Library, New York, 1960, pp. 21–23.

[45] Brown, Marcia, *Peter Piper's Alphabet,* Charles Scribner's Sons, New York, 1959.

[46] Merriam, *It Doesn't Always Have to Rhyme,* op. cit., p. 58.

[47] Rockowitz, op. cit., pp. 18–19.

[48] Sage, Michael, *If You Talked to a Boar,* J. B. Lippincott Company, Philadelphia, 1960.

[49] Wertenbaker, Lael, and Gleaves, Suzanne, *Rhyming Word Games,* Simon and Schuster, New York, 1964.

[50] Hymes and Hymes, op. cit., pp. 18, 31.

[51] Rockowitz, op. cit., p. 27.

[52] White, M. S., *Word Twins,* Abingdon Press, New York, 1961.

[53] Van Gelder, Rosalind, *Monkeys Have Tails,* David McKay Company, Inc., New York, 1966.

[54] Shipley, op. cit., pp. 118–119.

[55] Merriam, *It Doesn't Always Have to Rhyme,* op. cit., pp. 54–55.

[56] Merriam, *There Is No Rhyme for Silver,* op. cit., p. 25.

[57] Ibid., p. 28.

[58] Rees, Ennis, *Pick-A-Riddle,* Scholastic Book Services, New York, 1966, p. 6.

[59] Newell, Peter, *The Hole Book,* Harper and Row, Publishers, New York, 1908, unpaged.

[60] Keane, Bil, *Jest in Pun,* Scholastic Book Services, New York, 1965.

[61] Rockowitz, Murray, *X-Word Fun!,* Scholastic Book Services, New York, 1965

[62] Parish, Peggy, *Amelia Bedelia,* Harper and Row, Publishers, New York, 1963; *Thank You, Amelia Bedelia,* Harper and Row, Publishers, New York, 1964; *Amelia Bedelia and the Surprise Shower,* Harper and Row, Publishers, New York, 1966; *Come Back, Amelia Bedelia,* Harper and Row, Publishers, New York, 1971; *Play Ball, Amelia Bedelia,* Harper and Row, Publishers, New York, 1972.

[63] Shipley, op. cit., p. 143.

[64] Merriam, *It Doesn't Always Have to Rhyme,* op. cit., p. 59.

[65] Gardner, Martin, *The Arrow Book of Brain Teasers,* Scholastic Book Services, New York, 1959, pp. 30–31.

[66] Rockowitz, *X-Word Fun!,* op. cit., pp. 91–92.

[67] Provensen, A., and Provensen, M., *Karen's Opposites,* Golden Press, New York, n.d., unpaged.

[68] Ciardi, op. cit., pp. 68–74.

[69] Bach, Mickey, *Word-a-Day,* Scholastic Book Services, New York, 1963.

[70] O'Neill, Mary, *Words, Words, Words,* Doubleday and Company, Inc., New York, 1966, p. 27.

Chapter 6

[1] Bruner, J. S., *Toward a Theory of Instruction,* The Belknap Press of Harvard University, Cambridge, 1966, p. 125.

[2] Weir, R. H., *Language in the Crib,* Mouton and Company, The Hague, 1962, pp. 82–84, 109, 144, 100, 145, 123.

[3] Chukovsky, Kornei, *From Two to Five,* translated and edited by Miriam Morton, University of California Press, Berkeley, 1965, p. 7.

[4] Bruner, op. cit., p. 123.

[5] Chukovsky, op. cit., 170 pp.

[6] Piaget, Jean, *The Language and Thought of the Child,* translated by Marjorie Gabain, Routledge and Kegan Paul Ltd., London, 1959, pp. 11, 27.

[7] Petty, W. F., and Starkey, Roberta J., "Oral Language and Personal and Social Development," *Elementary English,* 43: 386–394, April 1966.

[8] Wilt, Miriam, "Talk-Talk-Talk," *The Reading Teacher,* 21: 611–617, April 1968.

[9] Strickland, R. G., *Language Arts,* D. C. Heath and Company, Boston, 1951, 370 pp.

[10] Lefevre, C. A., "Language and Self: Fulfillment or Trauma? Part I," *Elementary English,* 43: 128, February 1966.

[11] Davies, H. S., *Grammar Without Tears,* The John Day Company, New York, 1953, pp. 14, 19.

[12] Mearns, Hughes, *Creative Power: The Education of Youth in the Creative Arts,* Dover Publications, Inc., New York, 1958, pp. 221, 30, 218.

[13] Martin, Bill, Jr., "Helping Children Claim Language through Literature," *Elementary English,* 45: 583–591, May 1968.

[14] Brown, Roger, *Social Psychology,* The Free Press, New York, 1965 (citing "Language and Communication." In *Handbook of Research Methods in Child Development,* edited by P. H. Mussen, John Wiley and Sons, Inc., Publishers, New York, 1960), pp. 249–250.

[15] McCullough, C. M., "Implications of Research on Children's Concepts," *The Reading Teacher, 13:* 100–07, December 1959.

[16] Clegg, A. B., editor, *The Excitement of Writing,* Chatto and Windus, London, 1965, p. 19.

[17] Piaget, op. cit., 288 pp.

[18] Lloyd, Donald J., and Warfel, Harry R., *American English in Its Cultural Setting,* Alfred A. Knopf, New York, 1957.

[19] Cohen, D. H., "The Effect of Literature on Vocabulary and Reading Achievement," *Elementary English, 45:* 209–213, 217, February 1968.

[20] Burns, P. C., "The Elementary School Language Arts Library," *Elementary English, 41:* 879–884, December 1964.

[21] Delmare, Maxine, "Language Books for the Library," *Elementary English, 45:* 55–66, January 1968.

[22] Tiedt, Iris M., and Tiedt, Sidney W., "A Linguistic Library for Students," *Elementary English,* 45:38–40, January, 1968.

[23] Heys, Frank, Jr., "Means of Vocabulary Development," *Journal of Developmental Reading, 6:* 140–143, Summer 1963.

[24] Martin, op. cit., pp. 583–591.

[25] Bissett, D. J., editor, *Poems and Verses About the City,* Chandler Publishing Company, San Francisco, 1968, p. 18.

[26] Malmstrom, Jean, and Ashley, Annabel, *Dialects U.S.A.,* National Council of Teachers of English, Champaign, Ill., 1963, 62 pp.

[27] Petty, W. F., Herold, C. P., and Stoll, Earline, *The State of Knowledge About the Teaching of Vocabulary,* National Council of Teachers of English, Champaign, Ill., 1968, p. 58.

[28] The Enrichment Unit Project Staff under Title I (ESEA), *Access to Learning,* Dr. Harold H. Eibling, Superintendent, Columbus Public Schools, Columbus, Ohio, 1967, 269 pp.

[29] McCullough, C. M., "Balanced Reading Development." In *Innovation and Change in Reading Instruction,* edited by H. M. Robinson, The Sixty-Seventh Yearbook of the National Society for the Study of Education, Part 2, University of Chicago Press, Chicago, 1968, pp. 334–335.

[30] Russell, D. H., "Qualitative Levels in Children's Vocabularies," *Journal of Educational Psychology, 53:* 170, August 1962.

[31] Loree, M. R., *Psychology of Education,* The Ronald Press Company, New York, 1965, p. 320.

[32] Beckman, Jan, "Trying Words on for Size," *Elementary English, 44:* 846–848, 912, December 1967.

[33] Dolch, E. V., "Vocabulary Development," *Elementary English, 30:* 71, March 1953.

[34] Ausubel, D. P., "The Use of Advance Organizers in the Learning and Retention of Meaningful Verbal Material," *Journal of Educational Psychology, 51:* 267–272, October 1960; Burns, P. C., "Means of Developing Vocabularies," *Education, 85:* 533–538, May 1965; Cohen, op. cit.; Deighton, L. C., *Vocabulary Development in the Classroom,* Bureau of Publications, Teachers College, Columbia University, New York, 1959, 62 pp.; Deighton, L. C., "Developing Vocabulary: Another Look at the Problem," *English Journal, 49:* 82–88, February 1960; Lindner, Mabel, "Vitalizing Vocabulary Study," *English Journal, 40:* 225–226, April 1951.

[35] Petty, Herold, and Stoll, op. cit., p. 109.

[36] Ibid., pp. 27–29, 47–48, 65, 66, 67, 70.

[37] Ruddell, R. B., "Oral Language Skills and the Development of Other Language Skills," *Elementary English, 53:* 489–498, May 1966.

[38] Deighton, *Vocabulary Development in the Classroom,* op. cit., pp. 52–54.

[39] Eastman, P.D., *Go, Dog, Go!,* Random House, Inc., New York, 1961, 64 pp.

[40] Lopshire, Robert, *Put Me in the Zoo,* Random House, Inc., New York, 1960, 61 pp.

[41] O'Neill, Mary, *Hailstones and Halibut Bones: Adventures in Color,* Doubleday and Co., Inc., New York, 1961, 59 pp.

[42] Bissett, Donald J., editor, *Poems and Verses About the City,* Chandler Publishing Co., San Francisco, 1968, p. 31.

[43] Ashley, Rosalind, "Linguistic Games and Fun Exercises," *Elementary English, 44:* 765–767, November 1967.

[44] Deighton, *Vocabulary Development in the Classroom,* op. cit., pp. 46–50, 54.

[45] Blake, H. E., and Cohen, Gabriel, "Innovations in Oral Language," *The Reading Teacher, 21:* 653, April 1968.

[46] Tiedt and Tiedt, "Word Play," *Elementary English,* 42.189–190, 196, February 1965.

[47] O'Leary, Helen F, "Vocabulary Presentation and Enrichment," *Elementary English,* 41:613–615, October 1964.

[48] Cutts, N. E., and Mosely, Nicholas, *Teaching the Bright and Gifted,* Prentice-Hall, Inc., Englewood Cliffs, N.J., 1957, p. 22.

[49] Beggs, Bernice B., "Speak the Word Trippingly," *English Journal,* 40:39–40, January 1951.

[50] Dawson, M. A., Zollinger, Marion, and Elwell, Ordell, *Guiding Language Learning,* Harcourt, Brace and World, Inc., New York, 1963, pp. 61–79.

[51] Lake, Mary Louise, "First Aid for Vocabularies," *Elementary English,* 44:783–784, November 1967.

[52] Swatts, F. I., "Seniors Will Play—With Words," *English Journal, 43:* 322–323, September 1954.

[53] McKee, Paul, and McCowen, Annie, *English for Meaning,* Teacher's Annotated Edition, 6, Houghton Mifflin, Boston, 1962, p. 365.

54 Smith, D. V., *Selected Essays*, The Macmillan Company, New York, 1964, pp. 53–55.

55 Pilon, A. Barbara, "Culturally Divergent Children and Creative Language Activities." In *Language Differences: Do They Interfere?*, edited by J. L. Laffey and Roger Shuy, International Reading Association, Newark, Del., 1973, pp. 127–146.

56 Pilon, A. Barbara, and Sims, Rudine, *Dialects and Reading: Implications for Change*, Elementary Language Arts Conference, National Council of Teachers of English, Boston, April 1975, NCTE Stock 71281.

57 Hymes, Lucia, and Hymes, James L., Jr., *Hooray for Chocolate*, William R. Scott, Inc., Publisher, New York, 1960, p. 42.

Chapter 7

1 McCormack, Jo Ann, *The Story of Our Language*, Charles E. Merrill, Columbus, Ohio, 1967, pp. 21–25.

2 Smith, Frank, *Understanding Reading*, Holt, Rinehart and Winston, New York, 1971.

3 Epstein, Sam, and Epstein, Beryl, *What's Behind the Word?*, Scholastic Book Services, New York, 1964, 64 pp.

4 Kohn, Bernice, *What a Funny Thing to Say!*, The Dial Press, New York, 1974.

5 Stewart, George R., *Names on the Land*, Houghton Mifflin Company, Boston, 1958, 511 pp.

Chapter 8

1 Society for Visual Education, Inc., *Black ABC's*, Chicago, 1970.

2 Slepian, Jan, and Seidler, Ann, *The Hungry Thing*, Scholastic Book Services, New York, 1971.

Chapter 9

1 Pfloog, Jan, *The Cat Book*, Golden Press, Inc., New York, 1964.

2 Pfloog, Jan, *The Fish Book*, Golden Press, Inc., New York, 1964.

3 Martin, Dick, *The Apple Book*, Golden Press, Inc., New York, 1964.

4 Sendak, Maurice, *Nutshell Library*, Harper and Row, Publishers, n.p., 1962.

5 Ibid.

6 Ibid.

7 Joslin, Sesyle, *What Do You Say, Dear?*, Young Scott Books, New York, 1958.

8 Joslin, Sesyle, *What Do You Do, Dear?*, William R. Scott, Inc., New York, 1961.

9 McCloskey, Robert, *Burt Dow: Deep-Water Man*, The Viking Press, New York, 1963.

10 Adelson, Leone, *Please Pass the Grass*, David McKay Company, Inc., New York, 1960.

11 Williams, Garth, *The Rabbits' Wedding*, Harper and Brothers, Publishers, New York, 1958.

[12] Cleary, Beverly, *Henry Huggins,* Scholastic Book Services, New York, 1950, pp. 1–14.

[13] Myers, R. E., and Torrance, E. P., *Invitations to Speaking and Writing Creatively,* Ginn and Company, Boston, 1965, p. 45.

[14] Myers, R. E., and Torrance, E. P., *Invitations to Thinking and Doing,* Ginn and Company, Boston, 1964, pp. 93–95.

[15] Brown, Marcia, *Stone Soup,* Charles Scribner's Sons, New York, 1947.

[16] Kahl, Virginia, *The Perfect Pancake,* Charles Scribner's Sons, New York, 1960.

[17] Kahl, Virginia, *The Duchess Bakes a Cake,* Charles Scribner's Sons, New York, 1955.

[18] Hale, L. P., *Stories from the Peterkin Papers,* Scholastic Book Services, New York, 1964.

[19] Bishop, C. H., *Twenty and Ten,* The Viking Press, New York, 1952.

[20] Johnson, Edna, Sickels, E. R., and Sayers, F. C., editors, *Anthology of Children's Literature,* Houghton Mifflin Company, Boston, 1959, pp. 895–900.

[21] Twain, Mark, *The Adventures of Tom Sawyer,* The New American Library, New York, 1959, pp. 29–37, 135–141.

[22] Johnson, E. M., and Jacobs, L. B., editors, *Treat Shop,* Charles E. Merrill Books, Inc., Columbus, Ohio, 1960, pp. 237–241.

[23] Thayer, Jane, *The Puppy Who Wanted a Boy,* William Morrow and Co., New York, 1958, 48 pp.

[24] Nash, Ogden, *Custard the Dragon and the Wicked Knight,* Little, Brown and Company, Boston, 1961, 47 pp.

[25] Lampman, E. S., *The Shy Stegosaurus of Cricket Creek,* Scholastic Book Services, New York, 1955.

[26] Leaf, Munro, *The Story of Ferdinand,* Scholastic Book Services, New York, 1962.

[27] Johnson, E. M., and Jacobs, L. B., editors, *Treat Shop,* Charles E. Merrill Books, Inc., Columbus, Ohio, 1960, pp. 64–71.

[28] Simon, Tony, editor, *Ripsnorters and Ribticklers,* Scholastic Book Services, New York, 1958.

[29] Atwater, Richard, and Atwater, Florence, *Mr. Popper's Penguins,* Scholastic Book Services, New York, 1964, p. 7.

[30] Travers, P. L., *Mary Poppins,* Reynal and Hitchcock, New York, 1945, pp. 29–48.

[31] McCloskey, Robert, *Homer Price,* Scholastic Book Services, New York, 1962, pp. 100–130, 52–72.

[32] Lindgren, Astrid, *Pippi Longstocking,* Scholastic Book Services, New York, 1959, pp. 30–40.

[33] McSwigan, Marie, *Snow Treasure,* Scholastic Book Services, New York, 1958.

[34] Sperry, Armstrong, *Call It Courage,* The Macmillan Company, New York, 1964.

[35] Speare, E. G., *The Witch of Blackbird Pond,* Houghton Mifflin Company, Boston, 1958.

[36] Kramer, Nora, editor, *Arrow Book of Ghost Stories,* Scholastic Book Services, New York, 1960, pp. 32–68, 72–77.

[37] Kramer, Nora, editor, *Arrow Book of Spooky Stories,* Scholastic Book Services, New York, 1962, 90 pp.

Chapter 10

[1] Merriam, Eve, *It Doesn't Always Have to Rhyme,* Atheneum, New York, 1966.

[2] Summerfield, Geoffrey, editor, *First Voices,* Random House, New York, 1970.

[3] Dunning, Stephen, Lueders, Edward, Smith, Hugh, compilers, *Reflections on a Gift of Watermelon Pickle,* Scott, Foresman and Company, Glenview, Ill., 1966, pp. 58, 60, 17.

[4] Lewis, Richard, compiler, *Miracles,* Simon and Schuster, New York, 1966.

[5] Lewis, Richard, compiler, *Journeys,* Simon and Schuster, New York, 1969.

[6] Lewis, Richard, compiler, *The Wind and the Rain,* Simon and Schuster, New York, 1968.

[7] Pulsifer, S. N., *Children Are Poets,* Dresser, Chapman and Grimes, Cambridge, Mass., 1963.

[8] Koch, Kenneth, *Wishes, Lies and Dreams,* Chelsea House, New York, 1970.

[9] Pulsifer, op. cit., pp. 32, 59, 48.

[10] Applegate, Mauree, *Helping Children Write,* Row, Peterson and Co., Evanston, Ill., 1961, 173 pp.; *Easy in English,* Row, Peterson and Company, Evanston, Ill., 1962, 564 pp.; *Freeing Children to Write,* Harper and Row Publishers, New York, 1963, 184 pp.

[11] Holbrook, David, *The Secret Places,* University of Alabama Press, University, Ala., 1965; *Children's Writing,* Cambridge University Press, London, 1967.

[12] Mearns, Hughes, *Creative Power: The Education of Youth in the Creative Arts,* Dover Publications, Inc., New York, 1958.

[13] Arnstein, F. J., *Poetry in the Elementary Classroom,* Appleton-Century-Crofts, New York, 1962.

[14] Frost, Robert, *You Come Too,* Holt, Rinehart and Winston, New York, 1959.

[15] Pulsifer, op. cit., p. 11.

[16] Mearns, op. cit., pp. 131–132.

[17] Koch, op. cit.

[18] Dunning, Lueders, and Smith, op. cit.

[19] Ibid., p. 18.

[20] Pulsifer, op. cit., p. 4.

[21] Wolfe, D. M., *Language Arts and Life Patterns: Grades 2 through 8,* The Odyssey Press, Inc., New York, 1966, p. 266.

[22] Ibid., pp. 386–388.

[23] Osborn, A. F., *Applied Imagination,* Charles Scribner's Sons, New York, 1957, p. 66.

[24] Frye, Northrop, *The Educated Imagination,* Indiana University Press, Bloomington, 1964, p. 32.

[25] Merriam, *It Doesn't Always Have to Rhyme,* op. cit., p. 48.

[26] Glaus, Marlene, *From Thoughts to Words,* National Council of Teachers of English, Champaign, Ill., 1965, pp. 27–28.

[27] Orff, Carl, Keetman, Gunild, and Jelinek, Walter, *Music for Children,* Angel Records, New York, 1958, 33 3 rpm, Side 4, Band 1.

[28] Arbuthnot, M. H., compiler, *The Arbuthnot Anthology of Children's Literature,* Fourth Edition, Scott, Foresman and Company, Chicago, 1976, p. 134.

[29] Kuskin, Karla, *Square as a House,* Harper and Brothers, Publishers, New York, 1960.

[30] Koch, op. cit., pp. 105–06.

[31] Myers, R. E., and Torrance, E. P., *Invitations to Speaking and Writing Creatively,* Ginn and Company, Boston, 1965, pp. 29–31; R. E. Myers and E. P. Torrance, *Invitations to Thinking and Doing,* Ginn and Company, Boston, 1964, p. 29.

[32] Walter, N. W., *Let Them Write Poetry,* Holt, Rinehart and Winston, New York, 1962, pp. 34–51.

[33] Merriam, *It Doesn't Always Have to Rhyme,* op. cit., p. 27.

[34] Clifford, Eth, *A Bear Before Breakfast,* J. P. Putnam's Sons, New York, 1962.

[35] Ellentuck, Shan, *Did You See What I Said?,* Doubleday and Company, Inc., Garden City, New York, 1967.

[36] Kohn, Bernice, *One Day It Rained Cats and Dogs,* Coward-McCann, Inc., New York, 1965.

[37] Arbuthnot, op. cit., p. 50.

[38] Arbuthnot, M. H., et al., compilers, *Arbuthnot Anthology of Children's Literature,* Third Edition, Scott, Foresman and Company, Glenview, Ill., 1971, p 113.

[39] Dunning, Lueders, and Smith, op. cit., p. 110.

[40] Ibid., p. 37.

[41] Johnson, Edna, Sickels, Evelyn, and Sayers, Frances Clarke, editors, *Anthology of Children's Literature,* Houghton Mifflin Company, Boston, 1959, p. 1041.

[42] Behn, Harry, translator, *Cricket Songs,* Harcourt, Brace and World, Inc., New York, 1964.

[43] Lewis, Richard, editor, *The Moment of Wonder,* The Dial Press, New York, 1964.

[44] Bennett, George, and Molloy, Paul, *Cavalcade of Poems,* Scholastic Book Services, New York, 1965.

[45] Lewis, *The Moment of Wonder,* op. cit., p. xvi.

[46] Merriam, *It Doesn't Always Have to Rhyme,* op. cit., p. 32.

[47] Arbuthnot, M. H., et al., compilers, *Arbuthnot Anthology of Children's Literature,* Fourth Edition, op. cit., 1976, p. 63.

[48] Ibid., p. 39.

[49] Merriam, *It Doesn't Always Have to Rhyme,* op. cit., p. 33.

[50] Clymer, Eleanor, compiler, *Arrow Book of Funny Poems,* Scholastic Book Services, New York, 1961, p. 127.

[51] Arbuthnot, op. cit., p. 76.

[52] Ibid., p. 42.

[53] Clymer, op. cit., pp. 33–42.

[54] Corbett, Scott, *The Limerick Trick,* Little, Brown and Company, Boston, 1964.

[55] Merriam, *It Doesn't Always Have to Rhyme,* op. cit., p. 61.

[56] Applegate, *Freeing Children to Write,* op. cit., p. 39.

[57] Ciardi, John, *How Does a Poem Mean?,* Houghton Mifflin Company, Boston, 1959, p. 669.

Chapter 11

[1] Frye, Northrop, *The Educated Imagination,* Indiana University Press, Bloomington, 1964, p. 112.

[2] Coolidge, O. E., *Hercules and Other Tales from Greek Myths,* Scholastic Book Services, New York, 1961.

[3] Schwab, Gustav, *Gods and Heroes: Myths and Epics of Ancient Greece,* Fawcett, Greenwich, Conn., 1965.

[4] Hawthorne, Nathaniel, *Tanglewood Tales,* The Hampton Publishing Company, New York, 1921.

[5] Shafer, Burr, *The Wonderful World of J. Wesley Smith,* Scholastic Book Services, New York, 1960.

[6] Asimov, Isaac, *Words from the Myths,* Houghton Mifflin Company, Boston, 1961.

[7] Severn, Bill, *People Words,* Ives Washburn, Inc., New York, 1966.

[8] White, Anne Terry, *The Golden Treasury of Myths and Legends,* Golden Press, New York, 1965, 164 pp.

[9] D'Aulaire, Ingri, and D'Aulaire, Parin, *Norse Gods and Giants,* Doubleday and Company, Inc., Garden City, New York, 1967.

[10] Belting, Natalia, *The Moon Is a Crystal Ball,* Bobbs-Merrill, Indianapolis, 1952, pp. 33–38.

[11] Kipling, Rudyard, *Just So Stories,* Garden City Books, New York, 1912, pp. 69–76.

[12] Dasent, George, *Popular Tales from the Norse,* Appleton-Century-Crofts, New York, 1859.

[13] Benson, Sally, *Stories of the Gods and Heroes,* New York, Dial, 1940.

[14] Thompson, Stith, *Tales of the North American Indians,* Harvard University Press, Cambridge, 1969.

[15] DuBois, W. P., *Lion,* The Viking Press, New York, 1956.

[16] Le Grand, *The Amazing Adventures of Archie and the First Hot Dog,* Abingdon Press, New York, 1964.

[17] Le Grand, *Cap'n Dow and the Hole in the Doughnut,* Abingdon Press, New York, 1946.

[18] Gruenberg, S. M., compiler, *Let's Read More Stories,* Garden City Books, Garden City, New York, 1960, pp. 124–130.

[19] Le Grand, *How Baseball Began in Brooklyn,* Abingdon Press, New York, 1958.

[20] Barrie, J. M., *Peter Pan,* Charles Scribner's Sons, New York, 1928.

[21] Crowell, Pers, *First to Ride,* Scholastic Book Services, New York, 1959.

[22] White, Anne Terry, *The First Men in the World,* Scholastic Book Services, New York, 1961.

[23] Kramer, Nora, *Grimms' Fairy Tales,* Scholastic Book Services, New York, 1962, 154 pp.

[24] Lang, Andrew, editor, *Tales from the Red Fairy Book,* Scholastic Book Services, New York, 1955, 190 pp.

[25] Lang, Andrew, editor, *The Crimson Fairy Book,* Dover Publications, Inc., New York, 1967, 371 pp.

[26] Lang, Andrew, editor, *Tales from the Green Fairy Book,* Scholastic Book Services, New York, 1960, 113 pp.

[27] David, Alfred, and David, Mary Elizabeth, *The Twelve Dancing Princesses and Other Fairy Tales,* The New American Library, New York, 1964, 319 pp.

[28] French, R. A., "Working the Vineyard," In *Perspectives in Reading, No. 3: Children, Books and Reading,* compiled by Robert Karlin, Mildred Dawson, and W. J. Kalenius, Jr., International Reading Association, Newark, Del., 1964, p. 103.

[29] Lewis, C. S., *The Lion, the Witch, and the Wardrobe,* The Macmillan Company, New York, 1950.

[30] Johnson, Edna, Sickels, E. R., and Sayers, F. C., editors, *Anthology of Children's Literature,* Houghton Mifflin Company, Boston, 1959, pp. 652–663.

[31] Arbuthnot, M. H., compiler, *The Arbuthnot Anthology of Children's Literature: Time for Fairy Tales,* Scott, Foresman and Company, Chicago, 1961, p. 326.

[32] Wolfe, D. M., *Language Arts and Life Patterns: Grades 2 through 8,* The Odyssey Press, Inc., New York, 1961, pp. 104–105.

[33] Enright, Elizabeth, *The Saturdays,* Dell Publishing Company, New York, 1966.

[34] Holling, C. H., *Paddle-to-the-Sea,* Houghton Mifflin Company, Boston, 1941.

[35] Glaus, Marlene, *From Thoughts to Words,* National Council of Teachers of English, Champaign, Ill., 1965, pp. 13–14.

[36] Jacobs, L. B., and Turner, J. J., editors, *Happiness Hill,* Charles E. Merrill Books, Inc., Columbus, Ohio, 1960, p. 7.

[37] Arbuthnot, *The Arbuthnot Anthology of Children's Literature: Time for Poetry,* op. cit., p. 110.

[38] Applegate, Mauree, *Helping Children Write,* Row, Peterson and Company, Evanston, Ill., 1961, p. 23.

[39] Hollowell, Lillian, ed., *A Book of Children's Literature,* Holt, Rinehart and Winston, New York, 1964, p. 562.

[40] Travers, P. L., *Mary Poppins,* Reynal and Hitchcock, New York, 1945.

⁴¹ Arbuthnot, M. H., et al., compilers, *The Arbuthnot Anthology of Children's Literature*, Third Edition, Scott, Foresman and Company, Glenview, Ill., 1971, p. 7.

⁴² Ibid., p. 44.

⁴³ Ibid., p. 44.

⁴⁴ Ibid., p. 10.

⁴⁵ Ibid., p. 192.

⁴⁶ Glaser, Milton, and Glaser, Shirley, *If Apples Had Teeth*, Alfred A. Knopf, New York, 1960.

⁴⁷ Stover, J. A., *If Everybody Did*, David McKay Company, Inc., New York, 1960.

⁴⁸ Stover, J. A., *Why . . .? Because*, David McKay Company, Inc., New York, 1961.

⁴⁹ Reid, Alastair, *Supposing*, Little, Brown and Company, Boston, 1960.

⁵⁰ Applegate, Mauree, *Freeing Children to Write*, Harper and Row, Publishers, New York, 1963, pp. 48–49.

⁵¹ Gruenberg, op. cit., pp. 54–58.

⁵² De Regniers, B. S., *Something Special*, Harcourt Brace Jovanovich, New York, 1958.

⁵³ Hogarth, William, *The Arrow Book of Jokes and Riddles*, Scholastic Book Services, New York, 1962, pp. 52–53.

⁵⁴ Myers, R. E., and Torrance, E. P., *Can You Imagine?*, Ginn and Company, Boston, 1965, pp. 4–5.

⁵⁵ Myers, R. E., and Torrance, E. P., *Invitations to Speaking and Writing Creatively*, Ginn and Company, Boston, 1965, p. 45.

⁵⁶ Marksberry, M. L., *Foundation of Creativity*, Harper and Row, Publishers, New York, 1963, pp. 132–133.

⁵⁷ De Jong, D. C., *The Happy Birthday Umbrella*, Little, Brown and Company, Boston, 1959.

⁵⁸ Arbuthnot, M. H., compiler, *Arbuthnot Anthology of Children's Literature: Time for Poetry*, Revised Edition, op. cit., 1961, pp. 118, 119, 121.
119, 121.

⁵⁹ Palmer, Helen, *Why I Built the Boogle House*, Random House, Inc., New York, 1964.

⁶⁰ Seuss, Dr., *If I Ran the Zoo*, Random House, Inc., New York, 1950.

⁶¹ Seuss, Dr., *On Beyond Zebra*, Random House, Inc., New York, 1955.

⁶² Arbuthnot, *The Arbuthnot Anthology of Children's Literature: Time for Poetry*, op. cit., p. 130.

⁶³ Anglund, J. W., *What Color Is Love?*, Harcourt, Brace and World, Inc., New York 1966.

⁶⁴ Butterworth, Oliver, *The Enormous Egg*, Scholastic Book Services, New York, 1961.

⁶⁵ Sperry, Armstrong, *Call It Courage*, The Macmillan Company, New York, 1964.

[66] Speare, E. G., *The Witch of Blackbird Pond,* Houghton Mifflin Company, Boston, 1958.

[67] O'Dell, Scott, *Island of the Blue Dolphins,* Dell Publishing Company, Inc., New York, 1971.

[68] Krauss, Ruth, *A Hole Is to Dig,* Harper and Brothers, n.p., 1952.

[69] Glauss, op. cit., pp. 45–46.

[70] Penn, R. B., *Mommies Are for Loving,* G. P. Putnam's Sons, New York, 1962.

[71] Hymes, Lucia, and Hymes, L., Jr., *Hooray for Chocolate,* William R. Scott, Inc., Publisher, New York, 1960, p. 44.

[72] McGovern, Ann, compiler, *Arrow Book of Poetry,* Scholastic Book Services, New York, 1965, 96 pp.

[73] Nash, Ogden, *A Boy Is a Boy,* Franklin Watts, Inc., New York, 1960.

[74] Johnson, Sickels, and Sayers, op. cit., p. 1042.

[75] Nash, Ogden, *Girls Are Silly,* Franklin Watts, Inc., New York, 1962.

[76] McGinley, Phyllis, *Boys Are Awful,* Franklin Watts, Inc., New York, 1962.

[77] Schulz, C. M., *Happiness Is a Warm Puppy,* Determined Productions, Inc., San Francisco, 1962.

[78] Anglund, J. W., *A Friend Is Someone Who Likes You,* Harcourt, Brace and Company, New York, 1958.

[79] Anglund, J. W., *Love Is a Special Way of Feeling,* Harcourt, Brace and Company, New York, 1960.

[80] Anglund, J. W., *Spring Is a New Beginning,* Harcourt, Brace and World, Inc., New York, 1963.

[81] Munari, Bruno, *The Elephant's Wish,* The World Publishing Company, Cleveland, 1959.

[82] Arbuthnot, *The Arbuthnot Anthology of Children's Literature: Time for Poetry,* op. cit., pp. 121–122.

[83] Arbuthnot, M. H., et al., compilers, *Arbuthnot Anthology of Children's Literature,* Fourth Edition, Scott, Foresman and Company, Glenview, Ill., 1976, p. 86.

[84] Deutsch, Babette, *I Often Wish,* Funk and Wagnalls, New York, 1966.

[85] Huber, M. B., compiler, *Story and Verse for Children,* The Macmillan Company, New York, 1965, p. 95.

[86] Zolotow, Charlotte, *Someday,* Harper and Row, Publishers, New York, 1965.

[87] Dorian, Marguerite, *When the Snow Is Blue,* Lothrop, Lee and Shepard Company, Inc., New York, 1962.

[88] De Regniers, B. S., *A Child's Book of Dreams,* Harcourt, Brace and Company, New York, 1957.

[89] Merriam, Eve, *There is No Rhyme for Silver,* Atheneum, New York, 1962, p. 34.

[90] Warburg, S. S., *The Thinking Book,* Little, Brown and Company, Boston, 1960.

[91] Sendak, Maurice, *Where the Wild Things Are,* Harper and Row, Publishers, n.p., 1963.

AUTHOR AND ILLUSTRATOR INDEX

TITLE INDEX

SUBJECT INDEX

1150